COLD WAR COUNTERFEIT SPIES

TALES OF ESPIONAGE; GENUINE OR BOGUS?

COLD WAR COUNTERFEIT SPIES

TALES OF ESPIONAGE; GENUINE OR BOGUS?

Nigel West

Frontline Books

COLD WAR COUNTERFEIT SPIES
Tales of Espionage:
Genuine or Bogus?

This edition published in 2016 by Frontline Books,
an imprint of Pen & Sword Books Ltd,
47 Church Street, Barnsley, S. Yorkshire, S70 2AS

ISBN: 978-1-47387-955-3

For more information on our books, please visit
www.frontline-books.com,
email info@frontline-books.com
or write to us at the above address.

Printed and bound by CPI Group (UK) Ltd, Croydon, CR0 4YY

Contents

Abbreviations

ACC	Assistant Chief Constable	MEW	Ministry of Economic Warfare
AFSA	Armed Forces Security Agency	MGB	Soviet intelligence service
		MI5	British Security Service
ASIO	Australian Security Intelligence Organization	MI6	British Secret Intelligence Service
AVH	Hungarian intelligence service	MRF	Mobile Reconnaissance Force
AVO	Hungarian Security Service	NCB	Nuclear, Chemical, Biological
BND	Federal German Intelligence Service	NKVD	Soviet intelligence service
BOSS	South African Bureau of State Security	NSA	National Security Agency
		OPC	Office of Policy Coordination
BVA	Spanish Basque Battalion	OSS	Office of Strategic Services
CIA	Central Intelligence Agency	PFLP-GC	Patriotic Front for the Liberation of Palestine – General Command
DCI	Director of Central Intelligence		
DEA	Drug Enforcement Administration	PIRA	Provisional wing of the Irish Republican Army
EOKA	Greek Cypriot Separatist Movement	PRO	Public Record Office
ETA	Basque Separatist Movement	ROTC	Reserve Officer Training Cadet
FBI	Federal Bureau of investigation	RUC	Royal Ulster Constabulary
FFI	French Forces of the Interior	SAS	Special Air Service Regiment
FRU	Force Research Unit	SB	Polish Intelligence Service
GAL	Spanish Anti-Terrorist Group	SIS	British Secret Intelligence Service
GRU	Soviet Military Intelligence Service	SOE	Special Operations Executive
HVA	East German Foreign intelligence service	SVR	Russian Foreign Intelligence Service
INLA	Irish National Liberation Army	UB	Polish Secret Police
		UDR	Ulster Defence Regiment
IRA	Irish Republican Army	UVF	Ulster Volunteer Force
KPD	German Communist Party	WIN	Polish Freedom and Independence Movement
KGB	Soviet Intelligence Service		

Introduction

In 1998, *Counterfeit Spies* investigated two dozen books that purported to be non-fiction accounts of clandestine missions undertaken by secret agents during the Second World War. Some were obscure, such as John Cottell, who claimed to have been awarded numerous decorations for gallantry that mysteriously had not been recorded in any official archive, while others like the Countess of Romanones (*The Spy Wore Red*) appeared remarkably unembarrassed to be exposed as a fraud. A few, such as Lady Clarke (Elizabeth Denham, the pseudonymous author of *I Looked Right*), seemed to be deluded fantasists, whereas the historian Leonard Mosley must have known that he was fabricating material to support his tale of espionage, *The Druid*, and William Stevenson ought to have realised there were some serious problems about *A Man Called Intrepid*, not to mention doubts over the authenticity of the ostensibly genuine photographs that illustrated his best-selling book. Thus *Counterfeit Spies* addressed the issue of invention, fabrication and embroidery, rather than the much more common literary offence of plagiarism, wholesale theft or, in the case of Stephen Ambrose, an omission of attribution.

It is also fair to acknowledge that the scale of the difficulties presented by the fantasists is actually much greater than I had anticipated. For example, I always recognised that Dr Josephine Butler simply could not have undertaken all, or indeed any, of the clandestine missions she documented in *Churchill's Secret Agent*, but when I researched her story I had little idea of the true depth of her deception. Far from operating in Nazi-occupied France, she in fact she had spent much of the Second World War serving a sentence of hard labour in Holloway Prison, having been convicted of obtaining money under false pretences from four elderly, foreign sisters of their life savings.

Emphatically not a heroine of the French resistance, risking her life on numerous secret missions into enemy-occupied territory, she had manufactured an entire career for herself, of which I was only able to uncover a small proportion. Prior to her conviction Mrs Lily Butler (not *Lady Josephine* Butler, as she styled herself) had been forced to resign from the London Auxiliary Ambulance Service in 1942, following her involvement in fund-raising for a bogus charity boxing match, and had then found work as a clerk in the Ministry of Economic Warfare. Omitting her prison sentence from her memoirs, she had asserted that her role in the MEW merely had been cover for her covert activities abroad, a period that in fact she had spent in a north London prison cell.

Another woman I underestimated was Roxane Pitt, the author of *Operation Double Life*, who turned out to be Albertina Crico, also the author as Tina Crico of *Berretto Rosso*. At the time of *Counterfeit Spies'* publication, she was married to her fourth husband, Dudley Tudor, a retired British diplomat. Her own astonishing story included a bigamous marriage to an intelligence officer, Edward Wickens, testimony agaist an Italian war criminal, General Nicolo Bellomo, and a hasty escape from Rome in May 1950 after her life had been threatened.

I soon discovered that, as demonstrated in the Josephine Butler case, my research had scarcely scratched the surface, and there were plenty of egregious examples of downright fabrication in the publication of wartime memoirs. One award-winning, harrowing memoir of the Holocaust, *Fragments*, by Binjamin Wilkomirski, turned out to have been written, not by a Jewish survivor of the Nazi death-camps as the author claimed, but by a Swiss musician who had spent his entire life in the safety of a wealthy gentile family in Zurich. Far from having trekked from Riga through Poland to escape extermination in Auschwitz, Bruno Doessekker had duped Israeli researchers and international academics to complete a speaking tour of American universities and be feted as a writer of genius. In reality, the entire book turned out to be a total fiction.

Equally surprising was the willingness of some fraudsters, for there can be no more appropriate adjective for William Stevenson, to return to the scene of their original crime and perpetrate yet another confidence trick. In his case, having been mauled over the misrepresentations in *A Man Called Intrepid*, he adopted many of the same dubious techniques in 2007 with the publication of *Spymistress*, purportedly a biography of Vera Atkins, the intelligence officer for F

Section of Special Operations Executive. Just as Stevenson's first subject, Sir William Stephenson, had really existed, even if his authentic lifetime achievements never came close to matching what his biographer attributed to him, so Vera Atkins had indeed served in SOE, if only from April 1941 until the end of hostilities, and in a relatively subordinate position. However, according to Stevenson, she was really the mysterious guiding hand behind numerous wartime intelligence coups, the confidante of any number of political and military leaders, and the hitherto undisclosed participant in, or planner of, dozens of clandestine operations. The truth, alas, was that Stevenson's undoubted talent for narrative, reported speech and sheer invention had outstripped both his subject's life and authenticated fact. The result was *Spymistress*, a completely artifical blend of misreported quotations, non-existent organisations, impossible chronology and phony secret missions. To cap it all, Stevenson then endorsed his product with invented quotations from John le Carré, who was at least alive, whereas Ian Fleming had died forty-three years earlier and therefore was hardly in a position to offer the remarks attributed to him on the dustjacket.

At the other end of the scale *Bravo Two Zero*, written by Steve Mitchell under the pseudonym Andy McNab, proved to be a hugely successful account of an SAS patrol's ill-fated mission into Iraq during the 1992 Gulf War. Two of McNab's men died, Geordie Armstrong only just managed to escape to Syria (and later write *The One Who Got Away* as 'Chris Ryan') while the rest suffered imprisonment and appalling physical maltreatment in Baghdad. But was McNab's version, which included ferocious gun battles with vastly superior enemy forces in which hundreds of casualties were inflicted, really true? According to *The Real Bravo Two Zero*, a meticulous investigation by a fellow SAS soldier, Michael Asher, both *The One That Got Away* and McNab's tale were equally embroidered fictions that departed considerably from the after-action combat reports which had been videotaped upon their safe return to Hereford. Asher's revisionism was also supported by 'Mike Coburn', another member of McNab's patrol, a New Zealander who initially struggled to published *Soldier Five*, his version of what had really happened. Clearly the potentially lucrative business of passing off fiction as fact was not a phenomenon limited to purported experiences of the Second World War.

Since the publication of *Counterfeit Spies* I have been prompted to examine some of the titles dealing with the post-war era, and it was only while I was researching the background to *The Nemesis File* that I realised the extraordinary harm that these books can inflict. They are often circulated across the globe and even when their initial release attracts some adverse criticism, such reports rarely receive international media attention. Accordingly, often years after a book has hit the headlines, it is still being quoted as an accepted, reliable account of the events it claims to document. Much the same can be said of Sean McPhilemy's *The Committee*, another apparently non-fiction contribution to the debate about British dirty tricks in Northern Ireland. My purpose, in the pages that follow, is to set the record straight in an area that is notoriously difficult to obtain reliable corroboration. Where a writer, such as Gary Murray, has claimed to have worked for the security or intelligence services, I have attempted to analyse the book, and the writer's background.

At one time it was almost as though various security and intelligence agencies almost conspired to encourage the fantasists and crooks by sticking to an almost universally-adopted rigid rule that no official comment could ever be made regarding such matters so as to avoid setting a precedent and perhaps compromising security. Such policies served to enhance the reputations of the claimants and simultaneously handicapped those who were suspicious of them. Happily, in these more enlightened times, many services have introduced public affairs offices to handle such enquiries, and often are generous in giving off-the-record background briefings to correct potentially damaging allegations. The CIA has an impressively-staffed Office of Public Affairs, as does the Federal Bureau of Investigation and the National Security Agency, and also sponsors a more academically-orientated Center for the Study of Intelligence, staffed by historians and intelligence professionals. The SVR in Moscow, successor to the KGB, runs an enthusiastic press office, and even the British Secret Intelligence Service (MI6) and Security Service (MI5) have accepted the need to appoint senior personnel to liaise with the media and bona-fide researchers. Equally, at the end of the Cold War, there is a greater willingness within these organisations to ensure its history is not left to those who seem determined to perpetuate the myths. Indeed, both superpowers have adopted the principles of declassification and have released previously top secret documents to public scrutiny.

It is in this new era of openness that it is possible to place some well-established stories under a microscope, compare the once headline-grabbing tales of *sub-rosa* operations and unravel a few mysteries of the Cold War. Did Greville Wynne really exfiltrate a GRU defector from

Odessa? Was the frogman Buster Crabb abducted during a mission in Portsmouth Harbour? Did the KGB run a close-guarded training facility, as described by J. Bernard Hutton in *School for Spies*, which was modelled on a typical town in the American mid-west, so agents could be acclimatised to a non-Soviet environment? Only with the help of witnesses with first-hand experience, and recently declassified documents, can answers be found to some vexed questions.

Acknowledgements

I am indebted to the Director of the CIA's Office of Public Affairs and his highly professional staff, as well as to his counterparts at the NSA and FBI.

Chapter 1

Official Assassin

At the end of the Second World War, as the public became aware of the horrors of the Nazi extermination camps, there was a widespread and understandable outcry for revenge and retribution. The United Nations War Crimes Commission had been created in November 1943 to dispense justice to those convicted of atrocities, and various Allied military units were established to identify and pursue those responsible for the worst of the outrages. One such organisation was the War Crimes Investigation Unit, the work of which was recounted in *The Secret Hunters*, written by the historian Anthony Kemp.[1] He described how, following the liberation of the notorious Belsen concentration camp, the No. 1 War Crimes Investigation Team was headed by a barrister, General Leo Genn, and a second unit, detached from the Special Air Service regiment, had been despatched to Germany separately to establish the fate of the participants in Operation *Loyton*.

Loyton had been a parachute drop in August 1944 into the Vosges mountains by a Jedburgh team and fifteen SAS men who intended to liaise with the local maquis and harass the enemy behind the front line. However, the French resistance was riddled with informers and the well-equipped German forces launched numerous punitive sweeps around the town of Moussey to destroy the British troops. By October, when the commander of 1 SAS, Colonel Brian Franks withdrew his men and made contact with American forces, thirty-one of them were unaccounted for. Numerous rumours of executions and mass graves circulated, and Franks was determined to establish what had happened to the missing soldiers, although it was well known that the Nazis regarded Allied special forces as being outside the provisions of the Geneva Convention and treated them accordingly. There had been numerous examples of British personnel being executed soon after their

1

capture, one prominent atrocity being the murder in Norway of the survivors of *Gunnerside*, an SOE mission in November 1942 to destroy the hydro-electric plant at Vermork. On that occasion seventeen survivors of a glider-borne force had been shot by their captors, although the full details of the atrocity would not become known until the end of hostilities. The elimination of the *Loyton* prisoners followed an episode in which a Jedburgh team, *Giles*, had failed to prevent French FFI irregulars from exacting revenge on prisoners from the 2nd SS Parachute Division captured around Carhaix in Finisterre in early August 1944. As the American commander of GILES subsequently reported,

> Even if we had wished to prevent this shooting, we would have been powerless. These men had burned farms and farmers with their wives and children all the way along the main road.[2]

At the end of May 1945, Major Bill Barkworth took Company Sergeant Major Fred Rhodes and four men to Gaggenau, a Black Forest town deep in the French Sector, to exhume bodies buried in the vicinity.

Within two months Barkworth had identified a few of the corpses, confirmed that some *Loyton* prisoners were among them, and arrested one of their murderers, *Oberwachmeister* Heinrich Neuschwanger. Barkworth's methods were unorthodox, often cutting across British and French occupation protocol, but he did achieve results, circulating a list of Nazis implicated by Neuschwanger, and his unit remained in Germany after October 1945 when officially the SAS was disbanded.

Instead of maintaining contact with the SAS, at their headquarters at Wivenhoe in Essex, he communicated direct to the War Crimes Investigation Branch headquarters, then located at 20 Eaton Square, and on 15 November 1945, wrote a summary of his activities and named sixteen Germans, all subordinates of a Gestapo officer, Dr Hans Ernst, based at Saales, who had been responsible for the deaths. Ernst had commanded the *Kommando* zbV6 that, according to witnesses, had arranged for some of the 1 SAS survivors kept at a camp Schirmeck to be imprisoned at Strasbourg, and then taken to his headquarters at St Die, where they were shot.

For twelve months Barkworth's team remained based at Gaggenau, searching prison camps and pursuing leads in an attempt to track down the Ernst's *Kommando*, and in May 1946 eleven defendants were tried at Hamelin. Five were sentenced to death and the remainder received long terms of imprisonment. Altogether, British courts sentenced 240 war criminals to death, out of a total of 1,085 individual prosecutions.

In addition to Barkworth, there were a couple of other similar units. Vera Atkins, formerly the intelligence officer for SOE's F Section, conducted a semi-official investigation to discover the fate of her organisation's women agents who had perished at the Natzweiler and Ravensbruck concentration camps, and in September 1945 a second War Office unit was established to look into the deaths of captured RAF personnel. Additionally, 12 Force, drawn mainly from ex-SOE personnel, often German-Jewish in origin, ranged across the country gathering suspects and housing them in Minden where witness statements were taken prior to charges being brought.

By the end of 1945 the War Crimes Unit had accumulated 1,281prisoners, of whom ninety had been brought to trial, a statistic which suggests that the limited resources devoted to finding, arresting and prosecuting Nazi war criminals were quite effective. Certainly they were legal, for the units' operations were supervised by Colonel Gerald Draper of the Judge Advocate-General's staff, a distinguished solicitor and barrister who after the war was Professor of Law at Sussex University.

This then raises the issue of why the British government allegedly sanctioned the murder of Germans suspected, but not convicted, of war crimes, as alleged by Captain Peter Mason, who describes himself as a veteran of the SAS, having had first-hand experience 'of the fighting in France and the Low Countries'.[3] This is the central charge, or confession, made by Mason in his autobiography, *Official Assassin*, published in 1996, in which he related a series of what he asserted were officially-sponsored murders. The first was of SS *Unterscharfuhrer* Helmut Fokken, in June 1945, by two unnamed British NCOs, supposedly taking revenge for Folken's murder of two maquis guides and an SAS trooper in Strasbourg, and his participation in the removal and disappearance of 130 prisoners from the Natzweiler concentration camp. Mason relates that a corporal and sergeant removed Fokken from a PoW camp, drove him into the countryside and shot him with a single bullet from a pistol into the back of his neck. 'This was the first such act carried out by a team of the 1st Special Service Unit, with the knowledge, but not official sanction of "AG-3- VW", the branch of the War Office charged with the detection and arraignment of Nazi War Criminals.'[4]

Evidently Mason had read Kemp's *The Secret Hunters*, although he made no direct reference to it. His story is about a secret 'search and destroy' hunter team, known as 'Baker'. This was 'loosely attached to the Intelligence Section of the 2nd Special Air Service Regiment, consisting of an anonymous 'Major 'X' of the Field Intelligence Unit',

Corporal Taffy Evans, Corporal Josep Garlinsky, three others, and Sergeant Pete Mason himself. Not to be confused with the distinguished Polish historian Professor Jozef Garlisky, Corporal Garlinsky is described as a talented linguist and Pole who had fought with X Troop of No. 10 Commando.[5]

This unit, drawn from the Pioneer Corps, is itself the stuff of legend, not to mention myth (see *Counterfeit Spies*) and it is curious that such a talented individual, with 'a command of five written and spoken languages'[6] should have gone unnoticed, especially in X Troop which consisted almost entirely of Germans. There was a separate troop, designated No. 6, which was raised in August 1942 from within No 10 (Inter-Allied) Commando and was reserved for Polish personnel, comprising of five officers and eighty-seven other ranks. Initially based at Fairbourne, it was transferred in February 1943 to Caernarvon and was deployed operationally in September to Algiers and then in Italy with XIII Corps. In August 1944, having fought with the 2nd Polish Armoured Brigade at Monte Cassino, No. 6 Troop was designated the Polish Motorized Battalion and participated in the battle to liberate Bologna. In short, the possibility that there was a Polish member of X troop is highly improbable, and tends to cast some doubt on the very existence of 'Team Baker', the seek-and-strike unit described by Mason which supposedly was based at Wildbad, 'a few kilometres to the east' of Gaggenau.[7]

Mason's second victim was Klaus Baur, 'a minor official in the Political Section of the "Abwehr" and for two years had specialised in Soviet Communications, in particular radio signals to front line troops' whose 'termination had been authorised by an unnamed, uniformed brigadier, and an SIS officer named Symes, who stammered and wore a Cambridge University tie.[8] While Garlinsky and Evans gripped Baur's arms, Mason says he killed him with a single shot to the head and comments that by his death, 'British Intelligence had suffered its worse blow, the effect of which would be felt for a decade to come. Of all the ex-Nazi Intelligence people now throwing in their lot with the West, only the now dead Baur had had the key that would have exposed the Soviet mole.'[9]

Upon his return to Gaggenau Mason recalls that Major Barkworth introduced him to an MI5 officer, accompanied by a Special Branch detective who, during two days of debriefing, asked him to identify 'Symes' from a Cambridge University group photograph of undergraduates, but nothing more was said of the matter.

Mason's next mission was to arrest *Standartenfuhrer* Walter Rauff, whom he discovered in an SS camp close to the Italian frontier. After a successful ambush, all the Germans were killed, and a tribunal from Salzburg conducted a brief court of enquiry to confirm Rauff's death, and that of Dr Rudolf Funk. Later Mason was to learn that Funk, Rauff and his assistant Franz Thyssen, had made their escape to South America, leaving behind the bodies of substitutes to be found.

After this episode Mason was sent to Munich to kill SS *Unterscharfuhrer* Leopold Opelt, alias Leopold Segev, formerly a guard at Natzweiler, and latterly a black marketeer trading in penicillin. Mason traced Opelt without difficulty, garotted one of his minders while Garlinsky shot the other one, and then after a brief struggle killed Opelt with a bullet through the heart.

Following this incident Mason, ostensibly still a sergeant, was recruited in London into an unnamed military intelligence organisation by a Major Smyth, based at a barracks near Horse Guards Parade, and instructed to sign the 'Official Secrets Act (1929)'.[10] After training at the Intelligence Corps camp at Maresfield, in Sussex, Mason learned that Smyth was 'on the SIS Training Staff' and that his assistant, an Irish Guardsman named Mike Savage, 'had served with Mr Smyth for five years, accompanying the Norway and Channel Island raids (to take out Quislings)'.[11]

Mason's first mission for Smyth was to Germany, 'to accompany an emissary of the Crown to a location in the American zone of Germany' who would be unaware of his presence. His task was to provide 'security at a distance' for the 'tall, thin, cadaverous man' and travel to the Schloss Kronberg, the ancestral home of the Hesse family, 'to retrieve a quantity of sensitive British papers'.[12] The date of this adventure can be fixed with some certainty, for Mason recalled that the *Daily Herald* had reported on the trial on a charge of treason of John Amery, which had taken place at the Old Bailey on 28 November 1945.

Disguised as a British Army photographer, Mason and Nobby Clarke kept a watch on their quarry as he met Colonel Leo Long and, with his assistance, loaded 'seven or eight heavy trunks' into his car at the castle and then drove them back, via Newhaven, to deliver them to MI5's headquarters in St James's Street.[13]

Exactly what Mason did after this final adventure, and after the unit had been disbanded, can only be guessed at, based on hints contained in the book. For example, he refers to 'being on the "team"' swanning around Europe, looking after Anthony Blunt on what turned out to be a '"Royal" cover up; The Windsor letters!'[14] and recalls that he participated in a NATO exercise in Anglesey, which suggests that he was employed as a soldier until the late 1940s. The only reference to his earlier military career is a single mention of his training at Achnacarry, where he had been taught close combat skills by the legendary Captain Sykes, formerly of the Shanghai police.

The second part of Mason's autobiography is a fascinating account of his post-war recruitment by the Security Service, and his rather curious assignment to penetrate a unit of the Irish Republican Army which was suspected of being in contact with the Czech intelligence service and the Communist Party of Great Britain. According to Mason, he had 'worked closely with Five in the past' and had been recommended to a sub-division of MI5's A Section, which was then headed by a man who 'lived in Sussex and had a fairly large estate nearby' and drove a Rolls-Royce.[15] '"A-1" handled all the equipment needs, from surveillance cameras to untraceable firearms, while "A-2" supplied the personnel to utilize A-1's resources.' Unusually, Mason was interviewed by the Director-General, described as looking 'a little like Douglas Fairbanks' and was 'a yachting man', and then underwent a bizarre initiative test in which he and four other members of the new intake were dropped off in the countryside, in disguise, and set a series of tasks to perform while on the run from the police who had been informed that the group had escaped from a mental institution.[16] Overnight Mason succeeded in eluding the police, avoided arrest for passing counterfeit five pound notes, and bluffed his way into the Post Office's Special Investigations Unit headquarters in Fleet Street where he acquired a special stamp on a document to prove his visit and pass the test.

However, after just two weeks in A-2, Mason was invited to MI5's 'operational department' and was selected for a special mission. He was briefed by Cyril Mills, 'a senior Officer from MI6', and then adopted the identity of another trainee, a Canadian and ex-RCMP officer named Pat O'Shea.[17] Transferred to Hooke House, a former SOE training establishment at Chailey Camp, near Crowborough, where coincidentally Mason had been taught Russian sometime after the war, he was briefed on how to masquerade as a Canadian and then was infiltrated into the CPGB (Communist Party of Great Britain) while the real O'Shea, who had completed his 'entrance paper for the Security Service based on the transcripts from the Gourzenko debriefing' was posted to the 'Government Communication Establishment at Cheltenham'.[18] Before being deployed into the field, in Newhaven, Mason was briefed by 'Dennis Cholmondeley from F-Branch' who had displayed photographs of CPGB members who had 'been observed associating with low-level STB (Czechoslovakia State Security) agents abroad, and are known IRA sympathisers'.[19]

Mason's adventures as 'O'Shea', a fugitive Canadian who had been charged with an unspecified breach of security, are remarkable. Posing as a member of the Communist Party of Canada, he was passed along an underground network through London to Ireland, and joined a group of IRA activists who used the cover of a travelling circus to acquire weapons in Europe. Mason joins them and embarks on an adventure which takes him to Germany, and ends back in Ireland on the border with Ulster. The IRA cell is wiped out in a mysterious explosion which destroys their headquarters, a farm 'located a few miles south of the Irish border between Armagh and Monaghan in Eire', and Mason returns to England as a hero.[20]

Mason's mission takes him to London where, despite MI5 surveillance, he establishes contact with an IRA family, and travels to Fishguard with Sheila Collins, a twenty-year-old Sinn Feiner. Once in Dublin they acquired a pre-arranged, two-year-old Mini, and drove to the Collins family farm, two hours from Dundalk, which provided pasture for a particular breed of circus ponies, and also housed an impressive IRA arsenal of weapons, including machine-guns from the First World War and 'Semtex Z, a fairly recently developed odourless plastic of a very stable nature'.[21] He learned that two of Sheila's relatives were in prison in England, and then was introduced to another five IRA men, all of whom he knew from 'the files of "Known Terrorists."' The following day he was given a Travel Identity Card in the name of Brian Callaghan and was hidden in a horsebox for a journey to Rotterdam with three stallions.

Apparently this was a regular route for smuggling people and weapons from Eastern Europe, where the Collins circus had its winter quarters, to the Irish Republic. At a petrol station in Rheda, Mason was able to slip away from his companions and telephone a report to the British authorities in Bonn, and at Helmstedt they crossed into East Germany to continue their journey to Berlin. At Checkpoint Charlie they received clearance to drive into the East, and finally reach the circus's winter quarters early the following morning, where he was to remain for 'some weeks'.[22] After obtaining a work permit he was to travel further, into Poland, to deliver some horses to an equestrian centre housed in an old cavalry school, and conduct an affair with a Countess Olga von Hapsburg, an accomplished horsewoman who had tried out for the West German Olympic equestrian team, and accompanied him to an SS reunion and to a museum dedicated to the SS and the *Sicherheitsdienst*.

Here he was able to murder, with a single shot to the head from a concealed 9mm PP Walther, Otto Ortgies, Hitler's chosen head of the *Werwolf* Nazi resistance organisation. Mason concealed the murder as a suicide and later learned that the Nazis were supplying the IRA with gold bullion. Retrieving a lock-picking kit from his innersole, he gained entry into the museum's archive to photograph the content (together with the rest of a Nazi filing-cabinet) with a miniature Riga-Minox camera he had hidden in his hairbrush. Having exhausted three Air Ministry high resolution films, Mason posted them from Frankfurt, via registered mail, to a 'safe-drop' in East Berlin.

Precisely dating Mason's adventures is a difficult task, but there are several clues in his account, and a photograph of him, pictured as a circus hand, is captioned in the '1950s'. A better indication is a reference to Ian Fleming's *Live and Let Die*, the James Bond novel which was first published in 1954, so clearly the events described could not have taken place any earlier. However, he also mentions the American AR-15 rifle, which was not introduced into the U.S. Army as the M-16 until 1962. Curiously, the context of the reference is to an eighteen-year-old British 'National Serviceman' shot dead while on patrol with just such a weapon on the streets of Belfast, but that would have been impossible as National Service ended in Britain in 1961, and British troops were not sent onto the streets of Belfast until 1969. The reference to the Czech-made Semtex Z is also curious, as this explosive was not developed until more than a decade after the events Mason describes.

Driving through Checkpoint Charlie would also have been difficult during the 1950s, as the Berlin Wall was only constructed in August 1960. Another clue is the reference to a 'two-year-old Mini',[23] which firmly places the time frame as being after 1961, as the Mini was not produced until 1959.

The author also mentions that during his trip to the Continent a strict log was maintained on the vehicle because of the Foot and Mouth regulations, then tightly enforced because of recent outbreaks. Unfortunately, this is not an especially reliable guide because in the post-war era (and, indeed, from 1917) there were outbreaks in every year in the UK, with the exception of the period from June 1962 to April 1965. Between 1954 and 1960 there were significant outbreaks, with more than 101 cases reported in the first four months of 1961. If, on the evidence of the Mini and the Armalite, Mason's experience is pinned down to the year 1962, then the reference to Foot and Mouth is odd.

There is also a puzzle about why MI5 should have been taking an interest in the activities of the IRA in the 1950s, when the organisation was virtually dormant, apart from an unsuccessful 'border campaign' between 1956 and 1962. The only major incident that occurred during the period, which involved a significant explosion, took place in November 1957 at Edentubber when five republicans were killed when their landmine exploded prematurely. The role of the Security Service is quite peculiar because at that time responsibility for monitoring Irish republicanism rested with the Special Branch of the Royal Ulster Constabulary, and it was to be more than a decade before MI5 established a single permanent liaison officer in Belfast.

Even on the assumption that Mason's confusing timeframe is essentially correct, his details about the Security Service are hopelessly wrong, and such information as he retails appear to have been gleaned from identifiable, published sources, such as Peter Wright's *SpyCatcher*.[24] Although Wright had spent much of his professional career in the Security Service, his ghost-writer, Paul Greengrass, did not, and the speed with which he completed the manuscript meant he failed to avoid some errors, some of which Mason evidently picked up. For example, Mason recalls a visit to the GPO's mail interception office 'just off Fleet Street',[25] which corresponds to Wright's mistaken description of the identical unit which actually was located a considerable distance away, at Mount Pleasant. Thus Mason seems to have relied on Wright's error to perpetuate the misidentification. Similarly, Mason refers to the Soviet defector Igor Gouzenko as 'Gourzenko'[26], a blunder that nobody with a knowledge of Canada's most famous espionage case, which occurred in September 1945, could make. None of the other details mentioned concerning the Security Service stand any scrutiny. The Director of A Branch was not a millionaire Sussex landowner, but actually Malcolm Cumming, a former Rifle Brigade officer. There was never a Dennis Cholmondeley in MI5, and although there was a Charles Cholmondeley, he never served in the section attributed to him by Mason. Nor was the Director-General (then Sir Dick White, until 1956 when he was succeeded by Sir Roger Hollis) a 'Douglas Fairbanks lookalike' and certainly not 'a yachting man'.[27] Cyril Mills, described as 'an MI6 officer', certainly never was (he had been a wartime MI5 case officer) and after the war he was running his family business, the Bertram Mills Circus, and no Whitehall insider would ever refer to the 'Government Communications Establishment', when GCHQ's true name is the Government Communications Headquarters, a title unchanged since 1943. Equally, MI5 did not, as claimed, buy up the leases of 'any adjacent buildings' to its headquarters at Leconfield House. Although it did possess three other properties in the neighbourhood (being the old Ministry of Education site in Curzon Street, a mews off South Audley Street and a flat used as a safe-house on the corner of Mount Street) the Security Service's office accommodation was deliberately dispersed across London.

Leaving aside the tell-tale details, could any of the rest of the narrative be genuine? Mason's own claimed career is hopelessly flawed, and his admission to having murdered Helmut Fokken, Klaus Baur, Leopold Opelt and Otto Ortgies does not stand much scrutiny either. Of the four, there is only a record, or reference in an official War Office file, from the Judge Advocate General's department dated April 1946, to *Unterscharsfuhrer* Opelt as a suspect wanted in connection with the murder of four women and thirty SAS, and in another file as being linked to the murder of sixteen British parachutists. There is no trace of Fokken, Baur or Ortieges ever having existed.

Given the myriad inconsistencies and contradictions in Mason's account, and in the absence of any corroboration, it must be unlikely that any of his tale is true. Such information about him that can be verified suggests that he once owned an antiques business in Lewes, Sussex, and ran a riding business with his wife, Pru Mason, until they moved to rural Bluffton in Alberta, Canada, where he traded in military memorabilia. Aside from these vague details of his post-war life, nothing more can be verified.

Chapter 2

Nemesis in Northern Ireland

The allegation that the 22nd Special Air Service regiment had been conducting a policy of abduction and murder in Northern Ireland, leaving bodies buried in shallow graves, was one that might have been calculated to inflame public opinion in a province already overburdened by crime, tragedy, terrorism and personal loss, and concerns about an unofficial 'shoot-to-kill' policy. Throughout the 'troubles' in Northern Ireland much attention had focused on the myriad security and intelligence agencies engaged in combating terrorism, but their methods inevitably have been the source of controversy and speculation, and two charges have recurred frequently, that of 'freelancing', and collusion. The first claim is based on the proposition that SAS personnel often operate outside the law, and take it into their own hands, while the basis of the second is that it is partisan, and has conspired to help the loyalists against the nationalists. In a divided, sectarian community such as Northern Ireland, where it takes very little to raise suspicions, such issues are extremely sensitive, but the fact that they are frequently raised does not necessarily make them true.

Naturally the role of the Special Air Service regiment, which invariably is to be found at the forefront of counter-terrorist operations, has been a focus of attention as their intervention tends to leave rather more visible results than the activities of MI5, SIS or GCHQ, which are also actively engaged across Ulster, targeting the Provisional IRA (PIRA) as well as the loyalist paramilitaries.

The SAS was deployed publicly to the province, actually to South Armagh, first in January 1976 at the request of Prime Minister Harold Wilson, following the murder of ten Protestant workmen in what became known as the Kingsmills massacre, and has gained an awesome reputation for conducting lengthy covert surveillance operations,

11

ambushing armed Provisional IRA terrorists before they can launch their own attacks. In addition, the regiment has trained other units, including specialist police squads and other components of the British Army, such as the 14th Intelligence Company and the Force Research Unit. '14 Int' or simply 'the Det', as it was known, was the successor of the Mobile Reaction Force (MRF), a clandestine unit created by Brigadier Frank Kitson, the Commander Land Forces, Northern Ireland, in 1971. Disbanded in early 1973, following a couple of operational failures and the exposure of the Four Square Laundry and a massage parlour as its commercial fronts, the Detachment had taken over responsibility for the Army's covert surveillance activities and operated in the province at three bases, under cover titles such as 4 Field Survey Troop, Royal Engineers, and 216 Signals Troop, based at Castledillon and Ballykelly.

At the outset, the Det consisted of almost half of the SAS's B Squadron, about thirty men, who were 'debadged' for the task. In parallel, the RUC Special Branch operated its own equivalent of the Det, a surveillance unit designated E4 within which a 'Bronze Section' undertook covert surveillance operations. The Bronze Section proved unsuccessful and in 1976 a specialist sub-group, E4A, was formed under the leadership of a Detective Chief Inspector. In addition, the SB ran a completely separate agent-handling organisation, E3. Thus, at the time the SAS was officially declared to be in the bandit country of South Armagh, both the Army and the RUC were competing to run (often overlapping) clandestine operations.

Only one passenger and the Catholic driver had survived the Kingsmills killings, an atrocity carried out by the self-styled 'South Armagh Republican Action Force', allegedly in retaliation for the recent murder of five local Catholics by loyalist gunmen. These incidents marked the official beginning of the SAS's operations in Northern Ireland, although individual members of the regiment had been operational in the province since 1969, when D Squadron was deployed briefly at Newtonards, in the Mourne Mountains, and other members of the regiment undertook some short, individual, intelligence-gathering missions,

The very first SAS mission to Northern Ireland had taken place two years earlier, at the end of January 1974, when eleven men from B Squadron, fresh from Oman, had been ill-prepared for their assignment. A former UDR soldier, William Black, had been shot and wounded when he chanced upon a six-man patrol hidden in a derelict cottage on land he rented at Tully West, County Down. As, at the time, he was carrying a .22

rifle, he was shot by a soldier armed with a Patchet silenced sub-machinegun, and subsequently was paid £17,000 damages by the Army in compensation. Black was not a terrorist, but had stumbled into a covert observation post manned by police and soldiers who had been on a surveillance operation for the past three days. Confronted with the unexpected appearance of an armed man, one of the soldiers had reacted with three shots which hit an innocent individual.

The arrival of sixty men from D Squadron at Bessbrook Mill, in a Protestant village four miles from the border, in January 1976, commanded by Major (later General Sir) Michael Rose, was intended to 'stamp out cross-border banditry and murder',[1] and was followed in rotation by troops from B Squadron, and then in April 1977 by A Squadron. Mike Rose's D Squadron had been selected for the task because it had just returned from Dhofar, the secret war conducted in southern Oman over the previous six years to protect the Anglophile Sultan from rebel insurgents. Their first success occurred on the night of 15 April 1976, after three days of covert surveillance, when a well-known PIRA terrorist, twenty-five-year-old Peter Cleary, was arrested as he visited the home of his girlfriend's sister at Tievecrum, near Forkhill. His appearance had followed soon after a helicopter had been fired on as it came in to land at Crossmaglen. Intelligence had suggested that Cleary had been meeting his fiancé Shirley Hulme there, and the young man, known to hold the rank of a PIRA 'staff captain' was captured without a gunfight, although he had attempted unsuccessfully to make a break for the Irish border, just sixty yards from the house. However, as the four soldiers waited in a neighbouring field for a Puma helicopter to collect them, Cleary made another bid to escape and was hit by three rounds fired from a Self-Loading Rifle by the SAS officer standing guard over him. At the subsequent coroner's inquest, the soldier said that Cleary had leapt to his feet as the helicopter approached, and had made a grab for him, so he had responded instinctively by shooting him dead.

This episode, together with a less lethal incident the previous month, showed that the SAS, with its reputation for 'firepower, speed and aggression', meant business. A twenty-three year-old PIRA activist, Sean McKenna, was arrested at Killeen, but he insisted, shortly before he received a twenty-five-year prison sentence for attempted murder, that he had been abducted in the middle of the night, at gunpoint, from his home at Edentubber, North Louth, across the border in the Republic. The Army denied that any incursion into Eire had been made, and insisted the SAS had stumbled across McKenna who was drunk, and emphatically north of the frontier.

13

Early the following year, in January 1977, the SAS's lethal reputation was fully established when a twenty-year-old labourer, Seamus Harvey, was shot dead as he emerged on a Sunday afternoon near Drummakaval from a dark blue Datsun wearing a balaclava hood and carrying an ammunition bandolier and a sawn-off shotgun. A waiting SAS G Squadron patrol had challenged him and as he raised his weapon he was killed, but a fierce firefight ensued with other hidden gunmen, one of whom was thought to have been wounded. The subsequent autopsy on Harvey showed that in the confusion of the battle he had also been hit by his own side.

There were no further 'contacts' with the SAS in South Armagh for the next twelve months, word having spread of the SAS's presence. Indeed, according to Sergeant Ken Connor of D Squadron, who is usually a reliable source on matters concerning the SAS, 'in the eight years after Harold Wilson's very public deployment of the Regiment only nine IRA had been shot by the SAS, and in the five years from December 1978 to December 1983, not a single IRA man was killed in SAS operations'.[2] During that period two PIRA gunmen had been killed in Londonderry, but the plain-clothes officer who shot them on 28 May 1981 had been a member of 'the Det'. Also, the RUC had shot five republicans in late 1982 (and one innocent civilian, caught in the crossfire), but again these incidents were not related to the SAS. To understand the fuller picture, it is worth noting that between 1969 and 1993 the RUC was responsible for the deaths of fifty-one people, of whom eighteen were paramilitaries. The Army figures were 294 dead, of whom 136 were paramilitaries, whereas the republicans had killed 749 civilians, and the loyalists had claimed the lives of 899 civilians. These statistics are contradicted by other, partisan observers, such as Raymond Murray who claimed in *The SAS in Ireland* that between 'December 1977 and the end of 1978 the SAS and undercover soldiers shot dead 11 people'.[3]

Whereas there have been occasions when SAS personnel have been criticised for the use of excessive force, such as when in March 1988 three well-known IRA bombers were interdicted in Gibraltar and shot dead, these incidents invariably have been the subject of rigorous independent investigation, and even a criminal trial, thereby demonstrating that the regiment is not above the rule of law. Furthermore, the SAS successfully apprehend alive three times the number of terrorists that died in their meticulously planned and well-executed ambushes.

Almost inevitably SAS operations have been regarded by some as controversial, partly because of the necessary secrecy that surrounds their techniques, but often because of the unorthodox weaponry and high level of firepower they bring to bear on their adversaries. Few Irish republican terrorists have survived a direct encounter with the SAS, and in contrast the regiment has suffered minimal casualties in Ulster, with the loss of a single officer, Captain Herbert Westmacott of G Squadron, in a firefight in the Antrim Road, Belfast, in May 1980. Not surprisingly, much mythology surrounds the well-armed, impressively trained troops, and occasionally the speculation acquires some currency, such as when Captain Robert Nairac was murdered by a PIRA gunman in May 1977, partly in the mistaken belief that he was an undercover SAS officer. In fact, contrary to so much of what has been written about him, Nairac, who was awarded a posthumous George Cross, never served in the regiment, but had acted in a liaison role with the Royal Ulster Constabulary.

Nairac's murder raised much speculation about his background and career, and in particular linked him to the mysterious death in the Republic in January 1975 of James Green, a twenty-eight year-old father of three and a senior figure in the PIRA in Lurgan. An escapee from Long Kesh in 1973, when he had walked out of the prison dressed as his brother, a priest, and on the run, Green had been shot dead in an isolated farmhouse on a mountainside deep inside the Republic, and the original allegation, made in 1989 by Captain Fred Holroyd in *War Without Honour*,[4] that Nairac had participated in the unauthorised shooting, had always been denied. Holroyd had been an Army undercover officer in Lisburn who had served as a liaison officer at Portadown with the RUC Special Branch, and claimed that he had been shown a Polaroid photograph of the Green murder scene. He insisted that it had been Nairac who had produced the photo at the Army's Mahon Road camp in Portadown as proof of his boast that he had participated in the murder. Others retorted that several forensic photos, taken of the crime scene by the Gardai, had circulated within the Northern Ireland Headquarters. After he had been removed from his job Holroyd had undergone psychiatric treatment, but has always insisted that this was to prevent him from making some unwelcome allegations and disclosures about the Army's undercover role in Northern Ireland's dirty war.

However, in 1994, Shaun Clarke wrote *Soldier E: SAS, Sniper Fire in Belfast*, in which the author gave a graphic description of the Green incident, naming 'Captain Dubois', Sergeants Blake and Harris of 14th Int, and 'Lieutenant Randolph Cranfield of the SAS' as having been the four killers who had driven into Eire in January 1975 in an unmarked red Morris Marina 14 Int Q car.[5] In Clarke's version, Green had been renamed 'O'Halloran' and, having shot a pair of Alsatian guard dogs with a silenced Sterling, the two officers broke into the house and emptied a magazine of thirteen 9mm rounds from Cranfield's Browning Hi-Power semi-automatic into O'Halloran as he ate his breakfast in his pyjamas.

According to Clarke, O'Halloran had been a source for 14 Int but somehow had learned the identities of ten other informants, and betrayed them. MI5 had then taken on O'Halloran as an informant, having ignored the Army's advice, and Nairac had been determined to take revenge for the ten agents, who supposedly had been assassinated by the PIRA 'within a week'.[6]

This disclosure, apparently from a former member of the SAS, completely undermines the official view, postulated whenever the issue was raised, that the murder of James F. Green, in County Monaghan, was nothing whatever to do with the British Army. Perhaps significantly, Clarke also noted that six months before the O'Halloran murder, the SAS had been responsible for the abduction of a PIRA suspect from Eire, who had been snatched in the Republic and brought back 'to be recaptured', an episode that matched what had happened to Sean McKenna. Clarke gives in reported speech the statement attributed to Cranfield that 'six months ago we crossed the border to pick up an IRA commander and deposit him back in Northern Ireland, to be arrested by the RUC and brought to trial'.[7]

Clarke obviously had changed the names of the two principal officers in his book, Lieutenant Cranfield and Captain Dubois, but his account of Cranfield's own murder, having been abducted while on an undercover visit to a pub in a remote, staunchly Republican area, is very close to what really happened to Robert Nairac, who was killed after he had been abducted as he left the crowded Three Steps Inn at Camlough and taken over the border to be interrogated, tortured and shot in a field. Clarke appears to have deliberately transposed some of Nairac's biographical details and attributed them to 'Dubois', who he described as 'a former Oxford boxing blue and Catholic Guards officer', which exactly matches Nairac's real background as he was a Roman Catholic, a Grenadier, and had won a boxing blue at Lincoln College, Oxford. Cranfield, on the other hand, is referred to as 'formerly of the King's Own Scottish Borderers and the Parachute Regiment, had gone to Ampleforth', actually the Benedictine monastery where Nairac in fact had been educated. Equally, 'Dubois' is obviously Julian 'Tony' Ball MBE MC, Nairac's senior officer in 14th Int and once a private soldier in the King's Own Scottish Borderers. He had later transferred to the Parachute Regiment and then served twice in 22 SAS, but was to be killed in a car accident in 1981 in Oman, where he was leading the Sultan's forces. Thus, twelve years after the death of Nairac, and eight years after Ball had been killed, Holroyd had linked Nairac to Green's murder, and a further five years later Clarke had claimed Nairac and Ball had acted together.

The picture offered by Clarke is of plenty of authentic detail, apparently mixed in with some fiction so as to present a slightly distorted account of true events. For example, Robert Nairac's body was never recovered from the murder scene and was thought to have been disposed of in a nearby pig farm or meat processing plant, but in Clarke's version he was found, lying close to two PIRA youths whom he had succeeded in shooting before he himself was killed. Another curiosity is Clarke's assertion that Cranfield had been 'one of a small number of SAS officers attached to' 14th Intelligence Company, whereas Nairac was never in the SAS, but had acted as a liaison officer between the SAS, the RUC Special Branch and the local brigade headquarters.

However, the real impact of Clarke's account is in the detail of his supposedly authentic account of the 'O'Halloran' murder, and his central charge that Robert Nairac had shot John Green. But was this really true? The facts that emerge shed some interesting light on Clarke, and clearly identify the source of his information, which could not possibly have come from the SAS or, as claimed, one of its members, the anonymous 'Soldier E'. As regards the Green murder itself, there were very detailed police investigations on both sides of the border during which a rather different set of circumstances was to be revealed. Green had been shot, not with a single automatic, but with two guns, a Luger and a Spanish-made Star pistol. The suspect car, in which the two (not four) killers had arrived on the scene was thought to have been a white Mercedes or Audi, and the gunmen were believed to have been well-known loyalists, and one of them was known to have been involved in the planning of the Miami Showband massacre, an atrocity in July 1975 in which a minivan carrying a group of Catholic pop musicians had been stopped at a bogus checkpoint and three of them shot. A survivor described having been pulled over at a vehicle checkpoint near Banbridge in County Down after a gig and questioned by a group of ten men in military uniforms who then attempted to place a bomb in the vehicle. The device exploded as two terrorists tried to prime it, and they were both killed. Shocked by this unplanned development, the other uniformed gunmen shot the musicians in a bungled attempt to eliminate any witnesses, and fled, leaving two survivors badly wounded to tell the story. Forensic examination of the bullets that were recovered from the body of trumpeter Brian McCoy, who had been driving the minibus, showed they had been fired from a Star pistol, the very same weapon that was to be used to shoot John Green six months later. Indeed, ballistic tests were to link the gun to four other loyalist killings. On this evidence it is extraordinarily unlikely that Nairac was implicated in any way in Green's murder, unless he was also involved in the Miami Showband massacre and the other loyalist murders. Indeed, further information that the police investigation turned up effectively rules him out completely. For example, the incriminating Polaroid photo, mentioned by Holroyd as having been circulated by Nairac as proof of his participation in the murder, was recovered by the police, and it turned out to be an official crime scene photo, not taken at the time of the murder (as Holroyd had claimed) but more than a dozen hours later, as indicated by the congealed blood around the body.

The police learned that Green had taken refuge that evening at the home of an elderly Republican sympathiser, Gerry Carville, and had been shot by a prominent figure in the Portadown branch of the Ulster Volunteer Force who suspected that Carville had been involved in the murder of his brother. Although the UVF man was definitely implicated in the Miami Showband atrocity, and he was questioned by the police, no admissible evidence could be found and he was not charged with either crime. However, on 17 March 1975, the UVF held a press conference in the Shankill Road and released a list of six recent murders that the organisation took responsibility for, and among them was Green's name. Apparently he had not been their intended victim, who actually had been Gerry Carville, the owner of the farm which the UVF believed had been used by the PIRA as a safe-house. According to the UVF, one of their own members had been abducted and murdered at the farm, and the revenge attack had killed Green by mistake, but since the younger man was an even more senior republican, the UVF had been happy to leave the impression that he had been their true target.

Having established the true motive for Green's murder, where does that leave Clarke's assertion that 'O'Halloran' had been an informer for the Army who had betrayed ten of its 'grade-one agents', and then had been taken over by MI5? The reality is that there never was a week in which the Provisionals executed ten Army informants, either in 1974 (or at any rate prior to Green's murder on 10 January 1975) or at any other time, and Green certainly was never an Army informant. Altogether, over the length of the troubles since 1969, the Provos are estimated to have killed approximately twenty-four of their own men whom they suspected to be 'touts' for the British but most, including a few disappearances that were considered particularly embarrassing for the republican movement, are now well-documented and acknowledged. However, none of these murders conform to the description of occurring during a week-long bloodbath as a result of an MI5 leak.

Clarke's tale undoubtedly comes from Fred Holroyd, who claimed that an SAS officer whom he had spoken to had shot himself when he had been overcome with grief at the news that ten agents had been murdered by the Provisionals. According to Holroyd, the officer had walked into a bunker at Lisburn and had committed suicide, but once again, there is no record of any such incident, Herbert Westmacott being the only SAS officer whose life was lost in Northern Ireland. However, this tale bears a resemblance to Clarke's version, in which an NCO, distraught at the betrayal of ten agents, is described as having hanged himself.

Clarke's version of the death of 'Captain Cranfield' is a further example of embroidery, for an intensive police investigation on both sides of the border resulted in the conviction of Liam Townson, a known Provisional aged twenty-four from Meigh, near Newry, who confessed to Gardai detectives in Dublin to having shot Nairac at a bridge over the river Flurry in the Ravensdale Forest. A joiner by trade, and the son of a former British soldier, Townson was sentenced in Dublin to life imprisonment but released in 1990 after thirteen years, and five others were arrested in Northern Ireland and charged with offences related to Nairac's abduction from the Three Steps pub, and his murder. All gave detailed statements about precisely what had happened, implicating each other, and described how Nairac had made two attempts to escape before he had been shot dead by Townson, following a savage beating by several of the men involved in the abduction. In the meleé, one of the main players, Terry McCormick, was accidentally shot by another PIRA man, Pat Maguire. At their trial in Belfast, Gerard Fearon and Thomas Morgan were convicted of murder and sentenced to life imprisonment, Danny O'Rourke received ten years for manslaughter, Michael McCoy five years for kidnapping and Owen Rocks received two years for withholding information from the RUC. McCormick and Patrick Maguire later fled to the United States and settled in New Jersey, where Maguire works in Dumont as a builder. In May 2008 Kevin Crilly returned to Northern Ireland where he was arrested and charged with Nairac's murder, but on May 2011 he was acquitted at his trial in Belfast, the judge ruling that the prosecution had failed to prove that Crilly had prior intent.

Close examination of Clarke's book suggests that, far from being the recollections of 'Soldier E', it is a compilation developed from just two sources, Fred Holroyd's controversial, but discredited, *War Without Honour*, and a second, entirely genuine memoir, *Soldier I: SAS Eighteen Years in the Elite Force*, by Michael Paul Kennedy.[8] This latter book is the wholly authentic biography of Sergeant Pete Warne of B Squadron and contains an episode in which his unmarked car, on patrol in West Belfast, is the subject of an attempted hijacking by two youths in the Springfield Road. Warne and his fellow soldier make their escape and later failed to pick out their would-be hijackers at an identification parade held at the Castlereagh police interrogation centre. Curiously, the almost identical scene is reproduced in *Soldier E*, with two significant differences. In Clarke's version the SAS men fire on their armed hijackers and kill one of them, and successfully spot the other at the subsequent identification parade. Whilst the first version, by Michael Paul Kennedy, was true, the second offering, from Shaun Clarke, was sheer invention. However, in 1998, a former soldier decorated with the Military Medal, Nick Curtis, published his memoirs of his service in Northern Ireland in *Faith and Duty*, and gave a further version on the controversy of Green's murder, and offered a completely new claim concerning the death of Peter Cleary.

A non-commissioned officer in the Green Howards who had joined up in 1964, Curtis had been transferred to the Intelligence Corps in 1974 for duty in Northern Ireland. According to him, 'the word on the grapevine was that Benny Green had been whacked not by the UVF but by a hit-quad comprising Nairac and two of the SAS'. There was 'a widely held belief that he supplied information to the UVF and the UDA, enabling them to take out Provos'.[9] But although Curtis recalled having been on undercover patrols with Nairac, his knowledge of the Green murder seems sketchy, recalling that the terrorist had 'finally holed up in the farmhouse of a Republican sympathiser. The "safe" house turned out to be more dangerous than expected. For Green it proved fatal as he was ambushed and shot dead.'[10] Yet Green had only been a visitor at the house, and was not 'ambushed', which implies he had been trapped by assailants who had been lying in wait for him.

This example of embroidery is not unique, and may be one of the reasons why the SAS takes exceptional measures to enforce the contracts signed by all SAS personnel in which they undertake not to publish details of their military service with the regiment. Because many of the SAS's real operations are sometimes so extraordinary that they become the stuff of legend, it is not entirely surprising that fantasists are drawn to invent imaginary careers for themselves. Most often their claims are fanciful and do no lasting damage, but in the case of Sergeant Paul

Bruce, the result in November 1995 was *The Nemesis File*,[11] supposedly an authentic account of how the SAS had murdered numerous terrorist suspects in Northern Ireland, and then buried the evidence.

Bruce claimed that in 1971, as a vehicle mechanic in the Royal Electrical and Mechanical Engineers, he was transferred to 22 SAS and sent to Northern Ireland where he operated in an undercover, four-man squad for twelve months, to kill PIRA suspects. His first murders allegedly took place in the Ardoyne area of north Belfast in October 1971 when he says he shot two men in the street in front of a shop.[12] Altogether twenty-seven targets were singled out for abduction and execution, with their bodies buried in shallow graves in the Tardree Forest, near Ballymena in County Antrim, and at another site near the Blackskull Road at Dromore outside Lurgan, in County Armagh. Bruce also insisted that he had been ordered to drive into Catholic districts and shoot innocent passers-by so as to stir up sectarian unrest.

The first question to be asked was whether the SAS had been deployed in Northern Ireland in 1971 and 1972, when Bruce claimed to have served there.[13] They were not, but it is true that the MRF occasionally had accommodated SAS personnel on temporary secondments. The second question was the identity of Paul Bruce, and the genesis of his book which included several photographs of the author pointing to various locations where he asserted bodies had been dumped in trenches.

Paul Bruce turned out to be a psychiatric patient named Paul Inman, a former soldier from Weston-Super-Mare who had a long history of mental illness. Furthermore, it turned out, during the course of an investigation conducted by the RUC, that *The Nemesis File* had been written not by Inman, but Nicholas Davies, a former *Daily Mirror* journalist who was the foreign news editor when he had been dismissed by the newspaper in 1991 following allegations that, as a sideline, he had been engaged in selling weapons to Third World countries from his home in south London. Davies had worked particularly closely with the newspaper's proprietor, Robert Maxwell and, according to the American investigative reporter Seymour Hersh, the pair had developed a business partnership together, trading in military equipment and negotiating huge contracts with foreign clients, such as the Sri Lankan government. Hersh supported his allegations, contained in *The Samson Option*,[14] with copies of invoices and other documents removed from Davies's home by his estranged wife. Despite convincing public denials, and the backing of his newspaper, Davies was exposed as a liar by an American arms dealer who confirmed that he had only known Davies as another supplier in the same market. Davies issued further robust denials, insisting he had not met the person in question and had not even been in America on the dates cited, but was floored when photographs were produced to prove the allegation. Davies was promptly sacked from the *Mirror*, and subsequently lost an action for wrongful dismissal brought against the editor, Richard Stott.

Significantly, Davies had written *The Nemesis File* as a work of fiction, but had been put in touch with Inman by his publisher, John Blake, another tabloid journalist. The result of this collaboration was the book described as 'the true story of an SAS execution squad',[15] but under interrogation Inman acknowledged that the entire tale was fiction. Not so his sequel, a more factually-based account of the work of the Force Research Unit, a clandestine military intelligence organisation which employed a former soldier, Brian Nelson, as an agent to penetrate the loyalist paramilitaries. Codenamed 1033, Brian Nelson had been born in Belfast and had served, until he was discharged at the age of nineteen, in the Black Watch. In 1975 he served three years of a five-year sentence for possession of weapons and explosives, and by then he was a well-established member of the Ulster Defence Association. By September 1986, when he was working as a decorator in Germany, Nelson had been approached by the FRU to act as an agent, and when he returned to Belfast, and the UDA, he was working as a taxi-driver, had bought a house just off the Springmartin Road, with money ostensibly won on the German lottery, and had been appointed the UDA's 'intelligence officer'.

For the next three years Nelson and his handlers managed the delicate balance of keeping the FRU informed of the UDA's plans, while collecting sufficient information about republican suspects to sustain his position within the organisation. The extent to which Nelson exploited his relationship with the FRU to gain access to the Army's confidential lists of PIRA activists, and trade tips which saved the lives of potential targets for assassination, was to go to the heart of a police investigation later conducted by (Sir) John Stevens into allegations of collusion between the security forces and loyalist paramilitaries. Stevens wanted Nelson charged with conspiracy to murder, convinced that the FRU's agent had worked to his own agenda and had manipulated his handlers into supplying him with valuable information that had put lives at risk. The FRU believed Nelson had risked his life to produce 730 separate reports concerning 217 people, and had prevented numerous acts of terrorism by allowing the Army and police to mount apparently random vehicle checkpoints in the path of UDA gunmen on their way to murder a target. Was Nelson, as the FRU's senior officer, Colonel Gordon Kerr, testified at his trial in January 1992, an exceptionally brave man who had saved many lives or, as the prosecution insisted, a ruthless opportunist who played one side off against the other? Whatever the truth, Nelson was sentenced to ten years' imprisonment, to be served in Bristol, and released in 1994, with fifteen other charges, including two of murder, dropped. He died while visiting Florida, of a brain haemorrhage, in January 2003.

The controversy surrounding the FRU's relationship with Nelson, and the allegations of collusion, were to continue for years after Nelson's release, for when Stevens was appointed Commissioner of the Metropolis he reopened an investigation into a fire that had all but destroyed his inquiry team's office, inside the RUC's supposedly secure compound at Knock, on the eve of Nelson's arrest. Stevens learned that the arson had been a deliberate attempt by the FRU to protect Nelson, and had succeeded in destroying much of the evidence accumulated in Belfast, not realising that it had all been duplicated at another secure location, in the Cambridgeshire Police's headquarters.

Concerns about collusion were to be exacerbated by a Channel 4 television documentary on the subject made in 1991 in the *Dispatches* series, by a Belfast journalist, Sean McPhilemy, who subsequently wrote *The Committee: Political Assassination in Northern Ireland*[16] in 1998 for publication in the United States. As we have seen, rumours of collusion between the security forces and the loyalists had circulated in Ulster since John Green's murder back in 1975, or certainly since Holroyd's allegations in 1989, but there had never been any real evidence, and certainly no creditable eye-witness testimony until McPhilemy announced that he had found a disaffected loyalist willing to reveal the existence of a massive conspiracy that included, among others, an unnamed currently serving Assistant Chief Constable; Graham Long, a British Telecom engineer and former SAS soldier; Assistant Chief Constable Trevor Forbes, until recently the head of the RUC Special Branch, and more than fifty other influential Protestants, among them prominent businessmen, churchmen and politicians.

According to McPhilemy's witness, who was recorded in silhouette on screen and was kept anonymous, a hitherto unknown body, the 'Ulster Loyalist Central Coordinating Committee'[17] had planned numerous loyalist murders and directed the activities of a notorious killer, Billy Wright (who was himself later to be shot by an INLA assassin in the Maze Prison in December 1997). The Committee had been created in 1986 but had become active in the summer of 1990 and was headed by an executive at the Ulster Bank, William Abernethy, whose brother Colin had been murdered by the PIRA in 1988, and could rely on Forbes, who ran a small group of police sympathisers known as the 'Inner Force'. When the Committee selected a target, Wright was the triggerman, and Forbes's men covered his tracks, or so 'Source A' claimed. In a filmed interview McPhilemy's star witness recalled how, as a member of the Committee, he actually had been present at a meeting held at the Dolphin Bar in Lurgan at the end of September 1991 when a young Catholic, Denis Carville, had been selected for a reprisal killing following the PIRA's recent murder of an Ulster Defence Regiment soldier, Colin McCullough.

McPhilemy's documentary threw yet more petrol onto the smoldering embers of allegations of collusion, not least because Forbes had run the RUC Special Branch since September 1982 and had been at the epicentre of an incident that had been regarded as the most devastating example of an undeclared, deliberate 'shoot-to-kill' policy adopted by the police in Northern Ireland. The case which became known simply as 'the hayshed', concerned a cache of PIRA weapons and 1,000 pounds of explosives hidden in 1982 in a farm building outside Lurgan owned by the widow of a well-known republican. The RUC Special Branch had tried to maintain a watch on the hayshed but, because of the lack of cover in a predominantly hostile, republican area, had relied on listening devices which had been installed with help from MI5. Unfortunately, the technical equipment failed, and allowed a PIRA team to remove some of the explosives undetected in October 1982 to prepare a culvert bomb at Kinnego, near Lurgan, that killed three policemen as they drove by it, having been lured to the scene by a hoax telephone call. MI5 rectified the technical problem, and when the arms dump was next visited, six weeks later, by two youths, an RUC Special Branch team rushed to scene and fired on them. Michael Tighe was killed and Martin McCauley was wounded, and although both had handled the ancient rifles in the hayshed, there was no ammunition for them so the police were accused of participating in a shoot-to-kill policy, an allegation supported by McCauley who insisted that there had been no shouted warnings before the police had opened fire, and that after he had been wounded he had heard one of the policemen urge another to 'finish off' Tighe with a single shot to the head. Under normal circumstances such a charge would have amounted to evidence contradicted by other witnesses at the scene, but when word circulated that a surveillance tape existed of everything that had occurred in the hayshed, a struggle took place for possession of it. John Stalker, the Deputy Chief Constable of Manchester, sent to investigate the incident, one of three recent shootings in which unarmed republicans had died, failed to find it, and was informed that it had been routinely destroyed by MI5. Not surprisingly, the Security Service feared the consequences for future cooperation with the RUC if their recording was used to prosecute their Special Branch colleagues, so it was wiped.

The Special Branch, then headed by Forbes, was unenthusiastic about Stalker's investigation, and his team complained of constant obstruction while the RUC protested that information was leaking to the media from members of the enquiry, if not actually from its leader. When Stalker was withdrawn, to face quite separate internal disciplinary charges at his own force, and was replaced by the Chief Constable of Yorkshire, Colin Sampson, the RUC's hostility continued, and although Stalker believed he had been framed to remove him from Northern Ireland, Sampson's final report, delivered in March 1987, recommended the prosecution of two MI5 officers for conspiracy to pervert the course of justice, proved devastating, and certainly no whitewash. Ultimately, it was the Attorney-General, Sir Patrick Mayhew, who decided, bearing in mind the national security implications, that it was not in the public interest for any further prosecutions to be brought against either the police or the Security Service.

It was in these extremely delicate circumstances that Sean McPhilemy's book, *The Committee*, sought to prove that the 'Inner Force' had institutionalised collusion between the loyalist gunmen and the RUC, a charge that was probably the most damaging that could be made against the police at a particularly difficult time. However, as other journalists and the police sought to identify McPhilemy's key eye-witness, Source A, some surprising angles emerged, among them the assertion that the Committee had organised the death of the Belfast solicitor Patrick Finucane who had been shot at his home in front of his family on a Sunday evening in February 1989. According to McPhilemy's source, the lawyer, who had represented several republican clients and was widely believed to have other links to the Provos, was shot after his death had been sanctioned at a meeting of the Committee held at the Finaghy Orange Hall at the end of January. Finucane had been sentenced to death, not just because of his supposed PIRA connections, but because he had represented the family of James McKerr, a known terrorist who had been unarmed when he had been shot, together with two other unarmed companions, by an RUC mobile patrol following a car chase in November 1983. The pursuit had ended in McKerr, Sean Burns and Eugene Toman dying in a hail of 117 bullets as their car crashed at a roundabout near Lurgan. Significantly, Burns and Toman, both aged twenty-nine, had been the principal suspects in the culvert bombing at Kinnego which had killed three policemen, and subsequently had taken refuge in the Republic. The pair had returned later to Lurgan, only to be spotted by E4A surveillance on McKerr's home, and the chase had commenced at night when McKerr's green Ford Escort had sped away from a vehicle checkpoint arranged to stop it. Thus there was a continuous thread, from the hayshed, through the culvert bomb, to the deaths of the three PIRA men, and to Pat Finucane's murder. It was as a result of Finucane's advocacy at the coroner's inquest that the RUC had been forced to give detailed evidence about the chase, and this had led to the prosecution for murder of the three E4A men involved, Constables David Brannigan and Frederick Robinson, and Sergeant William Montgomery. All the trio were eventually acquitted in June 1985, with the judge, Lord Justice Maurice Gibson praising 'their courage and determination in bringing the three deceased men, in this case to the final court of justice'.[18] These controversial remarks were interpreted by some to suggest that the judiciary endorsed a shoot-to-kill policy, and were to cost the judge and his wife Cicely their lives nearly two years later, in April 1987, when their car was blown up by a massive bomb at Killeen, close to the border with the Republic, as they drove home from Dublin after a holiday abroad.

The acquittal of the three E4A men, combined with the judge's comments, reinforced the belief held by many that there was indeed a secret agenda in operation in Ulster, but the full truth was rather more complicated than any of the conspiracy theorists had anticipated. There were, in particular, two fundamental misunderstandings about clandestine operations conducted in the province. The first was that throughout the troubles there was always a principle of 'police primacy' which meant that in any circumstances the police always retained responsibility for everything that occurred in combating terrorism. For example, from the outset the second-in-command of the FRU was always the 'police adviser' (actually a member of the Security Service who liaised with the Special Branch), cleared the names of potential informants through the police, and ensured there were no operational overlaps. While the FRU recruited and ran agents, 14th Int limited its activities to surveillance and self-defence, and although its personnel underwent training with the SAS to Pontrilas on the Welsh border, their role was essentially passive. As for collusion with the loyalists, the FRU had been created precisely because the Army had always regarded the RUC as tainted by being too close to the protestant community. Indeed, the FRU soon discovered that there were plenty of Catholics with an abiding distrust of the police who were perfectly willing to cooperate with the Army. It was by exploiting the Army's reputation for being even-handed that the FRU had gained its early successes, including the cultivation of STAKE KNIFE, the unit's star source inside PIRA. STAKE KNIFE, now known to be the Belfast builder and PIRA enforcer Freddi Scappaticci, was a senior republican who had tired of the violence but could not bring himself to deal with the RUC. By working with the FRU, STAKE KNIFE and others salved their consciences and ensured the Army scored many impressive intelligence coups.

Clearly the accusations of collusion made by Sean McPhilemy were as controversial as could be made in the circumstances, and much attention was focused on his mysterious informant, whom he identified only as 'Source A'.[19] Indeed, when the veracity of 'Source A' was challenged, McPhilemy's television company went to considerable trouble and expense to protect his identity, with Channel 4 paying a fine of £75,000 after being found in contempt when a court order requiring the witness to be named was ignored.

'Source's A's' evidence could hardly have been more explosive, for he not only provided McPhilemy with a list of the Committee's membership, which was passed on to the police, but he also identified specific murders which, he claimed, he knew personally had been sanctioned and carried out by the Committee. In particular, the witness identified five loyalist attacks, in which ten Catholics had died, the most controversial of which was Pat Finucane's. The others, in chronological order, included the shooting of Sam Marshall, a PIRA terrorist suspect on 7 March 1990 soon after he had left Lurgan's police station where he had reported, with two other terrorist suspects, as part of their bail conditions; the murder of Denis Carville, a youth shot dead in his car outside Lurgan on 1 October 1990; the attack on a mobile sweetshop at Craigavon in March 1991 in which three people had died; and the murder of four customers in Boyle's Bar, a pub in Cappagh, later the same month.

Naturally, the RUC was interested in McPhilemy's allegations for two reasons. Firstly, there was the assertion that two very senior officers (Forbes, and another ACC) were masterminding loyalist death squads, and secondly, 'Source A' appeared to be a vital but hitherto undiscovered witness to all five incidents. The fact that the RUC was to obtain a conviction in the Marshall murder (with a UVF supporter, Victor Graham, being imprisoned for life in June 1992), identify Billy Wright as the gunman in deaths of Carville, and the Cuppagh atrocity, and identify Robin 'the Jackal' Jackson (imprisoned in January 1981 for seven years on firearms offences) as the leader of the Craigavon shooting, seemed immaterial, and apparently did nothing to undermine 'Source A's' credibility. Far from having colluded with the perpetrators of these crimes, the RUC seemed to have obtained convictions against the very men who supposedly were under the protection of 'the Inner Force'.

The exception, of course, was the death of Pat Finucane, the republican solicitor who was to be identified by Sean O'Callaghan (an informer and one-time head of the PIRA's Southern Command) as an important and influential member of PIRA whom he had first met in 1980 at one of their finance meetings in Letterkenny. Finucane had been shot by three masked intruders at his north Belfast home on 12 February 1989, and his death has been rigorously investigated precisely because there were, from the outset, allegations of collusion. This makes the incident a very worthwhile subject for analysis to compare the version given by 'Source A' to McPhilemy, and what was subsequently discovered by the external enquiry conducted by Sir John Stevens.

According to 'Source A', speaking during his filmed interview on 3 May 1991, Finucane had been murdered by 'people connected with the Ulster Resistance, and with help from Brian Nelson and the Inner Force'.[20] On this occasion, although he claimed that he had participated in the meeting held at the Finaghy Orange Hall at the end of January 1989 at which the decision had been taken to kill the solicitor, he was unable to name any of the gunmen. As for identifying Brian Nelson, he was simply naming someone who was already in police custody, for 'Agent 1033', as he had been known for the past four years, had been arrested on 18 January 1990, and was to be sentenced in January 1992 to ten years' imprisonment. A former Black Watch soldier, Nelson had returned to his native Belfast to operate as an agent for the FRU. Designated '1033', and ostensibly a self-employed taxi-driver, Nelson had supplied his Army handlers with a wealth of information from the very heart of the banned Ulster Defence Association for whom he had acted as its chief intelligence officer, a role that had included sifting reports on suspected republicans as potential targets for assassination. Evidence given at his trial by the FRU's commander, Colonel Gordon Kerr, suggested that Nelson had tipped off the Army to dozens of planned atrocities and had saved numerous lives by allowing the terrorists to be interdicted. So was it true that Nelson had conspired to kill Finucane or, worse, had he received instructions from the FRU to do so?

Nelson pleaded guilty to five charges of conspiracy to murder, fourteen of collecting information likely to assist in acts of terrorism, and a single charge of possession of a sub-machinegun, but was not charged with Finucane's murder. Of the two people linked to it, William Stobie, the quartermaster believed to have supplied the weapons, was himself shot dead by the UDA in December 1991, and another UDA man, Ken Barrett, made an admission on tape, while speaking to a

Special Branch detective, but was never charged because there was no other evidence against him. Thus, until Mc Philemy's interview with 'Source A' in May 1991, nobody had breathed a word about 'the Committee' or 'the Inner Force'. And although collusion had been suspected, and investigated in Finucane's murder, the suspicion had centred on Brian Nelson's relationship with his Army handlers, and not on any shadowy group with the RUC. Clearly 'Source A' was a potentially important witness, even if he had never mentioned Stobie or Barrett, and eventually a new enquiry, led by Detective Chief Superintendent Jimmy Nesbitt and Detective Inspector Chris Webster, in the face of McPhilemy's obstruction, was able to track him down. In September 1992 the Metropolitan Police had raided the London home of McPhilemy's main researcher, Ben Hamilton, and detectives had recovered sufficient documentation for the RUC to narrow their search to a council house in Portadown and arrest Jim Sands in November.

Questioned by the RUC, Sands admitted that he had absolutely no connection with terrorism, and that he had invented the story about 'the Committee' so as 'to make foreign journalists look stupid'. Sands was the manager of a woman's football team and a born-again Christian who had been a member of an entirely legitimate, harmless political group, the Ulster Independence Movement. He had known Billy Wright when they had attended the same school in Portadown, but apart from that he knew absolutely nothing about terrorism, collusion between loyalist paramilitaries or an organisation such as 'the Inner Force'. According to Sands, he had participated in the hoax at the request of a tabloid journalist, Martin O'Hagan, who allegedly had persuaded him to back the existence of the Committee so as to extract some money from the television company. The Nesbitt report into the affair concluded that there was not a shred of truth in the entire tale. The venues where Sands had claimed 'the Committee' had met had never been used for loyalist terrorist activities and none of those named as members had even the slightest connection to loyalist paramilitaries. If anything, the police concluded, the TV project had been a deliberate scam intended to milk Channel 4 out of large sums they had invested in an entirely spurious story that the programme makers knew to be fabricated.

Further research revealed that Martin O'Hagan had an interesting background, for in 1972 he had been an active member of the IRA and had participated in a shoot-out with the RUC in Lurgan, in which two policemen had been wounded, and PC William Chambers had been killed. O'Hagan had been convicted of possession of firearms and sentenced to seven years' imprisonment, and his brother Rory had gone on the run to the Republic, where he too subsequently had been convicted of terrorist offences. After his release O'Hagan had contributed articles to a tabloid, the *Sunday World*, and in 1985 had reported than an anonymous source, whom he identified only as 'Mr X', had told him about a mysterious organisation known as 'the Committee' which had been masterminding loyalist terrorism. It was this that had caught the attention of McPhilemy's young South African television researcher, and O'Hagan had obligingly introduced Hamilton, not to Mr X, who had turned out to be a hoaxer named Metcalfe, but to Jim Sands. Surprisingly, Sands had confirmed the existence of 'the Committee' and 'the Inner Force', and even had agreed to give McPhilemy a videotaped interview for *Dispatches*. When interviewed while detained by the police, in November 1992, Sands claimed he had been coached to give the required answers about loyalist collusion before he went on camera. Quite simply, he had been one of many in Northern Ireland who had tried to scrape a living by exploiting completely invented tales about terrorism in the Province.

As might be expected, the saga ended before the High Court in London where McPhilemy brought an action for defamation against *The Sunday Times* which had undermined the veracity of McPhilemy's programme and the integrity and motives of those involved in making it. He won in London against the newspaper in 1998, but was obliged to back down in the United States where he was sued by individuals named in his book as members of 'the Committee'.

Whatever the motives of those involved in making *The Committee*, there can be no doubt that Sands was a mischief-making hoaxer, but the implications of the film were to be far-reaching, even to the point of being used in evidence to support a defence in California against an extradition application brought against a fugitive PIRA gunman who claimed, on the basis of the content of the book, that he would be at risk of persecution from 'The Committee' if he was returned to Northern Ireland to resume serving his prison sentence. No such organisation ever existed, but many were duped into the belief that Sands had proved that the RUC had conspired with the loyalist paramilitaries to murder Catholics. The extent to which O'Hagan and McPhilemy were taken in remains unclear, but both turned out to have had family links to the republicans. O'Hagan had served a prison sentence for terrorist offences, and in August 1988 McPhilemy's nephew James died in Londonderry's Altmagelvin Hospital after he had been shot during an INLA attack on British troops at an Army vehicle checkpoint at Clady, outside Strabane. Armed with only a handgun McPhilemy, had been one of three masked gunmen to fire on the soldiers, but he had received fatal wounds when the fire had been returned.

It is against this background that the claims and counter-claims of collusion should be judged. The proposition that Robert Nairac and Tony Ball murdered John Green to revenge the loss of ten sources run by 14 Int makes no sense because the unit never handled agents, just as the assertion that MI5 had taken on Green as a mole after he had been rejected by 14 Int betrays a fundamental misunderstanding about how the various security agencies operated in the province.

While it is clear to most independent observers who studied the Green case that he was murdered by loyalists, and certainly not by Nairac and Ball, the issue of collusion is an especially corrosive one in the hothouse atmosphere of Northern Ireland politics. Perhaps the ripples of *The Nemesis File* did not travel very far, and maybe *Soldier E* was not taken too seriously by very many, but the impact of *The Committee* on the open wound of sectarianism will last for many years, not least because of the way it has influenced American public opinion.

Chapter 3

Sir Ranulph and the Feathermen

'The cloak and dagger world of espionage is
permanently awash with contradictions and false trails,
many of which have been set up by evil individuals
seeking to distort the truth.'

Gary Murray in *Enemies of the State*

Sir Ranulph Twisleton-Wyckham-Fiennes Bt. is one of the more remarkable eccentrics to have made newspaper headlines around the world as a daring explorer and adventurer who has endured appalling hardship to break numerous world records. He has trekked across icecaps, reached both Poles on foot, and lost several of his toes to frostbite. His army career in the Royal Scots Greys was almost as colourful, being thrown out of the Special Air Service regiment in 1970 for using military explosives[1] to blown up a dam in Castle Combe built by the film company making *Doctor Doolittle*. Apparently Fiennes had taken exception to Hollywood's visit to rural Somerset, and had exacted his unique brand of revenge. Even the ever-patient British Army, well-used to accommodating high-risk individuals with unusual talents and unorthodox skills, felt it would accomplish more without him.

Much admired and decorated for his astonishing achievements, Sir Ranulph fought in Oman and in 1975 wrote a well-received account of the conflict, *Where Soldiers Fear To Tread*.[2] What baffles his many friends is how he ever came to write *The Feathermen*,[3] a strange tale involving the mysterious deaths of four British soldiers whom, he alleged, had participated in an ambush at Qum in October 1969, during the 'secret war' fought in the mountains of Dhofar, to protect the Gulf states from Communist insurgents. Largely unacknowledged in England, and scarcely mentioned in Parliament, Britain engaged, and defeated, a guerrilla force intent on ousting the Anglophile rulers of the oil-rich countries which stretch along the Gulf of Arabia. Fiennes says that following one firefight, in which the son of a rich Dubai merchant was killed, his father hired a group of hitmen, known collectively as 'the clinic', which spent $5,000,000 and seventeen years tracking down all the British soldiers involved. The first victim was a former Royal Marine commando, John Milling, who died in March 1977 when the helicopter he was flying for the Royal Omani Police plunged into the sea, killing the pilot and his passenger. Fiennes says this was no accident, but was caused by a time-bomb placed in the aircraft. After this incident the SAS's wartime founder, David Stirling, apparently recruited a group of volunteers dedicated to tracing the Clinic's hitmen and protecting their targets, among the latter category being Fiennes himself who, unarmed at his remote farmhouse in Somerset, was dramatically saved from murder at the last moment by their intervention.

The Feathermen has more than a veneer of authenticity, not just because of the author's stature, but because almost all the names in the book are authentic, much to the irritation of some SAS officers who had served in Northern Ireland and judged themselves and their families' likely targets for a Provisional IRA attack. Fiennes describes in some detail the death of Michael Marman, formerly of the 9/21st Lancers, who was killed in November 1986 while driving his Citroen 2CV along the A303 in Wiltshire to meet one of his former commanding officers. According to Fiennes, this was a murder, but the police investigation conducted at the time showed that a BMW, driven by Sir Peter Horsley, a retired Air Marshal and former equerry to the Queen, then aged sixty-five, crossed the central reservation and hit Marman's car head-on. There was no question of this being anything other than a tragic accident on a road still notorious for fatal collisions. No-one else knew that Marman was to be driving along that road at that particular moment, although it was well-known that his divorce had left him reliant on a car that offers minimal protection to those inside. Actually, Marman did not take part in the ambush in Oman, although he was serving in the country at the time, and was later seconded to the Sultan's army. However, according to Fiennes, Horsley's car had been fitted with a remote-controlled electronic device that caused the BMW to swerve into Marman.

Similarly, Fiennes alleged that Major Mike Kealy DSO, the hero of Mirbat, was the target of an assassination, but the reality is that he died of hypothermia in February 1979 while on a training exercise on the Brecon Beacons, having returned to Hereford after a tour in Northern Ireland to command G Squadron. Although aged only thirty-three, he was not sufficiently fit to have participated in the gruelling exercise, often undertaken in the most difficult weather conditions, but had done so to make a point to the troops he was about to command. Instead of carrying waterproof clothing, like the other twenty-nine men being tested, Kealy's Bergen contained only fifty-five pounds of bricks. In truly dreadful weather the men set off after midnight, but the cold wind and rain quickly took its toll. Kealy eventually stumbled into a snow drift, where he was found, barely alive, by an SAS trooper who remained with him while a companion went for help. Nineteen hours later the pair were found by a rescue helicopter, delayed by bad visibility, but by that time Kealy had succumbed from hypothermia. According to Fiennes, Kealy's tragic death was the result of drugged tea and an injection of insulin while he was unconscious.

Any background check conducted on Ranulph Fiennes reveals much of his very public career, and while his friends regard *The Feathermen* as an aberration, they are tolerant of his eccentricity because of his many accomplishments. But what of Gary Murray, a man who describes himself as 'a former MI5 undercover agent'?

Murray's principal achievement is *Enemies of the State*, an exposé of the clandestine work of the British security and intelligence services written in 1993 by an insider who became a private detective in 1968, founding his own business called Euro-Tec, after service in the RAF Provost Police as a 'Special Investigator (Crime and Security)', and for the next seventeen years 'worked on many special assignments for the government'.[4] Murray's revelations seemed to be extraordinarily important in England where members and former members of the security and intelligence services are banned from making any unauthorised disclosures. How could Murray, if he really had been employed by MI5, have managed to avoid prosecution, or at least an injunction? The ease with which he succeeded in making his allegations seemed remarkable, and all the more so because of the gravity of his charges. In particular, Murray concentrated on the unsolved murder of Hilda Murrell, an elderly anti-nuclear campaigner who had been abducted from her house in Shrewsbury in March 1984 and brutally murdered. Her half-naked body was recovered from a field, six miles away from her home, was bruised, as if she had been kicked, stabbed repeatedly with a knife, and there was also evidence that she had been the victim of a sexual assault. Despite these injuries, the actual cause of death had been hypothermia, with the septuagenarian left in the open to die alone. According to Murray 'a number of illegal acts, including violence and murder, have been committed by agents of British Intelligence – in some cases with the connivance of members of her

Majesty's Government'.[5] Indeed, it was Murray's contention that private investigators like himself routinely engage in 'unorthodox, and at times highly illegal, covert intelligence operations on behalf of the Security Services (MI5) and foreign governments':

> The intelligence services of the erstwhile Soviet Union were also known to utilise the expertise of western private investigators. The GRU as well as the KGB found established detective agencies an excellent method of expanding soviet covert operations. Past soviet intelligence operations, contracted out to British detective and security agencies, penetrated the very heart of the British Defence Ministry and other official departments.[6]

The author could state this with some authority because, as a private detective himself, he had undertaken plenty of 'freelance work with MI5' and in January 1982 had mounted a surveillance operation on 'a group of anti-war protestors suspected of planning a raid on a top secret Ministry of Defence base in Berkshire'.[7] The basis of his book is that another private investigator, collecting information about anti-nuclear activists for the Atomic Energy Authority, was responsible for Hilda Murrell's death. While the West Mercia police had concluded that she had encountered a lone burglar who stole some cash she had drawn out of her bank account earlier in the day, Murray claimed that the peace campaigner and professional rose-grower had been the target of a botched operation intended to steal or copy a report she had compiled into nuclear safety, which she was to submit to the public enquiry then considering a controversial application to expand an atomic power station at Sizewell in Suffolk.

Murray says he was enrolled as an MI5 agent after an interview in Whitehall at the end of February 1980, and resigned exactly two years later, in 1982. In the intervening period he says he 'was nothing more than an informer, helping the Security Service to monitor the activities of ordinary citizens voicing their opinions on nuclear weapons … I had failed to uncover any evidence of criminal espionage or subversion and was now of the opinion that innocent people, especially those engaged in sincere anti-nuclear protests, were being hounded. I not only found this distasteful, but I sympathised and agreed with the majority of the protestors I investigated. This new emotionally changed state of mind had turned me into ideal double agent material'.[8] Whatever his mental state, Murray must have been busy, for as well as compiling reports on the protestors, he was also 'investigating the business and personal lifestyles of journalists and TV producers. My reports contained details of Members of Parliament, British Telecom officers, former RAF officers – I even extended my research to the friends and relatives of targets of investigation'.[9]

Although Murray says he did not participate in any MI5 investigation of Hilda Murrell, he did claim to know who the killer was, and in an interview conducted in central London to promote his book in August 1983, he claimed that 'he's about five minutes from where we're sitting now'. Later he added that the person who had supervised the attack was 'a former MI5 agent who has left the service to run a private detective agency'.[10] However, in his book Murray's evidence amounted to an affidavit sworn by Catriona Guthrie, a friend of Hilda Murrell's who also a prison visitor, related that during a series of meetings with a prisoner in Lincoln she had been told about an armed robber serving a fifteen-year sentence 'who had been engaged in regular freelance work for some kind of secret intelligence department. One of their assignments had been to search Hilda Murrell's house for papers or information relating to signals intelligence, specific mention was made of the *Belgrano* and the Falklands. The most frightening aspect of the informant's story is that the leader of the group was said to be reporting to the Cabinet Office via an MI5 Liaison Officer and that the team, in addition to their government work, were also engaged in all manner of other illegal activity, including armed robbery'.[11] According to the prisoner, three men and a woman had been searching Murrell's house when she returned unexpectedly and surprised them. 'Confusion and panic ensued and one of the perpetrators became very unstable and subjected Hilda to violence and threatened her with a knife, accompanied by obscene sexual acts involving masturbation'.[12] Guthrie had been 'specifically briefed by Mr Murray in methods of cross-examination' who was told of her source's true name, but he omitted it from *Enemies of the State*. Thus, according to the armed robber, MI5 had commissioned a search for classified material relating to the sinking of the Argentine warship ASA *General Belgrano* during the Falklands conflict two years earlier. This incident had indeed become a political *cause celebre* in March 1984 because the Prime Minister Margaret Thatcher and the Secretary of State for Defence, Michael Heseltine, had been accused of making misleading statements concerning the exact circumstances in which HMS *Conqueror* had torpedoed the cruiser on 2 May 1982. Opposition MPs had raised various queries concerned discrepancies between the official British version of the sinking of the *General Belgrano*, and two recently published books in which rather different accounts had been given. Had the Prime Minister lied, and was the Ministry of Defence engaged in a cover-up to conceal the possibility that the cruiser either had been sunk illegally (while outside a declared 'exclusion zone'), or had been attacked for political purposes, to sabotage Peruvian peace negotiations?

In August 1984, a senior MoD civil servant, Clive Ponting, was arrested and charged with having breached the Official Secrets Act by leaking classified information about the episode, but he was acquitted at his trial at the Old Bailey in February 1985. This is only relevant because Ponting acknowledged having written an anonymous note, on 24 April 1982, encouraging a Labour MP to press the government on certain points where he believed the replies given had been misleading. This chronology is important, for prior to April 1982 there had been no leaks, and the questions raised in the House of Commons the previous month had been as a result of the books that had been published. In other words, there was no leak enquiry underway at the time Hilda Murrell had been murdered, and the first had been conducted by the Cabinet Secretary, Sir Robert Armstrong, in December 1983.

Guthrie's source, of course, had alleged that the Murrell home had been searched, not for information relating to her Sizewell submissions, but because it had been suspected that she was in possession of secrets relating to the Falklands conflict. The basis of this assertion was the fact that Murrell's nephew, Robert Green, had been an officer in the Royal Navy until his resignation the previous year, and during the *Belgrano* incident had served at the Fleet Headquarters at Northwood where he routinely had handled classified data, including signals intelligence. So, whereas Murray had opted for a bungled MI5 search for subversive literature, Guthrie's prison source had claimed that the team led by the convicted armed robber had been after military secrets. Either way, MI5 ultimately had been responsible.

Devoid of any other clues, having pursued 3,600 possible leads, West Mercia detectives took Murray's charges seriously, and Chief Inspector Peter Herbert conducted a further investigation to track down Guthrie's informant, and quickly discovered that neither Special Branch nor MI5 had ever heard of Hilda Murrell before her murder. Of the six people mentioned in Guthrie's affidavit, all were traced by the police and five were interviewed. It turned out that the principal figure referred to in *Enemies of the State* was a well-known informer who had been serving a long prison sentence for drug dealing when, in late 1989, he had read a newspaper article about the murder and seized the opportunity to fabricate his participation in the case in order to draw the media's attention to what he considered to be his own wrongful conviction. Subsequently he had abandoned this strategy, but by then he had mentioned it to a fellow prisoner who had passed on the information to Guthrie, who then had confided in Murray. Apart from one of the purported participants, a ruthless armed robber and police killer named David Graecity, who had shot himself accidentally when cornered by detectives, all those involved were re-interviewed by the police, and confirmed the content of their original statements, and denied 'communicating any revised version to Gary Murray'. Finally, in February 1994, the police announced that there was no truth in *Enemies of the State*, and that 'the book should not be considered as a serious authoritative work on the murder of Hilda Murrell'.

Given this damning verdict, how could such an experienced expert, as Murray claimed to be, have been duped by uncorroborated prison whispers? The answer may lie in some of Murray's other assertions. For example, he says he 'unexpectedly joined' the Operational Intelligence cadres of 21 SAS, but no such unit exists in the territorial regiment.[13] Trying to check on his two years with MI5 is also complicated by what he has said about the organisation which, he claimed, in 1980 had its headquarters in Curzon Street, whereas the true location at that time was in Gower Street. His 'first operational controller' was frequently drunk and was unavailable when Murray wanted to deliver his report on 'suspected Russian agents'.[14] His next assignment was to investigate 'a journalist who was suspected of passing on restricted documents to CND', and then in September 1981 he had worked as a helicopter pilot on a project filming secret nuclear bases from the air. By the end of 1981 he had 'suffered at the hands of several controllers' and when he attempted to resign he had experienced 'a weak attempt to blackmail' him.[15]

Murray's antipathy towards the Security Service, which he incorrectly asserts is 'controlled by the Ministry of Defence', stems from the unprofessionalism of the staff he encountered, and the suggestion made by an MI5 officer that he should 'take a subject of investigation, who was described as "a menace", for a ride in my private aircraft and drop him out over the North Sea'.[16] Acknowledging that 'assassination is of special interest to me', Murray revealed that 'over the years there had been a number of mysterious deaths said to be attributed to MI5, including that of Sir Maurice Oldfield, former boss of MI6'.[17] If this allegation is bizarre (as there was absolutely nothing mysterious about the death of Sir Maurice in the Edward VII Hospital in March 1981 after a long battle against stomach cancer misdiagnosed as diverticulitis), Murray claimed 'rebel MI5 agents who wanted a change in government' had 'used sex, forgery and drugs in what became a seriously bungled operation'.[18]

One of the key figures in the plot was brought out of retirement in 1987 to act as an adviser to the services. He was previously a member of the section which drew up secret files on MPs, trade unionists and journalists. This officer was the chief to whom all my own reports were delivered by my handler; no wonder I was asked to take one of my targets of investigation for a no-return flight over the North Sea. Names from the abovementioned hit list make interesting reading: Edward Heath, Reginald Maudling, Francis Pym, Norman St John Stevas, Harold Wilson, Tony Benn, David Owen, along with numerous other well-known MPs and trade unionists, were listed for special attention.[19]

But could any of this really be true? Of the seven, only David Owen is still alive, but if there really had been such a plot, it must have been in existence prior to Maudling's resignation as Home Secretary in 1972. And what retiree was brought back to MI5 by the Director-General, Sir Antony Duff, in 1987 to supervise operations when his two deputies, Patrick Walker and David Ranson, fulfilled those duties? The answer is that there was no such plot, and no such individual. From all the evidence provided by Murray, the only conclusion to be reached is that whatever link he may have had to the Security Service, it was at best very peripheral. As for the murder of Hilda Murrell, a local labourer, Andrew George, was arrested in May 2003 and charged with the offence. George had been sixteen-years-old at the time of the murder, and was linked to the crime by fingerprint and DNA evidence. At his trial George admitted participating in the crime, but claimed that he had broken into the house with his brother, who had been responsible for the sexual assault and the killing. In May 2005 George was convicted of kidnap, sexual assault and murder, and was sentenced to life imprisonment with a recommended minimum term of fifteen years.

The need for 'wannabe spies' to create exotic backgrounds for themselves in the world of security affects a variety of authors, ranging from former dog-handlers like Gary Murray, to some more plausible authors, such as Patrick Meehan, who wrote *Framed by M.I.5* in 1982. Meehan's motive for inventing his relationship with the Security Service was not dissimilar to the one fabricated by the prisoner who claimed to have inside knowledge of Hilda Murrell's murder, for in October 1969 the career criminal from Glasgow had been convicted of killing an elderly woman, Rachel Ross, in her home in Ayr. She and her husband, a wealthy scrap-metal merchant, had been tied up while their wall-safe had been emptied of £13,000 by two Glaswegian intruders, but after they had left the couple had been unable to free themselves and the following day Mrs Ross, who was aged seventy-two and in poor health, died.

However, in March 1976 another criminal, William 'Tank' McGuinness, died in a street fight, and his solicitor issued a confession in which McGuinness confessed to having murdered Rachel Ross. Two months later Meehan was granted a Royal Pardon, and £50,000 compensation for the seven years of a life sentence he had been imprisoned.

Meehan had established his criminal reputation in August 1963 when he had escaped from Nottingham prison during a cricket practice, while serving a sentence for safe-cracking, having arranged the escape of Terry 'Scarface' Martin from Peterhead in 1955. A former Communist, he was known as an explosives specialist and an expert on prison escapes, and claimed that when he had fled to East Germany in 1963 he had learned of the HVA's interest in springing George Blake, who was then serving a forty-two-year sentence at Wormwoods Scrubs. According to his version of events, MI5 had framed him for the Ayr murder to keep him quiet about his knowledge of Blake's escape.

In Meehan's account, he had reached East Berlin on a false passport but had been imprisoned for sixteen months and then deported back to England in December 1964, where he was placed in Wandsworth prison, before being transferred to Blundeston in Suffolk in February 1965. After his return he had been interviewed by MI5 officers and Special Branch detectives, and he had mentioned to both the interest expressed by the East Germans in freeing Blake.

In September 1966 Meehan had been moved to Saughton prison, in Edinburgh, and he was here when, a month later, George Blake made his daring escape from Wormwood Scrubs and hit the headlines. Bearing in mind his own warnings, Meehan deduced that Blake's escape 'had been manipulated by the British Security Service'. This revelation prompted him to write to the *Daily Express* journalist Chapman Pincher who visited him at the end of November 1966 at Blundeston and published an article on 5 December about Meehan's warning, reporting that he had obtained confirmation from his MI5 contacts that Prisoner 519 had indeed predicted the spy's escape, but this assertion was contradicted by Lord Mountbatten's subsequent enquiry which observed that 'there is no evidence that this prisoner who escaped to East Germany warned the Security Service, as is now alleged, that the Communists intended to rescue George Blake from prison in England'. The Inquiry conceded that Meehan had been interrogated at length by MI5 at Blundeston but asserted that the prisoner had suggested that if the East Germans wanted to arrange an escape, perhaps of Blake or Gordon Lonsdale, a transfer should be arranged to Scotland where he would be able to advise on corrupt prison officers who might be bribed.

Meehan had been released from Parkhurst in August 1968, and on 5 July the following year, according to his account, Meehan had been driving around Stranraer with a fellow criminal, James Griffiths, to plan a robbery on the local motor tax office which he knew contained a safe he could open with ease, and he insists he had no idea the bungalow belong to Abraham Ross was being robbed fifty miles away in Ayr. Nine days later the police arrested Meehan at his home, placed him in an identity parade where his voice was recognised by Ross, and charged with murder. At this point Meehan remained confident that he would not be convicted because he had an alibi, but when James Griffiths was shot dead, his conviction became a certainty. When the police had called to arrest Griffiths at his flat in Glasgow he had responded with a shotgun, and as he attempted to make his escape he had killed a bystander and wounded thirteen others before he was finally felled by a single round fired by a detective. With Griffiths dead, Meehan's conviction for murder in October 1969 was a mere formality and, after a trial lasting four days, he was sentenced to life imprisonment. Impressed by Meehan's protests that he 'had been framed on the orders of MI5', and accusing the head of Glasgow's Special Branch, Detective Chief Superintendent Thomas Goodall, of rigging the crucial identification parade, the journalist Ludovic Kennedy wrote *Presumption of Innocence*, a detailed analysis of the whole prosecution, drawing attention to what he described as a monumental miscarriage of justice. Kennedy continued to campaign for Meehan while the prisoner spent much of the next six years in solitary confinement in Peterhead prison's punishment block.

Following Meehan's Royal Pardon in May 1976, a judicial enquiry was conducted into the case by a Scottish High Court judge, Lord Hunter, who took five years to produce a report in four volumes, covering 1,600 pages. The final document, published in August 1982, concluded that there was no substance in Meehan's allegation of MI5's involvement in a plot to frame him and, astonishingly, suggested that Meehan probably had been present at the home of Mr and Mrs Ross when it was robbed by four, not two intruders. Naturally, Meehan had been outraged by the Hunter Report, and wrote *Framed by M.I.5* in an attempt to redress the balance. He died in 1994, aged sixty-seven, having spent his last years devoted to a business selling burglar alarms.

Chapter 4

Espionage in Korea

Despite the curious title, *Sing a Song to Jenny Next* is 'the incredible true account' of a secret mission into China in May 1952, is based on a message found on the body of an American agent, which was interpreted as being a hidden reference to Sŏngjin, a port in North Korea where six ships had been sunk. How did this come about? The story, recounted by Lawrence Gardella shortly before his death from leukemia in February 1981, was remarkable. Soon after transferring to the U.S. Marine Corps from the Massachusetts National Guard, Gardella had been selected for a special assignment. At the height of the Korean War, he was to join six others and be parachuted into Manchuria with the objective of attacking a nuclear facility beneath the Sungari Resevoir. Having achieved his objective, in the face of overwhelming odds, Gardella had trekked across a thousand miles of China in just twenty-two days and had made contact with American forces which arranged for him alone to be collected off the beach by a U.S. Navy submarine. Upon his return the lone marine was congratulated by President Harry Truman, on 28 June 1952 at the U.S. Navy hospital at Annapolis, who swore him to secrecy.

Gardella changed his mind about maintaining secrecy when he learned in May 1977, while working as the foreman of a construction site in Danbury, Connecticut, that he had contracted leukaemia, and he was undeterred when he was threatened and even offered a bribe not to publish his story two years later. Part of Gardella's motive, aside from wishing to explain his brief military career to his two daughters, his grandson and friends, was his belief that his illness had been caused by an exposure to radiation at the experimental atomic laboratory at Sungari twenty-five years earlier.

Gardella's adventure had begun in April 1952, when he was seventeen years old, just out of boot camp at Parris Island, South

Carolina, and a new arrival at the marine barracks at Annapolis with two months' experience in the U.S. Marine Corps. Originally from New York, he had been taken by his parents, with his brother, from New Jersey in 1947 to Boston to be near his grandparents. Previously he had served in the 180th Field Artillery Battalion of the Massachusetts National Guard, but was found to have altered his birth certificate to join up under-age, and to have concealed his childhood asthma. Discharged on 31 February 1952, he had been inducted into the marines the following day, with the help of a mysterious civilian who would later to play a key role in Gardella's story.

At Annapolis Gardella had volunteered for combat duty and had been flown to a training facility in a barren area about an hour's flight away, accompanied by the civilian. For the next two weeks he underwent gruelling parachute and live firing exercises for up to twenty hours a day with five other marines, among them a Lieutenant Kenneth F. Damon, in his mid-twenties, and Gunnery Sergeant Robert Masters, a thirty-six year-old with nineteen years' service in the Corps. Dressed in Oriental clothes, and armed with Soviet weaponry, Gardella had practised three low altitude parachute drops a day and been given hand-to-hand combat training before the six men were taken 'on a flight that never seemed to end' with windows that had been blacked out, to an airfield where they were transferred in a crate to another aircraft for a further flight that lasted 'six or seven hours'.[1] The men were uncertain about the length of their journey because their wristwatches had been removed, but when they arrived at their destination they were moved in another crate to a Quonset hut where they received a final briefing from 'a marine colonel with rows of ribbons on his chest'. They were allowed to have their 'first really good meal in days' and then, after four hours' sleep, were loaded back into the crate for a further journey back to the airstrip for another flight 'maybe three or four hours long' to another airfield where they climbed aboard their mission plane, an aircraft piloted by Chinese aircrew. This final flight took 'less than half an hour' and Gardella and his companions were dropped into 'a mountain meadow' on 9 May 1952, only moments before the aircraft was attacked by two fighters and blown out of the sky before the pilot had a chance to manoeuvre.[2]

Once on the ground the six men were joined by twenty-five Chinese nationalist guerrillas who revealed that they had landed in Manchuria, near the town of Hunchun, some 175 miles from their objective, the Sungari Reservoir, north of Hautien, where the Communists 'were using several large caves for experimental work on atomic weapons'.[3] Accompanying the guerrillas was a Scot, in his mid-forties, who had come to China in 1935 and had worked for Chiang Kai-shek during the Japanese occupation and then the civil war. The Scot divided the soldiers into two groups, headed by Sergeant Mike Holden and the lieutenant, and supervised the distribution to each American of food, a bandolier of ammunition, a pair of grenades, an animal skin full of water, a suicide pill and a Soviet machine-gun. Communications between the two groups was to be by 'lights that could be seen at night only if you wore special glasses' and, thus equipped, the guerrillas set off towards their target. However, on the second day, the team led by Lieutenant Damon encountered some Communists who took one of the guerrillas, a girl, prisoner. Gardella then described how he had been prevented by his more experienced companions from rescuing her, and had been obliged to listen all night to her harrowing screams as she was tortured. The following morning, she was still alive, but only just, and was finished off with a single bullet by one of the marines.

As the guerrillas approached the reservoir, on their fourth day in China, they discovered a Communist encampment, which they attacked silently, with Gardella cutting the throats of no less than four sentries. Having made the scene look as though it had been the handiwork of local bandits, by 'stripping the bodies and collecting the weapons', Gardella moved closer to his objective and killed another sentry, his knife having gone 'straight into an artery'.[4] At this point the two teams combined to discuss their strategy, and the Scot described how 'the laboratories had been built for the Japanese by Chinese prisoners' and the only way into the caves was through a single tunnel. He announced that they would capture a truck, which was quickly accomplished by two of their number dressing in captured uniforms and stopping a lorry on the road. In 'a minute or two' the driver and passenger were quickly despatched and the dozen soldiers clambered aboard. They bluffed their way past the guards at the main entrance to the complex and then drove past 'barracks, several small buildings, and dozens, maybe even hundreds of soldiers' and a radio tower. The truck reached a second gate, at the mouth of the caves, and again were able to enter unimpeded and proceed down a steep incline, underground. Finally, as the Scot prepared an explosive charge, the truck came to a halt 'in front of a gigantic steel door' where they were challenged by four armed guards. All were killed in the ensuing firefight, and 'we must have knocked over fifty of them in those first few minutes, while we still had the advantage of surprise'.

Gardella then fought his way into a laboratory 'with tables, test-tubes and other apparatus', and tossed grenades into it while the Scot attached his explosives and timer on 'a big boiler'. He was wounded in the legs, and Lieutenant Damon was hit in the shoulder and the neck, and had his left ear shot off. But they were able to take refuge in a bunker filled with crates of American weapons and ammunition. Seizing a bazooka, Gardella fired at some tanks that were advancing down the tunnel, and when two were disabled the access was blocked. He then picked up an American flamethrower and was able to deter some more tanks and troops that had assembled at the tunnel entrance. Having suffered six casualties, the guerrillas retreated back into the tunnel as two Chinese aircraft made strafing attacks and dropped 'incendiary bombs, possibly napalm'. A third then dropped 'conventional bombs' but they were ineffective, and the guerrillas were able to make their escape. The smoke helped to conceal them, although the Scot mentioned that it might be radioactive. 'The stuff that's used to make atomic bombs. I think it was in the labs you blew up' he explained. When Gardella asked if he could read Chinese, the Scot had explained that the bunker doors had borne warnings of radioactivity. 'I've been here seventeen years, you know.' he replied.[5]

The half dozen survivors fought their way out of the tunnel and Gardella again used the flamethrower to great effect against troops advancing upon them from trucks, backed with mortars. As the Chinese fell back, another group of guerrillas arrived on the scene to give covering fire, and they were able to withdraw to a cave twenty-five miles away. Here some thirty guerrillas gathered, and there was medical care for the wounded, and an unexpected surprise. Sergeant Holden's group had ambushed a convoy of trucks and captured a man in denims, 'the same civilian who had put us through our training for this mission' who was found to be carrying a blue identification card bearing the words 'United States of America, Central Intelligence Agency' and a photograph of Joseph Roberts. He was questioned by Sergeant Masters and the Scot but they 'had been unable to learn anything new, either from talking to his men or through the radio transmitter he carried'. However, they did find among various scraps of paper he was carrying a message bearing the enigmatic words:

> Six ships sunk. They will not return. They feel the same as most of us.
> But hung his name on anyway. Sing a song to Jenny next.[6]

According to the Scot, this could be interpreted to mean that the six survivors would not return, and there were references to Hungnam and Sŏngjin in North Korea. However, as the group was discussing the implications of this, they learned than Communist troops were less than two hours away, so they decided to move on, in two groups, with

Gardella taking another marine, named White, ten Chinese 'friendlies' and three stretchers. Together they trekked to another campsite, evading four fighters on the way, but were attacked in a canyon by troops armed with rifles, machine-guns and mortars. Lieutenant Damon was killed by a mortar fragment, and White's stomach was blown open by another. As all but one of his companions were picked off Gardella reached for his suicide pill, but at the last moment saw that the unexpected arrival of a large force of guerrillas, led by a tiny, English-speaking Chinese woman, had put the Communists to flight. The leader introduced herself and was dubbed 'the Dragon Lady' by Gardella, who then witnessed her shoot twenty communist prisoners, and decapitate an officer with a 'thick-bladed sword like a machete'.[7]

The Dragon Lady agreed to lead Gardella to the rendezvous where he had arranged to meet his American friends, and on the way they were attacked by a couple of hundred Chinese troops, backed by four tanks. One of the tanks was destroyed by a mortar, and the crew of two others were eliminated by Gardella who tossed a grenade inside the open turrets. After yet more fierce fighting, the Communists were beaten off, and Gardella was reunited with Masters and the Scot, who explained that Roberts and Sergeant Holden had been killed by Chinese fighter planes. They then made a plan to reach Port Arthur, taking as a route one that would mislead their pursuers. They would cross the plain of Changchun, and head south for the Great Wall which they would cross between Kalgan and Changteh. Skirting Peking to the west, they would head for Cheng-ting and reach Laichow Bay where they would find a boat for Weihai, a port some two hundred miles from Seoul. To avoid the Chinese troops, they would march through a pair of tunnels, linked by a stone bridge, which would take them to another valley, and relative safety.

Gardella's epic, thousand-mile trek to the coast was to involve many further adventures, including a horseback, night attack on an airbase in which ten Russian military advisers, 'five officers in black uniforms, five enlisted men whose uniforms were brown' were killed, planes were set ablaze, a radio transmitter destroyed and several trucks commandeered. A hundred horsemen made the successful attack and 'had not suffered a single casualty'.[8] He also met Andy, an Australian, a former coastwatcher in Burma who had been in China since the Second World War, who was known to the Scot and had ridden a camel from the Gobi Desert with a band of Mongol tribesmen. Together they made a two-pronged, night attack on a Chinese underground nuclear test facility, 'between Chihfeng and the mountains' which they destroyed with explosive charges, but suffered the loss of forty tribesmen 'plus about a dozen more wounded, only one of them seriously'. After this success Gardella and Masters set off for the Great Wall, 150 miles away, accompanied by Andy on his camel and another 'thirty or forty' horsemen. On the way they engaged a force of a 1,000 Communist troops but were able to outwit them and reach the Great Wall on 24 or 25 May. Disguised by wearing hats pulled down over their heads, Gardella and Masters then rode into Peking, on a holiday, when Mao was scheduled to make a speech on the Great Wall. Their objective was to help the Dragon Lady assassinate a Communist, Sing Yet-soo, who had been snubbed by her, and then in retaliation had killed members of her family. Swapping their horses for bicycles, the group made their way to a particular house where they stabbed to death ten men, shot one in the throat with an arrow, and cut the head off and castrated the Dragon Lady's principal target. The one person to escape with his life later turned out to be Mao.

While on their way out of the city Gardella came across 'about half a dozen cages' three feet square and 'three feet high made of strong wood' in which some emaciated prisoners were being held. Gardella heard one say 'Lieutenant-Commander, United States Navy' but then was hustled away by the Dragon Lady anxious to make their escape. Reunited with the main party of Mongols, at a rendezvous outside the city, they continued their journey south towards Loshan, and met John O'Malley, a huge, armed Irishman and former Foreign Legionnaire who declared he was walking from Burma to Indochina to fight with the French.

Together they made their way along the Grand Canal to Hwang Ho where the Dragon Lady knew there was a boat equipped with a radio. Gardella was keen to use the transceiver to make contact with an American voice he heard over the airwaves, but he was persuaded not to do so for fear of monitoring by the Communists. Deterred by the news that gunboats were patrolling the mouth of river in Laichow Bay, they abandoned the boat and walked to a nearby village. Another radio, this one portable with a hand-powered generator, was found and the Scot used the original password used by Lieutenant Damon to identify his group of parachutists to the guerrillas to make contact over a voice channel with an unknown American station with the call-sign 'Spec One'. The owner of the transceiver made a gift of it to the group, and Sergeant Masters used the open code of 'onion', and masqueraded as the dead CIA officer Joseph Roberts to identify their position as being close to Lienyun, a town that the Scot estimated to be about two days' march away.[9]

Over the next few days Gardella and his eight companions maintained contact with the American wireless station, to arrange a rendezvous on the coast, and Masters announced that he would remain in China. Dismayed, Gardella decided to try and make it home, but when the group learned that Communist troops were plundering a nearby village they opted to go onto the offensive. By the time they reached the village more than 100 of the inhabitants had been butchered, but they were able to save some children who had been imprisoned in a school. In freeing the children, the Australian was shot twice in the back and badly wounded, but the rest of the group killed the remaining Communist soldiers and then withdrew.

That same night Gardella found time to sleep with the Dragon Lady, and then made contact with the American radio station to request a delay in the pick-up arranged on the coast. Twenty-four hours later the group reach Lienyun and silently climbed aboard a junk moored at one of the piers. Inside the cabin they found three Americans, one of who was the other civilian who had trained them with Roberts. As one made a desperate lunge for a weapon, Gardella killed him with a knife, and the Scot and Masters finished off the other pair. This was evidence, to Gardella, that 'a calculated breaking of faith by our own people had caused the deaths of our comrades. We were trained, sent on a mission, and abandoned – purposely.'[10] When searched, the bodies revealed two photo identity cards, of James Strong of the CIA, and Aleksei Kutuzov of the U.S. Foreign Service but, as Gardella acknowledged, 'To this day, I have no clearer idea that I had then about who trained us or where their orders came from.'[11]

Having disposed of the three American corpses, by tossing them into the South China Sea, Masters used the junk's radio to make contact with the American station and demand a pick-up, explaining that Roberts and Strong were 'gone', and threatening to defect to Mao unless they received assistance. Using the call-sign 'Eagles Nest', they were tested by a query concerning the star of the movie *The Outlaw*, and when the correct reply of 'Jane Russell' was given, a rendezvous was agreed, two miles east of Lienyun. While the others in the group made their way ashore by a small boat, Gardella drifted out to sea in the junk, and was intercepted two hours later by an American submarine.

Gardella's remarkable odyssey lasted until 30 May 1952, when he says he was drugged while aboard a U.S. Navy submarine, and he did not regain consciousness until he was being interrogated by American personnel in a hospital. He recalls being visited by his mother at Annapolis on 5 July 1952, when she was told that he was suffering from 'a severe allergic reaction to poison ivy in the field', and was given an honourable discharge ten days later, on 24 July 1952. During his meeting with Truman, the president had apologised to him and, when observing that there would be no record of the operation, nor any medals, asked him 'to forgive our country' as though some shameful event had occurred.

In a curious sequel to the story, Gardella explains that Sergeant Masters had threatened to 'take matters into our own hands' and go to the Communists if Gardella was badly treated upon his return to the United States, and revealed that although the Australian, Andy, 'never really recovered from the wounds he suffered', he was still alive in 1981, as was Sergeant Masters, the Scot, and the Dragon Lady, who subsequently had given birth to Gardella's two twin sons.

Gardella's story raises many issues, going to the heart of its authenticity, and one is bound to ask why the United States decided to launch a clandestine attack on China in 1952, and why such unconventional tactics were adopted. For example, what was the logic in selecting Gardella, an inexperienced, under-age asthmatic, for such a mission, and why were his companions all coerced into participating? Gardella admitted that he had 'volunteered so as not to be thrown out of the Corps' while Sergeant Holden had been caught stealing food in Korea and 'had been given the same kind of choice'. Even Sergeant Masters had been pressured, because he 'punched an officer in Korea'.[12] Corporal J.F. White had gone absent without leave and got a 'choice of this or a court-martial', making Private First Class Jake Craig the only true volunteer, for he had simply been offered the opportunity to volunteer by an officer, while on a ship bound for Korea. Thus Craig, who took part in the fortnight's training with the others, must have been brought back from Korea to undergo his training. Apart from Lieutenant Damon, about whom Gardella appears to have learned little, none of the other members of his team possessed any obvious qualifications for such a mission. Sergeant Masters had nineteen years' experience in the marines, but little else, and none apart from the officer even knew details of their objective prior to their landing, nor any understanding of how they were to be exfiltrated, nor any means of communicating with whoever was in overall command of the mission.

The proposition that the parachutists would be dropped, unarmed and unsupported, some 175 miles from their target, and in any event would be entirely dependent upon a Scot who had lived in China since 1935 seems odd, as it the team's determination to continue with its assignment after it obviously had been compromised, firstly by the loss of their aircraft that had dropped them into Manchuria, and then by their first encounter and firefight with a Chinese patrol.

Gardella clearly implies that he believes his mission was deliberately betrayed, and this was the essence of President Truman's apology. But if it was always intended to be a suicide assignment, with no prospect of success, why had the two civilians who had supervised their training turned up in China too? Was President Truman's apology intended to be an admission that Gardella was never intended to return from China, or that his mission had been betrayed? Gardella himself claims that all the U.S. Marine Corps records relating to Damon. Holden, Masters, Craig and White have been destroyed, and that his own file shows he never left the United States, with his medical record lost in a fire, so it is hard to check on his version of events. Suffice to say that upon close analysis his tale makes little sense, and no aspect of it bears any scrutiny whatever. The drop zone near Hunchun is in the extreme north-east of China, well to the north of North Korea, and the alleged journey to the Great Wall, via Kalgan, and then through Peking to Eitai, across the Yellow Sea from Seoul, truly defies belief.

Sing a Song to Jenny Next was published in 1981, and in the following years documents declassified and released by the National Archive revealed that some military units, including several Ranger companies, had indeed infiltrated North Korea during the conflict, penetrating far behind enemy lines and invariably landed by sea. However, none of the units mentioned, nor the missions listed, bore any resemblence to Gardella's tale, at least until 2008 when Lieutenant-Colonel Arthur T. Boyd revealed in *Operation Broken Reed* that in 1952 he had been selected for a clandestine assignment.

Boyd's remarkable story is not so dissimilar from Gardella's experience, even to the author's apparent unsuitability for his mission. Despite being married with a child, and being an expert on cipher systems he had been chosen for an exceptionally dangerous undertaking in which, he was warned by a mysterious officer whom he knew only as 'George Brown', that there was only a '50 percent chance' he would survive.[13] Barely aged eighteen when he had been commissioned at Fort Benning, Georgia in 1946 'as the youngest second lieutenant in the United States Army' he had been sent to the Signal Corps at Fort Monmouth and then posted to the 7772nd Signal Battalion in Frankfurt, Germany, the headquarters of the Armed Forces Security Agency with regular access to 'top secret, cryptographic, eyes-only messages addressed to General Lucius Clay.[14]

After the Berlin Airlift Boyd was posted back to Fort Bliss, Texas, and then in 1951 he was assigned to another signal battalion in Kaufbeuren,

Germany, in support of NATO, but in August he was summoned to a secret meeting in Munich. There he was invited to volunteer for Operation *Broken Reed*, a plan devised and named personally by President Truman to collect intelligence in Korea. According to 'George Brown'. Boyd had been chosen because he could 'transmit high speed international Morse code', knew cryptology, had been first in his officer candidate course and 'understood both COMINT and SIGINT'.[15] He also claimed that 'he wanted a young officer; younger men were willing to take more risks' and as Boyd was willing to take on anyone except 'the very nasty KGB' he accepted the mission. During his briefing Boyd was told that 'during the Second World War we broke the Japanese code and the British broke the German code'. The intention was 'to put men behind enemy lines. That's the HUMINT. We're going to insert a team into North Korea to determine enemy strengths. Relaying the information back is the COMINT.'[16]

The actual plan was extraordinarily complicated. A team of Americans, consisting of two CIA agents, a pair of Navy frogmen, two Rangers, a B-29 pilot, co-pilot and navigator, and Boyd as the 'communications specialist', would be delivered to North Korea by a submarine and rendezvous with a group of Nationalist Chinese soldiers masquerading as Communist troops who would escort the ten Americans across the whole peninsula, making contact on the way with twenty-two Chinese and Korean operatives who had no other way of reporting their vital information, and had been waiting since June to deliver their messages. The CIA personnel would translate their messages in English, Boyd would then encrypt them and transmit to an aircraft flying over the Sea of Japan which would act as a radio relay to Washington. This elaborate operation had an even more elaborate cover: the ten Americans would pretend to be the surviving aircrew of a B-29 crash, captured by Chinese Communists and on their way to China for interrogation. This ruse would be sufficient to bluff their way across the entire peninsula, to be picked up in the Yellow Sea by a Royal Navy helicopter five days later.

In August 1951, having accepted the high risk of not returning from *Broken Reed*, Boyd was sent back to his unit in Kaufbeuren, and it was not until December that he learned that his mission would take place. He then promptly told his wife Nell that he would be out of touch 'for a month or so', but did so in a curious way. His cover story, which he did not mention to her, was that he had been given leave to visit his father's ranch because fifteen of his cattle had 'died mysteriously'. Instead, his method of breaking his news to his wife was to place 'an amateur radio call to Nell that went through a ham station in Blytheville, Arkansas. It was New Year's Eve. Harold Sudsbury, manager of the radio station KLCN in Blytheville, patched me through to her.'[17]

Thus, according to Boyd, he was allowed to speak on a voice radio channel from Germany to the Arkansas. Then, having been flown in January to Japan, where he and the others underwent some last-moment first-aid medical training, they were taken by helicopter to the coast to board a submarine manned only with a skeleton crew for the journey to Korea. Once aboard they were informed that the submarine would only submerge fifty miles from their objective, and then 'surface after dark a few miles offshore' but only after they had made 'contact with the unit on shore'. They were invited onto the bridge because they could 'get a good view from the conning tower' and then proceeded on their thirty-two-hour voyage across the Sea of Japan to Yongjin Bay. Upon arrival they paddled ashore in two rubber boats while 'a diversion was created onshore by the Nationalist Chinese to cover the sound of the surfacing sub; eleven vehicles started their engines and men began to talk loudly and laugh to distract any attention from the sea'. However, when an enemy searchlight was illuminated 'a single shot rang out and the searchlight shattered and went dead'.[18]

When Boyd's team reached the beach they found their guide, a Lieutenant Lee, and sixty-six men accompanied by a pair of modified American armoured half-tracks, two stolen Soviet T-54 tanks, and half a dozen other trucks and reconnaissance vehicles. Having burned their wetsuits in some oildrums, and changed into clothes more appropriate for captured aircrew, the group moved off and spent the following five days undergoing frequent encounters with Korean forces, an air attack by UN aircraft and finally an ambush in which all but Boyd and two companions escaped to the west coast to be rescued by a Sikorsky HS-1 helicopter after he had spent 'nearly eight hours' flashing a light signal out to sea. Fortunately, the team was well fed, for their convoy included 'Chinese cooks' who prepared 'hot chow three times a day' of soups, rice, highly seasoned vegetables and 'chunks of unknown meat', plus 'snacks of rice cakes and sweet cookies' and, to vary the diet, there were standard issue C rations – ham and beans, beans and franks, canned bread, stew and crackers'.[19]

Boyd's role in the mission was essential, as he was the communications link between the numerous agents waiting to transmit their vital reports, on enemy strengths and positions. He was equipped with 'a sophisticated encryption machine' and another item, a 'high speed code key, known as a vibroflex or bug, to transmit the five-letter code groups using international Morse code'. Boyd recalled that 'the crypto machine spat out a paper tape with adhesive backing containing five-letter encoded word groups, identical to a stock market tickertape'. To ensure the valuable hardware could not fall into enemy hands, it was protected by 'six Thermite bombs' set to detonate six minutes after they had been activated. However, Boyd's transmitting technique was unusual, especially for a clandestine operator, for as soon as he landed on the beach he tested his radio and registered 'the emission of a strong radio frequency signal from the transmitter and a check for cryptographic operation proved that everything was ready to go'. His first exchange with the airborne operator lasted four hours but he 'changed frequencies several times to avoid anyone getting a fix on our position'. On another occasion Boyd transmitted for fifty-five minutes before he received news that the aircraft's crew had experienced 'trouble with their port engine and takeoff had been delayed'. Boyd also recalled that once it had taken 'several hours to complete the transmission'.[20] For an operator to have spent hours on the air while participating in a covert operation might strike many readers as rather odd, perhaps almost as strange as the idea of carrying classified crypto equipment on a secret mission into enemy-occupied territory. Most sensible planners would assume the worst and anticipate that all the members of the team, and any equipment they were carrying, would be compromised. Accordingly, in most covert missions, equipment is not put in jeopardy, and the participants are not briefed on matters that have no direct bearing on the mission. For someone with AFSA experience to be selected, and then to be briefed on the history of signals intelligence, and be given a detailed account of intelligence failures in Korea, seems highly unusual. Probably the very last person to be chosen for infiltration behind enemy lines, when there was a good chance of capture, would be anybody either with a knowledge of future plans, or experience of signals intelligence procedures and techniques. Evidently some thought had been given to the prospects of likely success for Boyd had been warned that he had 'only a 50 percent chance' of survival and says 'there's a good chance men will die on this mission' before issuing the team with cyanide pills.

One explanation for the very unorthodox arrangements made for *Broken Reed* might be Boyd's belief that the entire undertaking had been prepared by the president who had been emphatic that it should not be contaminated by the previous failures experienced by the conventional intelligence agencies on earlier attempts to gather information in Korea. All these efforts had failed, and President Truman had personally supervised this operation because he felt he had been let down so many times before. Indeed, George Brown had told Boyd that apart from the

Director of Central Intelligence, Walter Bedell Smith, the Defense Secretary George Marshall, the Chairman of the Joint Chiefs Omar Bradley, and Secretary of State Dean Acheson, nobody else knew of the plan, which was to be a 'top secret, out-of-channels operation'.[21] Brown knew all this because he had been briefed personally by Truman on 'numerous' occasions, and had access to him whenever he wanted. However, the secrecy was not intended to protect the personnel on the mission, but rather to insulate the White House from the embarrassment of other branches of his administration learning of Truman's scheme. 'he does not want any record of having gone over the heads of his military, civilian authorities, Congress or without consulting allies'.[22]

The lengths to which Truman had gone to preserve secrecy were remarkable. 'There will be no proof that this mission took place' warned Brown at the outset, 'None of this will be declassified until 1998', choosing the rather arbitrary length of time as forty-six years. And sure enough, Boyd says 'Operation Broken Reed was declassified in 1998', when he was undergoing psychiatric care, but his version of declassification does not mean the release of official documents, nor even the availability of a single archive file even referring to *Broken Reed*. Boyd recalled that he had been assured at the mission's conclusion: 'As far as military history goes, this operation did not take place. Every record of vessels and flights, including your rescue, will be erased, all files destroyed. No one will ever divulge anything about Broken Reed. There are no documents indicating the mission took place. That has been done on the orders of the president.'[23]

Although Boyd says twice that *Broken Reed* was declassified in 1998, his purported attempts to conduct searches with the CIA, the Department of Defense and the Truman Library 'encountered a dead-end', but that is not quite the same as his assertion that 'as Brown told me would happen, every record had been destroyed'. There is a distinction between an acknowledgment that a particular operation occurred, and a flat denial of any record of it. Boyd appears to have received the latter, but interpreted it as the former.

Furthermore, supposedly elaborate precautions had been taken to prevent news of the mission leaking in the event of the team suffering casualties. Perhaps indiscreetly, Boyd had been told that 'your wife will be informed you died in a plane crash while en route to your home on a military leave status. A cadaver burned beyond recognition will be substituted for your body and shipped to your hometown for funeral arrangements'.[24] Later he was told that CIA agents' deaths will not be connected in any way with the Korean War. They will be reported as missing or killed in the line of duty at some other geographical location. In addition, the dates of their deaths will be delayed and altered. The details, along with notification of their next of kin, are being handled by the agency.'[25]

It might be thought that Boyd's mission, to act as a communications channel, contained some contradictions and implausibilities. His task was to link up with an existing network of twenty-two agents who had been infiltrated behind enemy lines earlier, in June and July. 'Eight had parachuted or been dropped by helicopter. Six were inserted by boat' and another 'eight had slipped through the battle lines from South Korea'.[26] Although 'all carried radios', it seemed that 'because of distance and terrain' they were prevented from transmitting their reports directly, either to South Korea, Japan or even an aircraft, which was why Boyd's mission was required. But instead of opting for what might have appeared to have been the best and simplest solution, the infiltration of a single wireless operator, Truman had opted for a massive project involving nearly eighty men, most of whom perished. Furthermore, it was apparently dependent on 'a covert operative serving within the Chinese high command headquarters' who had been 'successful in preparing authentic-looking forged documents in such a way that there was little chance of' the group being challenged as it crossed the peninsula masquerading as a Chinese unit escorting ten handcuffed American aircrew. As a means of solving the problem for collecting and relaying reports from agents in Korea, *Broken Reed* seems a very strange solution. Why not simply offer the agents more powerful radios? Instead, President Truman opted for a bizarrely overt beach infiltration involving decoy noise, burning wetsuits and a destroyed enemy searchlight.

But did Boyd, or those briefing him, truly understand signals intelligence? There are indications in the text that Boyd's principal source of information, George Brown, had a less than perfect grasp of the discipline, and appeared not to know the difference between a code and a cipher, as suggested by his description of ULTRA: 'Without Ultra, the codename for Britain's greatest secret, and the cipher machine Enigma which broke Germany's code, Hitler might not have been defeated.'[27]

Boyd says the United States had enjoyed 'an almost complete and uninterrupted ability to decipher Japanese radio traffic throughout the Second World War. The order to attack Pearl Harbor had been decoded many hours before the first bombs were dropped. The long delay in transmitting the warning to Hawaii was the result of human error.'[28]

Several other clues in the text suggest that Boyd invented the tale many years after the Korean War. For example, he mentions 'the very nasty KGB', and organisation that simply did not exist in 1952. He also refers four times to the assurance that details of *Broken Reed* would not be declassified until 1998, which is curious because the concept of declassification did not exist during the Korean conflict. Boyd does not appear to know the true name of any of the other participants, nor the name of the submarine which delivered him to Korea, nor the ship which recovered him. According to Boyd, the submarine commander had been given exceptional orders, and would sail unarmed and with only a skeleton crew, but would proceed most of the way on the surface, submerging only for the very last part of the voyage. Boyd's description of this part of his mission sounds very odd indeed. Although he had never worn a wetsuit before, he was provided with one, for no apparent reason, which he put on over his other clothes, and then he burned it in a convenient oildrum upon his arrival. Paddling ashore, in two rubber boats, was supervised by two frogmen who sank their craft on the beach instead of returning to the submarine. Since they were redundant on the remainder of the mission, why did they not take the dinghies back to the submarine, instead of leaving evidence that might be found by the enemy?

One of the more baffling aspects of Boyd's tale is the willingness of an intelligence analyst, Jay T. Young, to add an afterword in which he appears to endorse the author's claims. Young says he is a former senior analyst at the CIA and a reserve naval intelligence officer, and appears to endorse Boyd's authenticity, observing that both the British and American governments had been handicapped by high-level Soviet penetration during the Korean War, noting that 'especially the British secret service' had been compromised. This seems an odd assertion to make, considering that Kim Philby, the only known Soviet penetration of SIS during the Korean War, had been dismissed in November 1951. So how had Young decided that SIS had been infiltrated? One possibility is that the suggestion came from Boyd himself who, when attempting to explain President Truman's enthusiasm for running 'black' out-of-channel operations, insisted that his 'distrust and concern' regarding 'almost daily revelations about communist infiltration of the U.S. and British intelligence communities' had been a major motive, citing in particular 'the defection of agents such as Donald Maclean and Guy Burgess'. Whilst it is true that both Soviet spies disappeared in May 1951, their whereabouts remained unknown until they materialised at a press conference held in Moscow in February 1956. In other words, in August 1951, when *Broken Reed* was being planned, it is unlikely that the cases of either Burgess or Maclean could have played any role in influencing Truman. Boyd also mentions Klaus Fuchs, and Ethel and

Julian Rosenberg as spies arrested by the FBI in 1950 who had undermined Truman's confidence in American intelligence, but in fact Fuchs, a natrualized Briton, was never arrested by the FBI, and the Rosenbergs were detained in New York in July 1950. Indeed, the capture of spies is usually regarded as a success by the counter-intelligence authorities, so it is hard to see how any of these incidents, which did not involve members of either the British or American intelligence communities, could have had the impact claimed.

It is Young, not Boyd, that tentatively named HMS *Cardigan Bay* as the likely rescue ship which retrieved the mission's survivors off the Korean coast, but no Sikorsky, nor any other helicopter, ever flew off the old Second World War frigate, so the identification would seem to be somewhat flawed. Apparently his view was not reached on any evidence beyond Boyd's version, and Young's own research which suggested that the *Cardigan Bay* had been engaged on a support mission for special forces.

In retrospect, Operation *Broken Reed* appears to have much in common with *Sing a Song to Jenny Next,* and each seems as bogus as the other, although Colonel Boyd at least has the excuse that he has suffered from a psychiatric disorder.

Chapter 5

The Soviet Conspiracy

'Neither can one talk to intelligence men about a subject like Operation Splinter Factor without at one point feeling oneself to be part of some enormous fantasy'

Stewart Steven

The sudden end of the Soviet Bloc took many by surprise, including most of the West's intelligence agencies. While the CIA had monitored the economic collapse of the Warsaw Pact members with some precision, it had certainly failed to predict the speed with which the Berlin Wall was to be dismantled, and hardly addressed the issue of German reunification. In April 2001, the CIA sponsored an academic conference at Princeton University to celebrate the declassification and release to the public of thousands of documents generated by the Directorate of Intelligence, and in the main they demonstrated that while the analysts had maintained a close watch on the impending implosion, they had never grasped the full implications.

In the years that followed the elimination of the Communist Party's grip on Eastern Europe, new democratic safeguards were introduced to supervise the activities of local security and intelligence structures, and in some countries provision was made to open and inspect the records of the previous regimes. In Germany the Gauck Commission was entrusted with the task of cataloguing and making available the copious files of the notorious Stasi, and similar exercises were undertaken in the Czech Republic, Hungary and Bulgaria. Even Romania and Slovakia paid lip service to the principle of exercising parliamentary control over the replacement organisations, but it was in Poland where closest attention was paid to the names emerging from the archives of the hated, ubiquitous UB. Had Lech Walesa once acted as an informant for the despised security apparatus? Who had been responsible for the penetration of the Solidarity movement? Which cabinet minister had ordered the murder of Father Popieluszko?

While these questions preoccupied the modern historians anxious to bring the supporters of the Communists to account, others were engaged in more long-term research, using the newly-released records to reassess the accuracy of what had been published in the West. Among the surprises was the doubt cast over *Operation Splinter Factor*, a book which in 1974 purported to document clandestine operations in Poland in the post-war era, written by the distinguished British journalist Stewart Steven, who later was to edit the *Mail on Sunday*. Married to a Pole, to whom he dedicated the book, Steven had long taken an interest in Poland and, relying on sources he never named, or people such as Colonel Jozef Swiatlo, whom he never interviewed, Steven blamed Allen Dulles, the DCI appointed in January 1953, for a Machiavellian CIA scheme intended to spread dissent across the Warsaw Pact, but actually resulted in the notorious post-war show-trials. Steven revealed that Dulles, who had died five years earlier in January 1969, had masterminded a ruthless plot, codenamed *Splinter Factor*, that had been intended to eliminate Eastern Europe's moderate Communist leadership with the objective of preventing its popularity from sweeping across the rest of the Continent and causing France and Italy to succumb to the Kremlin. According to the author, the plan had run out of control and its unexpected consequences 'destroyed the dreams of a generation and made the world a safer place for its secret police'.

> *Operation Splinter Factor* destroyed any hope of a genuine political dialogue between the governors and the governed in Eastern Europe for years to come, and it poisoned the relations of these countries with Russia and with each other.[1]

Nor Steven did pull his punches when he described the results of the diabolical plot developed and supervised personally by Dulles:

> Politically counterproductive, necessarily barbarous and unquestionably a failure, Operation Splinter Factor was part of that bleak period. It lies as an ugly stain upon the honour and integrity of the United States and must rank as one of the darkest chapters in the whole history of American diplomacy and espionage.[2]

These harsh words were followed by the author's conclusion, that 'Operation Splinter Factor has shown how deeply the foreign policies of a nation can be contaminated by the premise that a just cause often needs to be pursued by unjust means'.

According to Steven, Allen Dulles had used Colonel Swiatlo and an unsuspecting American Communist, Noel Field, to discredit the leaders of Hungary, Bulgaria and Poland, who then fell victim to show trials. Not pulling his punches, the author accused Dulles of responsibility for the arrest of 100,000 people, and the deaths of a thousand others who were tortured and killed. But could any of this be true?

The basis of Steven's story is that Jozef Swiatlo, a senior officer in the notorious Polish UB, approached the SIS with a view to defecting, and after an initial clandestine meeting in Warsaw with 'Captain Michael Sullivan', an undercover SIS officer, it was decided by the Foreign Secretary, Ernest Bevin, not to grant him political asylum. His reason was not Swiatlo's unpalatable reputation, but Bevin's disenchantment with SIS. Instead, the SIS station commander in Washington DC was instructed to hand Swiatlo over, not to the CIA, but to Allen Dulles, then practising as an attorney in New York. Then, under direction from Dulles, 'a special courier was sent to Warsaw to open negotiations with the Pole', and when he agreed to remain in Poland and spy for the Americans 'the most successful Western agent in the history of the Cold War had been activated'.[3] Swiatlo's very first message to Washington DC suggested that 'great damage could be done to the Party and to Party credibility within the country as a whole' if 'Noel Field, an American agent', could be shown to be 'actively collaborating' with certain senior Communists. Dulles had seized the opportunity and 'the Swiatlo-Field link could be so twisted, Dulles realized, that through it the Soviet empire could be torn apart'. Accordingly, Swiatlo was activated, although he 'was quite surprised when the reply he had been waiting for was personally delivered by his senior American controller'. His instructions were to 'find spies everywhere. He would denounce top Party leaders as American agents, and the evidence for such a denunciation would be provided by the Americans themselves'.

He would uncover a major Trotskyist conspiracy, financed by the United States, which was enveloping every country in Russia's satellite empire. He would prove that Titoism was rampant not only in Poland, but in Hungary, Bulgaria, Czechoslovakia, Rumania and East Germany. He would report to Beria himself that the centre of that conspiracy, the link man between these traitors and Washington, was a man named Noel Haviland Field, who, Beria was to be told, was the most important American intelligence man in Eastern and Western Europe.[4] He would show how Field had run the most successful American espionage operation during the Second World War, using the Unitarians as cover.

60

He would show how Field had used his position to attract members of the Communist Party to him and then recruit them as agents. He would show, ever since he had left Harvard, Field had worked for American intelligence, posing as a fellow traveller or a member of the Communist Party. He would show how, after the war, Field had infiltrated his agents into Eastern Europe into top positions in Party and government so quickly that the big jobs were seized before the Moscow loyalists had a chance of exerting their strength. He would show how, even now that Field's cover was deepening, the Senate investigation was a sham designed to help Field establish himself inside Eastern Europe.

So here we have the spymaster Allen Dulles deliberately sacrificing Noel Field in a scheme to implicate certain moderate Communists and thereby provoke a savage reaction from Stalin, all in the hope of provoking popular revulsion, and maybe a counter-revolution. To assist Swiatlo's ambitious scheme, Dulles played two further trump cards, both Soviet spies working under American and British control. The first 'who still cannot be named because of state security reasons', was 'the CIA's resident double agent'.

A desk officer working within CIA headquarters in Washington, he was thought by the Russians to be a Communist spy, but, as a junior State department official in the mid-thirties, he had immediately informed his superiors when he was approached by a Soviet agent. He had been carefully nurtured by the U.S. ever since. On no occasion had he sent deliberately false information to Russia. He was being saved for just such an event as this.[5]

This double agent's task, when he was asked by his Soviet controller for information about Noel Field, was to give an answer 'carefully guarded and subtly worded' which implied that Field was definitely a CIA asset. His report was 'dynamite. It was convincing because it was not specific. There could be little doubt any more in the Soviets' minds that Field was a U.S. agent'.[6]

Dulles' second ploy was to use 'an Englishman named Hathaway' who worked for Lieutenant-General Fedor Belkin, one of the most senior Soviet intelligence officers and was one of his regular informants'.[7] Allegedly Hathaway, also acting as a double agent, had been instructed to tell Belkin, while on a visit to Austria, that 'SIS and CIA people were quarrelling over the activities of a man called Field who, Hathaway said, was hiring SIS operatives into the CIA by offering them more money than the British could afford and thereby damaging the SIS network in Czechoslovakia'.[8]

Belkin, described as 'in charge of the Soviet secret police in Hungary, Austria, Germany, Czechoslovakia, Poland, Rumania, Bulgaria and

Albania' promptly 'flew to Moscow for consultations with Beria and also for a final pep talk from Stalin' who decreed that nothing 'was as important as destroying Field and the nest of vipers he controlled. Belkin was given a free hand to achieve this aim'.[9] Thus Stalin, Beria and Belkin all fell for the Dulles ploy and were provoked, on bogus evidence, to launch another savage purge that would rid the Eastern bloc of the Party's moderate leadership.

So who was Noel Field? Born in London to American parents living in Zurich, where his father was a psychiatrist, Field had graduated from Harvard and in 1926 had joined the State Department where he became friends with Alger Hiss and Lawrence Duggan. Both, of course, were already active Soviet agents and, according to his former Soviet controller, Field too worked as a spy during this period. After ten years in the State Department, and against the wishes of his controller, Field had moved to Geneva to work for the League of Nations, and while there he had in some way become implicated in the plot to murder Ignace Reiss, a senior Soviet illegal.

Like numerous other important Soviet intelligence organisers, Reiss had fallen victim to Stalin's purges, but instead of obeying his recall to Moscow he had gone into hiding in Switzerland, but had been lured out to meet his murderers in Lausanne in September 1937. It was at this point, following an intensive Swiss police investigation, that Field lost his usefulness to the NKVD and he had been cast adrift. However, as a committed ideologue, Field never lost his faith and even travelled, as a tourist, to Moscow the following year.

Upon his return from the Soviet Union, Field had been posted to undertake refugee relief work in Perpignan, then crowded with survivors of the Spanish Civil War, and in October 1940 left the League of Nations to continue his work for the Unitarian Service Committee, in Marseilles. He was obliged to flee to Switzerland in October 1942, when the Nazis extended their grip of France to take over the Vichy unoccupied zone, but by then Field had established contact with remnants of an underground KPD cell, and with Allen Dulles, the OSS representative in Berne. Whatever the precise nature of his covert courier activities for OSS and the KPD, Field during this period was to contaminate virtually every Communist he came into contact with, and when he travelled to Prague early in May 1949 to look for a post at the Charles University, he was arrested and taken to Budapest for interrogation.

Field himself was to remain in solitary confinement in an AVH prison, without charge but subject to frequent interrogation, until

November 1954 when he was released, without explanation. In the meantime, the Hungarian Foreign Minister, Laszlo Rajk, had been arrested, accused of having been a Soviet spy, convicted at a show trial, and hanged. The same fate befell Traicho Kostov, Bulgaria's deputy Prime Minister, and even the Polish Communist Party First Secretary, Wladyslaw Gomulka, was thrown into prison, but the thread connecting the three was the allegation, contained in their separate indictments, that each had been recruited and run on behalf of OSS by Field, described as 'one of the leaders of the American espionage service' headed by Allen Dulles. Even Rudolf Slansky, who himself, as the powerful Secretary of the Czech Communist Party, had overseen the purge in Czechoslovakia, was arrested, charged with espionage and executed. In fact, of course, Slansky, like Rajk and Gomulka had shown too much independence from Moscow, and had fallen victim to Stalin's paranoia, and it is likely that Field only survived, to be released twenty months after Stalin's death in March 1953, because, like his wife Herta and his brother Hermann, he held an American passport. Field had indeed aided Rajk's return to Hungary in 1943, having arranged his escape from an internment camp in France, doubtless with OSS's help, but his route through Yugoslavia served to compromise him when, four years later, Tito distanced himself from Stalin and the combination of links to OSS, Field and the Yugoslavs were considered highly incriminating. Dozens of other Communists, in Czechoslovakia, East Germany and Poland, whom Field had given assistance in the war, found themselves contaminated and purged. Some survived years of imprisonment and the *gulag*, many others were less fortunate.

Three months after Noel Field disappeared in Prague his brother Hermann, then living in Warsaw, started on a journey to find him, but he only reached Okecie Airport, where he was taken into custody by the UB. Noel's wife Herta, who had awaited Hermann's arrival in Prague, had been baffled by his failure to catch his flight, and later in August 1949 she too was arrested by the Czech police and sent to Budapest where she was imprisoned, isolated from her husband. Hermann would not be released from his confinement in a basement cell at Miedzyszyn, a secret UB facility outside Warsaw, until November 1954, only days before his brother and sister-in-law were freed in Budapest. Hermann promptly flew to Zurich, but Noel and Herta chose to seek political asylum in Hungary, apparently undaunted by their experience. One influence over their decision to make their permanent home on the Sashegy Hill, overlooking Budapest, may have been the eagerness of the FBI to question them about their links to the CPUSA.

Since the end of the war his friend Alger Hiss had been convicted of perjury for having lied about his espionage, Lawrence Duggan had committed suicide by throwing himself out of his Madison Avenue office window in December 1948 while under investigation by the FBI, and numerous former CPUSA members had denounced Noel Field as a spy who had betrayed secrets from inside the State Department. Field knew that he was of intense interest to the FBI because when he had sought to renew his American passport in 1949 he had been granted a short extension, and informed that the document was only good for travel back to the United States. Field must have known that a former CPUSA courier, J.B. Matthews, had named Field as a fellow Communist in testimony before the Dies Committee in November 1938, and perhaps that another FBI informant, Whittaker Chambers, had also denounced him, but what he did not know was that he had also been identified positively as a Soviet spy by a defector, Hede Massing, in 1947, and she had been in a position to know a great deal about his espionage because she had recruited him in the first place. She and her husband Paul had acted as Soviet illegals before the war but, disillusioned by Stalin's excesses, had broken with the Party and agreed to cooperate with the FBI to whom she had identified Field as one of her top sources. However, as the Fields had remained abroad, out of its jurisdiction, the FBI had been powerless to pursue them.

During his imprisonment in Budapest Field had been cross-examined by numerous interrogators, but one of the most brutal had been Colonel Josef Swiatlo, the UB officer who had arrested his brother Hermann at Warsaw Airport, and who had travelled to Hungary to question him. Even by the UB's standards Swiatlo was a ruthless individual with a terrifying reputation, and as deputy director of the feared 10th Department he had arrested the Party's General-Secretary, Wladyslaw Gomulka. None of this might have become public knowledge but in early December 1953, while on an official visit to East Berlin, Swiatlo had seized the opportunity to defect to the CIA, and late in September 1954 he announced at a press conference in Washington DC that he intended to expose the true, political nature of the show trials that had been held across Eastern Europe. Unaware that Swiatlo's nickname was 'the butcher', the CIA had sponsored him to broadcast to Poland over Radio Liberty, and his very detailed disclosures were considered to be extremely effective in that the Polish regime had been stunned to learn of the UB's malign activities. Swiatlo's 10th Department had been responsible for maintaining Party discipline, and this had given him the right to spy on the most senior officials on the land. Not surprisingly,

Swiatlo's broadcasts had proved devastating, as all his listeners recognised the authenticity of his remarks.

Whatever else the broadcasts achieved, Noel and Herta Field were to be released, and paid compensation, within weeks of Swiatlo's revelation confirming that he had interrogated them personally in Budapest where they had been incarcerated. Hitherto the Czech, Polish and Hungarian authorities had claimed complete ignorance of what might have happened to the three members of the Field family. However, once Swiatlo had exposed the truth, all three governments were forced to admit at least that the trio had been imprisoned.

Steven's interpretation of these events is remarkable, for he claimed that Swiatlo had been acting on the CIA's instructions when he had initiated Operation *Splinter Factor*, and that Dulles had conceived the entire stratagem, which had spun out of control with such dire consequences. Unfortunately, the two principal players in the drama, Field and Dulles, were both dead when Steven wrote his book. Dulles had died in 1969, and Field, whose health had never fully recovered from his incarceration, died three years later. As for Swiatlo, he was never interviewed by Steven who appears to have relied upon the defector's testimony before a Congressional committee in September 1954 for his biographical background. Strangely, if Steven is to be believed, Swiatlo not only lied in his evidence to Congress, but omitted to mention that he had been an agent of the CIA for more than three years before his defection. The chances of this being true seem very slim, especially when one considers that part of Swiatlo's tremendous value to the CIA was his disclosure that a long-running operation, the so-called Polish Freedom and Independence Movement, known by the Polish acronym WIN, was actually controlled by the UB. Organised from Nuremberg where the CIA's Ted Shackley drew volunteer agents from the nearby Camp Valka, a displaced persons camp housing up to 20,000 inmates, mainly from eastern Europe. Shackley had armed and trained them for infiltration home, never realising that the entire project had been penetrated, and that the Polish end was handled by the ubiquitous UB.

Completely duped, the CIA had been pouring resources into WIN right up until the moment Swiatlo revealed that the entire undertaking was nothing more than a sophisticated deception run from Warsaw. For two years, arms, money, ammunition and radios had been air-dropped to what the CIA had mistakenly believed had been an underground resistance movement, never suspecting that the entire organization had been manipulated from the outset by the Communists. The WIN fiasco was to prove a huge embarrassment to the CIA, but if Swiatlo, who had known of the project, had been working for the CIA since 1949, why had he kept quiet about it? The obvious explanation is that Swiatlo genuinely did not defect, nor make contact with the CIA, until 1953, exactly as he had said in his sworn evidence to Congress.

So who else did Steven, who asserted he 'was particularly well qualified to separate truth from fiction', rely upon for his astonishing information? The author says he spoke to 'former members of the CIA' who do not have 'any desire to see their names in print', 'past members of Eastern European security services and armies who have defected to the West' and cannot be named for fear 'the KGB will one day ring at their front doors and take its revenge'.[10] He also talked to 'current employees of government and governmental organizations in the West' who would 'risk losing their jobs if their identities are divulged' and finally 'current employees of governments in the East European bloc' who 'desired to remain anonymous'.[11] Thus Steven's book contains not a single identified source to verify the quite terrible charges he directs against Allen Dulles, Jozef Swiatlo and the CIA.

In the absence of any named witnesses, it is worth taking a closer look at some of the claims made in *Operation Splinter Factor*. For example, did the British SIS participate in such a plan? Steven makes three assertions that can be checked: Firstly, that Swiatlo approached the British, and was contacted by 'Captain Michael Sullivan' before his offer to defect was taken up by the CIA. Secondly, that SIS ran a source named 'Hathaway' who was in touch with General Belkin, and thirdly that the SIS station commander in Washington DC in 1949 took Swiatlo's offer straight to Dulles in New York.

Close scrutiny of Captain Michael Sullivan, 'the head of the Secret Intelligence Service operation in Poland' is illuminating. Steven describes him in some detail, as the son of a paper manufacturer with a business in Poland, having been educated at a minor public school, a graduate of Cambridge University with a degree in Eastern European languages, fluent in Polish who had joined SOE during the war but later had switched to SIS. However, SOE had kept him 'away from the Poles so he would not be compromised in any way' after the German surrender, and he had been sent to Poland 'as head of a British relief agency and, using charity as his cover, set up one of the most complex and sophisticated political intelligence networks then operating anywhere in the world'. From 1945 onwards Sullivan had acted as an illegal resident, maintaining contact with the legal resident who based in the British Embassy in Warsaw. Steven does not explain his rank of 'Captain', which under normal circumstances could be either military or naval. However, neither service allows its personnel to use this rank in civilian life unless they had served with a regular commission, and in any event regulars do not use their rank if below that of a major. Accordingly, the only possible explanation is that Sullivan had been a regular naval officer and achieved the rank of captain before he joined SOE, a career path which would have been quite unique for that organisation.

One might think, given the very comprehensive nature of this description, that it would be easy to confirm Sullivan's existence, or his real name if this was an alias (a point Steven leaves moot), but no such person ever existed. Only one SIS officer in the immediate post-war period spoke fluent Polish (the head of SIS's Polish section, Wilfred Dunderdale, having spoken fluent Russian) and Harold Perkins worked in SOE's Polish Section, liaising with the Poles in exile throughout the war, before he was transferred to SIS's southern Italian base at Bari to work in the Adriatic. In short, Perkins is the only person to even remotely match 'Sullivan', but they could not be the same person. So where did Steven learn about 'Sullivan'? According to his source notes, the author claims it came from 'a former employee of the CIA', which may account for its inherent improbability.[12]

But even if 'Sullivan' was an invention, what about the assertion that a single person, working under non-official cover in Poland, developed a huge network immediately after the war? Once again, this simply never happened, and the local sources were run from the SIS station at the embassy in Warsaw. According to Steven, Swiatlo had used an intermediary to contact the 'legal' to arrange a rendezvous, and this senior SIS official, protected by diplomatic immunity, had passed the task of meeting the UB officer to Sullivan who, of course, enjoyed no such protection and would have been extremely vulnerable. The idea that any intelligence organisation would endorse such a foolhardy procedure simply beggars belief, and the hazardous nature of the arrangement in which a well-known UB officer had insisted that 'he would meet with no-one but the resident himself'.[13] Evidently SIS, in acknowledging that 'the chances that the Soviets were setting a trap seemed disproportionately great' had taken out an insurance policy.[14] If Sullivan had been arrested, his masters in London 'had "boxed in" an active [Soviet] agent whom they would pick up and exchange for him if things went wrong'.[15]

But is this scenario really likely? Firstly, the concept of a 'spy-swap' did not develop until the American U-2 Francis Gary Powers was exchanged for Rudolf Abel in 1961. As far as Britain is concerned, the only similar bargain was struck in 1964, with the release of the KGB spy

Gordon Lonsdale in return for imprisoned SIS courier Greville Wynne. Thus any confidence in such a deal in 1949 seems to have been somewhat premature. Nevertheless, is it true that SIS had such a card up their sleeve, and there was just such a spy active in 1949 whom the Soviets would have been anxious to have returned to Moscow? The only way to assess this issue is to look at the espionage investigations then underway in England, and examine both the British and Soviet archives to see whether there were spies active at the time against whom, for some reason, no action was ever taken. In 1949 MI5's major preoccupation was the Soviet spy codenamed initially *Rest* and later *Charles* in the *Venona* project (a counter-intelligence programme). However, he was not to be identified as the atomic physicist Klaus Fuchs until many months after these events, and he was not to be arrested until 2 February 1950, which tends to eliminate him as the 'boxed-in' spy. As there were no other espionage convictions for several years before and after 1949, with the single exception of William Marshall, whose activities were not to be discovered by MI5 until 1952, and then only accidentally. A junior employee of the Diplomatic Wireless Service, Marshall had been spotted in London in the company of a suspected Soviet agent, Pavel Kuznetsov, who operated under diplomatic cover at the embassy. Marshall was subsequently convicted of breaches of the Official Secrets Act, and Kuznetsov was expelled, but neither person was under investigation in 1949. Accordingly, the assertion that SIS had someone to trade for Sullivan if he had been taken into custody seems open to very considerable doubt.

There are some other unusual aspects to Steven's account of Swiatlo's defection. For example, Steven claims that as a result of their encounter, on a bench at night in winter in the middle of Warsaw, Sullivan wrote a report on Swiatlo in which he said that the UB officer was in possession that was 'not only explosive but totally up-to-date. He had access to the most secret archives' but he also claimed that the decision to defect had been made 'almost on the spur of the moment', as he was 'an angry man, frustrated by thwarted ambition and the belief that the system he had fought for all his life was corrupted beyond repair'.[16] Apparently a committed ideologue, Swiatlo had recommended an investigation of a member of the Party's Central Committee, but he had been overruled by President Boleslaw Bierut who had 'ordered the arrest of one of Swiatlo's principal informants and had counselled Swiatlo to keep the whole affair to himself'.[17]

This complex explanation hardly seems to merit the description 'spur of the moment', but what is really strange about Sullivan's report about 'an invaluable find – an intelligence man's dream' is that the Foreign

Secretary, Ernest Bevin, was unimpressed and rejected Swiatlo. Steven insists that Bevin turned SIS's recommendation and 'scornfully attacked British intelligence methods inside Eastern Europe as embarrassingly worse than useless. The satellites were a lost cause, he said; political intelligence in capitals like Warsaw, Budapest and Bucharest was a waste of time'.[18] Steven notes that 'by withdrawing SIS from Eastern Europe, he weakened his organization immeasurably; it lacked the expertise to operate overnight as efficiently elsewhere and it began to spread its tentacles over too wide an area with too limited a budget'.[19]

This account seems quite at odds with Ernest Bevin's reputation as one of SIS's favourite Foreign Secretaries who greatly encouraged the organization's efforts to undermine Communism in Eastern Europe, and is probably best known for authorising his deputy, Christopher Mayhew, to supervise the creation of the Information Research Department, a specialist unit designed to counter Moscow's propaganda. Far from being sceptical about SIS, Bevin was a tremendous enthusiast about the organisation, always expounding on its virtues and encouraging numerous high-risk operations. Given that Bevin actually *expanded* SIS's operations in Eastern Europe, and certainly never withdrew from the arena, is it credible for him to have turned Swiatlo away, as alleged?

The background for the Foreign Secretary's decision in such matters has to be understood in its political and historical context, and although Steven gives the impression that at the time Whitehall was inundated with requests from 'hundreds of minor officials', the truth is that between 1945 and 1971 Britain received only a single Soviet intelligence defector, Grigori Tokaev.[20] Apart from one each received by Canada (Igor Gouzenko) and Australia (Vladimir Petrov) respectively, almost all the rest had headed to the United States, and invariably claimed that Britain was unsafe for defectors as its security and intelligence apparatus had been penetrated comprehensively. In such circumstances, a prize of the value of Swiatlo, 'one of the most important intelligence operatives of modern history' would have been a very significant coup, and the assertion that the Home Secretary, Herbert Morrison, had decreed that 'there were too many such defectors', and had refused permission to receive Swiatlo, is patently absurd.[21] Such decisions, of course, were not made by the Home Secretary as Steven claims, and intelligence defections were considered important novelties to be given the very maximum encouragement. In short, SIS would have jumped at the opportunity of landing a catch and the SIS Chief, Sir Stewart Menzies, would have dealt with his Secretary of State personally on such a crucial matter.

So if 'Captain Michael Sullivan' is an invention, what about 'the CIA's resident double agent', referred to by Steven as 'Agent X' whose identity still needed to be protected in 1974? This is an especially improbable scenario, for at that time the CIA's Counterintelligence Staff, headed by James Angleton, was very wary of any contact between CIA personnel and his Soviet adversaries. According to Steven, 'Agent X' had been recruited by the Soviets when 'a junior State Department official in the mid-thirties' and who had, by 1949, switched to the CIA and was working as a desk officer at headquarters.[22] But could there really be anyone with such a profile? Certainly there were Soviet spies active in the State Department in the 1930s, and the *Venona* decrypts proved that Lawrence Duggan, for example, had worked as a spy codenamed *Sherwood*, and Alger Hiss had appeared in the texts as the source known as *Ales*. But it was also the case that two of the Soviet spies responsible for handling such agents in Washington DC, Hede Massing and Elizabeth Bentley, had cooperated with the FBI and disclosed the members of their networks. They mentioned nobody fitting 'Agent X', and there does not appear to be such an individual in the *Venona* intercepts, so is it possible that such a person really existed? Not only is it highly improbable, but since the end of the Cold War, and the release of some Soviet archives, not even a hint of such a spy has emerged. As for the idea of running such a dangerous double agent operation from inside the CIA's headquarters, the suggestion is certainly novel, and if it had really happened, it would have been well documented by the end of the twentieth century. While it is hard to imagine the CIA undertaking such a project in 1949, it is equally difficult to think that the ever-vigilant Soviets would have fallen for such a scam.

In general terms it must be said that as Steven misidentifies the Chief of SIS as 'Sir Stuart Menzies'[23], not a great deal of confidence can be attached to his comments about this organisation, and Swiatlo himself denies having had any contact with SIS. The proposition that Swiatlo would have chosen the British first is certainly odd because, as we now know, and Swiatlo must have known at the time, the SIS network in Poland in 1949 was effectively run by the UB who had penetrated it at every level. So did SIS run a reliable source who was in touch with General Belkin? The problem with this scenario is that since Steven's book, much more information about Fedor Belkin has emerged.

Belkin was indeed the Soviet MGB adviser in south-east Europe, and had supervised a team of forty investigators who prepared Field's arrest and the show trials on instructions from Moscow. He had also personally supervised the interrogation of Rajk who initially had refused to confess but, according to Janos Kádár, the minister then in charge of the AVO who was interviewed after the Soviet collapse in 1989, had been persuaded to participate in the show trial in return for a promise that he and his family would be saved. Persuaded that the charade was in the best interests of the cause, and would help compromise Tito, Rajk had agreed to the ploy, only to find himself double-crossed, and on the gallows. Significantly, Belkin himself was also to be one of Stalin's victims, and perished when he was accused of having worked for British and Zionist intelligence services. This occurred at the height of Stalin's 'Doctors' Plot' during which he launched a savage campaign of anti-Semitism across eastern Europe. This critical detail was not learned until the publication of *Show Trials* by George Horos, and therefore was unavailable to Steven when he wrote *Operation Splinter Factor*.

With Steven's version of Belkin's true role in the so-called Field plot being so misunderstood, it is probable that 'Hathaway' is equally bogus. Finally, there is the curious assertion that SIS passed Swiatlo's offer to defect to Dulles. This is a strange claim, for the SIS head of station in Washington DC at the time, from 1949 to 1951, was Kim Philby, himself an experienced Soviet mole.

Back in September 1945 Philby had received an offer to defect from a GRU officer, Colonel Konstantin Volkov, who was then based under consular cover in Istanbul. Assigned to handle the delicate task of negotiating terms and ensuring his safe arrival in the West, Philby had instantly informed his Soviet contacts who ensured that the hapless Volkov was unceremoniously bundled aboard a plane home, where he was executed. It seems likely, given Philby's track record of eliminating potentially dangerous defectors, that he would have tipped off the Russians to the traitor in the ranks of the UB. In Steven's account he fails to name the SIS officer responsible for travelling down to New York to deliver the Swiatlo file to Dulles, but the fact that this person must have been Philby rather undermines the tale's veracity, especially as Philby omits the entire episode from his memoirs, *My Silent War*.

In terms of the book's chronology, Steven is frustratingly vague about precisely when Sullivan met Swiatlo on the bench in Warsaw, and says only that this took place in the winter, so some analysis is required to narrow the timeframe. The other dates that are known for certain are his visit to Warsaw in January 1949, the day when Noel Field arrived in Czechoslovakia from Paris, being 5 May 1949, the day he was last seen walking out of the Palace Hotel, on 22 May 1949, and Swiatlo's defection in Berlin on 22 December 1953. Whereas Swiatlo and the CIA insist that he had no contact with either the British or the Americans prior to his escape, Steven avers that the true story has him talking to Sullivan, and setting the stage for Operation *Splinter Factor* in the winter of 1948/49 at the latest. This version means that, following his decision to defect, Swiatlo remained in place, as a CIA agent, for up to four years, which suggests a few other problems with the chronology in Steven's account. For example, Swiatlo's very first message to Washington DC was on the subject of Field, yet we know he had been allowed to leave Warsaw in January 1949, and he did not enter Czechoslovakia until May. Thus, having let Field slip through his fingers in January, when he was in Poland, Swiatlo was obliged to wait for a further four months until he flew to Prague, and even then he was not arrested for a further fortnight, and taken, not to Warsaw, but to Budapest. Considering that Field was planning to return to Poland later in the year, and had even left some of his possessions in Warsaw, it is odd that Swiatlo did not wait for him to return. Indeed, Steven asserts that the Czechs had been reluctant to arrest Field, and had been pressured into doing so: 'They had not regarded Noel Field as being a particularly dangerous figure, and had had to be persuaded by General Belkin to arrange for his arrest. They had handed him over to the Hungarians with evident reluctance'.[24]

Another curiosity about Operation *Splinter Factor*, a codename which, incidentally, does not appear in any declassified CIA document, is its relationship with Allen Dulles, who did not join the CIA as Deputy Director until 1951, much more than a year *after* Field had been arrested in Prague. Steven's explanation for this is that Dulles's work as an attorney for the distinguished New York firm of Sullivan & Cromwell was mere cover for his clandestine activities, masterminding covert operations in Eastern Europe, but there is little to substantiate the claim that during his period on Wall Street Dulles acted as 'a consultant to the CIA on covert operations'.[25] In fact, Dulles had been commissioned, with a lawyer, William H. Jackson, and a leading New York Democrat Matthias F. Correa, to write a bipartisan survey on the CIA's first year of activity for the White House. Dulles had taken the lead in preparing the report which was delivered in January 1949 to President Truman's second administration. Dulles, of course, had campaigned against Truman and had backed Thomas Dewey in the expectation that a Republican electoral victory would ensure that his report would be accepted as a guide to the CIA's future, and he himself would be appointed DCI. Instead the survey was shelved, and Dulles had to wait a further three years before he was offered the post of General Bedell Smith's deputy.

In the meantime, Dulles had worked as an attorney in New York, promoting the interests of the Shah of Iran, and was active on the Council on Foreign Relations. It was not until November 1950 that he accepted the offer of a six weeks' consultancy at the CIA, working at its headquarters in Foggy Bottom, on the shore of the Potomac, two days a week. Thus, at the critical time in early 1949, when Stewart Steven says Dulles was handed the British file on Jozef Swiatlo, Dulles was definitely not working for the CIA. But what about the previous two years, when Steven says 'from 1946 until 1948 Dulles ran private intelligence operations inside Eastern Europe with funds collected from wealthy friends and companies'.[26] This was the period prior to Dulles's work on his survey of the CIA, and bridges the creation of its predecessor, the Central Intelligence Group in January 1946, and the passage of the National Security Act in March 1947. So what was Dulles really doing over these two years?

Dulles had resigned from government service on 7 December 1945, a little more than three months after President Truman had abolished the OSS, and as well as working at Sullivan & Cromwell in New York, wrote *Germany's Underground*, which was published in March 1947, and was engaged as the legal counsel for the United Nations committee seeking a permanent site for its headquarters. In addition, Dulles travelled widely, attended several academic conferences in Europe and was much in demand as a public speaker. In April 1947, shortly before a trip to Europe on the *Queen Elizabeth*, Dulles was invited to submit a paper on his ideas for a central intelligence organization to the Senate Armed Services Committee, and this he did in nine brief pages. Two months later he gave evidence before the House Committee on Expenditures in the Executive Departments to emphasise his view that the functions of intelligence collection and analysis should not be separated, as military orthodoxy demanded. This view prevailed, so that when the new Central Intelligence Agency was created on 26 July 1947, with a very loose remit for clandestine foreign collection, it took over the CIG's small staff of about one hundred, and then absorbed the two principal overseas networks, in Germany and Italy, then run under the umbrella of the War Department by OSS veterans Dick Helms and Jim Angleton respectively. Hitherto the CIG possessed not a single agent abroad, and the two embryonic structures in Europe had been operated independently, and certainly had not taken any direction from Dulles. Six months later, in February 1948, the Secretary of State, James Forrestal, invited Dulles to participate in the non-partisan review of the new Agency's first year record, and this was the 193-page document, containing fifty-seven recommendations, which was delivered to Forrestal in January 1949.

Whilst it is always hard to prove a negative, the evidence suggests that Steven's characterisation of Dulles's activities in the immediate post-war period was far from accurate. Certainly Dulles believed that a confrontation with the Communist bloc was inevitable, and he was anxious to challenge Soviet propaganda and political influence, but at that stage the United States simply did not possess the capacity to undertake what is now broadly termed 'covert action'. Indeed, the other significant adherent to the Dulles view was the former OSS officer Frank Wisner who was in 1947 languishing in the State Department, keen to rebuild an American ability to challenge Soviet hegemony, but his Office of Policy Coordination, which was to supervise the CIA's initial clandestine operations, was yet to be established, let alone employ staff and recruit agents. So what evidence does Steven have to substantiate his version of Dulles' career, with him being the CIA's effective 'director of operations'? The author says only that while his 'immediate post-war career is shrouded in some mystery, few experts who have studied the subject doubt that he was an active intelligence agent'.[27]

Steven claims correctly that in 1974 'the Dulles report remains a classified document and only its general outline is known' but he gives no indication of how he acquired his knowledge of it, claiming that it advocated the development of an agency capable of collecting and assessing political intelligence:

> It must be equipped to mount large-scale sophisticated covert political operations designed to destroy Stalin's grip on the satellites and turn back the tide of communism. The satellites, slave states all, must be encouraged to rise up and throw off the yoke of the oppressor. The mission of the CIA must be to create the conditions to make that possible.[28]

Thus, according to Steven, Dulles presented the Truman White House with a blueprint for confrontation, apparently in direct contradiction to the President's oft-stated policy of 'confinement'. Accordingly, there were two critical issues to be resolved. The first was whether it was desirable to combine the different disciplines of intelligence collection and intelligence analysis. Dulles argued that OSS's experiences demonstrated that centralisation was absolutely vital. The second issue was whether an intelligence agency should passively collect information about foreign governments, or if the CIA should actively influence those governments. Dulles took the latter view, and although the Dulles-Jackson-Correa report (now declassified and available at the National Archives) was shelved by Forrestal, who retired a month after his last meeting with Dulles, and killed himself soon afterwards, the report had a rather different emphasis. Dulles certainly wanted to extend the CIA's role to encompass covert action, but its purpose, as illustrated by the then-recent success in the Italian general election campaign, where the Communists had been defeated despite heavy Soviet intervention, was to contain Soviet pressure wherever it was manifested, but not to actively promote subversion in the Eastern Bloc. This is a fundamental distinction, but Moscow's spin was to present Dulles as a dangerous warmonger, and in April 1949 there were reports from the TASS news agency that the Americans had created a 'special European bureau' to spread sabotage and terrorism in Eastern Europe. Dulles own visit to Europe in that month was denounced as 'a sabotage mission'.

In reality President Truman had set out the U.S. policy of containment in the National Security Council Directive 10/2 in June 1948 which had extended the CIA's legal powers to plan and execute covert action. Steven records merely that the NSC 'gave the CIA the authority 'to carry through clandestine operations which the NSC directed' this abbreviation loses the true sense of NSC 10/2 which contains a preamble recognising that the Kremlin had embarked on a 'vicious' campaign 'to discredit and defeat the aims and activities of the United States and other Western powers' and defined covert action as,

> Propaganda, economic warfare, preventive direct action including sabotage, anti-sabotage, demolition and evacuation measures, subversion against hostile states including assistance to underground resistance movements, guerrillas, and refugee liberation groups.

The sponsor of NSC 10/2 was not Allen Dulles but the senior State Department official George Kennan who also ensured that the OPC, led by Frank Wisner, operated under the control of the State Department's Policy Planning Staff. Thus, although Steven gives the impression that Dulles was masterminding a clandestine offensive against the Soviet Union, based on his own report which was adopted as official policy in NSC 10/2, the reality is that Dulles certainly influenced Kennan and was a close friend of Wisner, he simply was not in a position in 1949 to supervise a Machiavellian plot in 1949 to subvert Poland, Hungary and Czechoslovakia, codenamed *Splinter Factor*.

Equally, Steven offers no explanation for why SIS would pass Swiatlo's offer to defect, not to the CIA, but to Dulles who was, after all, then a private individual. As for the codeword, Steven mentions in his source notes that an imminent book, billed as 'the memoirs of an ex-officer of Britain's Secret Intelligence Service' was to be released shortly, written by Robert Deindorfer, 'in which not only is the operation featured but its name is revealed'.[29] In fact, no such book has ever been published, and references to Operation *Splinter Factor* can be found only in Steven's work. While Robert Diebendorfer is indeed a published author, he is best known for writing *The Liars Club*, and some books on fishing.

Even if for a moment one accepts that Swiatlo really did try to defect to the British, and then the Americans in 1949, is it really likely that he would have been told to remain in place? There is a considerable difference between individuals who offer to spy for the West, and those who have already decided to defect. The history of modern espionage is littered with examples of spies, among them Oleg Penkovsky, Dmitri Polyakov and Oleg Gordievsky, who chose to return home and face the possibility of arrest, rather than remain in the West. Yet in Swiatlo's case, which if it were true would make it unique, is that having decided to defect, he then is somehow persuaded to stay in Poland for a further four years. Perhaps even more incredibly, during this period he was not, we are told, to 'work for the Americans, not provide them with intelligence appreciations, not warn them of political or military developments inside Eastern Europe'. Thus, according to Steven's account, Swiatlo's task for the CIA was to continue to 'do the work which his Polish and his Russian masters were paying him to do'.[30]

Although Dulles did not join the CIA until 1950, Steven says that in 1949 his work as a lawyer was 'a very subtle cover for his primary role as CIA head of special operations'[31] and, in the case of Rudolf Slansky, goes into some detail to demonstrate the personal responsibility of Dulles for his death.

As First Secretary of the Czech Communist Party and deputy Prime Minister, Slansky had been one of the most powerful men in the country and therefore, according to Steven, one of Dulles' principal targets. 'Slansky had to go. He was to be removed by the same methods which Dulles had ruthlessly used on so many others'.[32] Like other top Communists, Slansky had spent much of the war in the Soviet Union and had returned to Slovakia by parachute to fight with the partisans and eventually to seize power. What is well documented is that Slansky was arrested on 23 November 1952, imprisoned at Ruzyn, tried with a dozen other fellow conspirators in November 1952, and pleaded guilty to high treason, espionage, sabotage and military treason. He made an abject confession and, like ten of the other defendants, was sentenced to death and executed on 3 December 1952.

According to Stewart Steven, there was overwhelming proof that the CIA lay behind these events, and he revealed that the arrest of Slansky, 'the biggest catch of all', came about because 'Dulles sought to tighten the screws'.

Colonel Swiatlo, in Poland, was working overtime on the Czech affair. He personally saw the Czech security chief and demanded that members of Field's 'criminal gang' inside Czechoslovakia be arrested. He persuaded both President Bierut of Poland and Party Secretary Rakosi of Hungary to exert utmost pressure upon the seemingly reluctant Czech government.[33]

Thus Swiatlo 'tried to stoke up the flames' and in Washington DC 'it was agreed that Rudolf Slansky should become the target of a direct attack, many details of which are still obscure, but which had as its theme the complete destruction of the political and moral credibility of one of the most significant figures in Eastern Europe'.[34] Steven explains that 'not since the earliest days of Operation Splinter Factor, when the Fields were being set up as American agents, did the CIA have to use "direct action" – the actual planting of incriminating evidence' but the policy changed with the prospect of such an attractive quarry, and rumours were circulated among Czech émigrés in Germany that Slansky 'was talking about defecting to the West'.[35] On 4 November 1951 a double agent, a spy for the Soviets who had penetrated the CIA base in Munich, reported that 'arrangements were far advanced to lift Rudolf Slansky to the West'.[36] Himself a Czech Jew, the double agent passed another message on 9 November confirming that he had been appointed to run 'the Czech end of the operation and would be using his old network'. This news reached Stalin who ordered his representative in Prague, Anastas Mikoyan, to demand Slansky's immediate arrest. Simultaneously, compromising letters containing mysterious messages were sent to a supposed intermediary in Czechoslovakia where they were intercepted and copied, and Radio Free Europe began broadcasting some clumsily coded signals. The final touch was an invitation to certain leaders of the Czech émigré community to go to an American military airfield outside Munich to welcome an important visitor.

> They were not told, as they stood with senior American officers at the end of the runway night after night, who the 'important arrival' was to be. But they all guessed: Rudolf Slansky. Though they were all pledged to secrecy about their futile vigil, the news got out very quickly. Charles Katek, head of the CIA operation in Munich and former U.S. military attaché in Prague, made sure of that.[37]

One further contribution was made, according to Steven, by a spy run by General Reinhard Gehlen's BND. He was 'a Czech Swiatlo – who was firmly entrenched in the upper rungs of the Czech security apparatus. Although the identity of this agent is still not known today, there is no doubt that he existed; in fact, he was so much in control that at one stage in the operation he even deliberately ignored the direct orders of Marshal Stalin'.[38] This mysterious figure encouraged victims of the purge to name Slansky as a fellow-conspirator even after the Minister of the Interior, prompted by President Gottwald and Stalin, had banned 'anymore further questioning concerning Slansky'.

To Allen Dulles, Stalin's uncharacteristic intervention had interfered with an operation which was running very nicely. Admittedly he hadn't stopped it, for the security men involved, including principally Allen Dulles's German agent, simply ignored the order and continued asking their prisoners about Slansky.[39]

Having prepared the ground so ingeniously, with help from the BND's asset, Slansky was thrown into prison. Almost a year later he was hanged and 'Operation Splinter Factor died with him' added Steven. But does any of this really stand up to scrutiny? Those details than can be checked, such as the name of the CIA Chief of Base in Munich, turns out to be accurate, although there is a slight discrepancy in Steven's description as 'the former U.S. military attaché in Prague'. Actually he had been the CIA Chief of Station in Prague until the Communist coup of 1948. Nevertheless, overlooking these trifling details, one is left wondering why, if the BND really enjoyed the services of such a senior Czech security officer, Dulles and Swiatlo had found it so difficult for arrange for Field to be arrested in the first place. Then there is the central theme that Dulles masterminded his project to provoke and empower the Stalinists. But if this was indeed the case, why was Rudolf Slansky one of his targets? Slansky, after all, was one of Czechoslovakia's hardliners, and the person responsible for initiating the purge of his fellow comrades of the Communist Party, and carrying out the arrest of none-Party members in the terror of 1947. As an instrument for Dulles's mischief, there could hardly be a better candidate yet, according to Steven, he was yet another target. But does this really make sense? Two matters of historical fact suggest not. Firstly, there is the awkward point that Noel Field chose to remain in Hungary after his release from prison in 1954. This is very peculiar because if the Hungarians honestly believed him to be a CIA spy, why was he allowed to stay in the country? Under normal circumstances an enemy agent would be deported the moment he was freed, and it is hard to fathom a plausible explanation. Of course Field himself may have had plenty of motive for keeping away from the United States, one of which would have been his fear of what subpoenas or criminal charges may have awaited him.

The second matter to be considered is how these events were viewed in the countries in which they took place. One consequence of Dubcek's 'Prague spring' of 1968 was an enquiry conducted by the Communist Party into what had really happened during the era of the show trials. The result was the Piller Report which investigated the various prosecutions and concluded that they were a grotesque manifestation of Stalinism, and Field had been used merely as an excuse. Similarly, in Hungary it was the Party chief Matyas Rakosi who, in a report prepared in 1962, was blamed for having 'invented the slanders' to 'secure his personal power'. Thus the conclusions reached in Hungary and Czechoslovakia established where the blame should lie, and one cannot help wondering why the relevant Communist parties did not opt for the easier option of denouncing the CIA if there had been even a grain of truth in the allegation.

So is *Operation Splinter Factor* merely an example of skewed interpretation by a journalist who was either misinformed or misled, or was it an exercise in disinformation perpetrated deliberately by the Soviets? This latter suggestion is of particular interest because the KGB's disinformation department, known as Service A, did indeed attempt to perpetrate a hoax, claiming that Stalin's ruthless purges had been prompted by a devious scheme hatched by Dulles. When Tennent H. Bagley, a former senior CIA counter-intelligence officer who had headed the CIA's Polish branch, and had debriefed Swiatlo, attempted to track the provenance of this particular example of disinformation, the former Chief of the Polish UB, Rudolf Barak, proudly insisted to him that it had been developed and propagated by his service, and not the KGB. The entire *Splinter Factor* stratagem, as Barak proudly boasted, had been part of an orchestrated campaign directed against the CIA and Dulles. What made it so attractive was that it exploited the wartime connection between Field and Dulles, which was entirely authentic, and neatly explained the hideous excesses of Stalin's regime by passing the blame to the CIA. Steven explains Dulles' motive as a determination 'to show communism to be the evil that he thought it was. Nationalist Communists were making communism acceptable to the people, and so, accordingly, they had to be removed'.[40]

Incredibly, the author even says that Stalin 'was a victim of forces greater than he', which is an astonishing statement, as previous few historians regard Stalin as 'a victim'. This bizarre interpretation can now be seen as a somewhat crude device, but evidently it was considered sufficiently plausible to fool the gullible. Upon close scrutiny, *Operation Splinter Factor* bears all the hallmarks of a predetermined interpretation laid over a set of facts, not all of which, when examined carefully, quite fit. Dulles was not even in the CIA when Field was arrested, but he is described as an influential, external consultant, indeed one 'ranked at about the level of the CIA's head of operations'.[41] We are told that Swiatlo in Poland was the driving force behind Field's arrest in Czechoslovakia, and his subsequent transfer to Hungary, but if so why did the UB colonel not simply wait for Field to return, as he planned, to Poland, to arrest him? If Swiatlo really had wanted to defect in 1949, why did he wait for a further four years before fleeing to West Berlin? Quite simply, with so many unanswered questions, Steven's version does not stand any test of probability.

Whatever the explanation of how it came to be written, the book was condemned by the CIA analyst and bibliophile George Constantinides as 'one of the worst books to appear in years in the field of intelligence'[42] and, more importantly, no evidence has emerged in the post-Cold War era to support any part of story. Swiatlo never worked for Dulles, there was no Operation *Splinter Factor*, and the naïve Noel Field was not set up for arrest by the CIA. This was not 'the foremost intelligence battle of the Cold War', so how could Steven have come so unstuck? One possibility is his generous acknowledgment to the role played by Ladislas Farago, the controversial Hungarian-born journalist whom the author described as 'an invaluable source of detailed information' without whom the 'book could not have been written'. Soon afterwards his reputation suffered a serious blow when he backed his friend Farago in his sensational, but mistaken, identification of an innocent, penniless Argentine agricultural worker as Hitler's deputy führer, Martin Bormann.

It was unimaginable during the Cold War that there could ever be a time that historians could gain access to the Soviet Central Committee's most secret archives in Moscow, or apply to look at particular KGB records, but this has now happened, and this limited transparency has encouraged other agencies in the west to follow the Russian's lead. The British Security Service is undertaking a lengthy declassification programme, and hundreds of previously top secret files have been released to the Public Record Office (now the National Archive) at Kew. This has allowed researchers the opportunity to study particular cases from both perspectives, East and West, and make comparisons between the way the same topics were handled, East and West.

The new openness has also allowed readers to re-examine the claims made decades earlier by authors who insisted they had been privy to inside information, and there are two good examples of how embroidery or worse influenced perceptions of the Soviet conspiracy. We now know, from first-hand testimony and detailed scrutiny of hitherto secret documents, that Nikita Khrushchev's boasts about Soviet missile strengths were simply a bluff. The same can also be said for Soviet bomber numbers, and much else, including some aspects of the Cuban missile crisis. Deception and disinformation played key roles in Soviet foreign policy, and the skill with which the West was manipulated, under the euphemism 'active measures', helped support a regime that was economically, militarily and morally bankrupt. In some cases, there was active collaboration with sympathetic figures in the media who consciously followed the Kremlin's line, but there were others, often virulent anti-Communists, whose flawed interpretation of events served only to exaggerate Moscow's power.

A good example of this latter trait is to be found in *School for Spies*, a book published in 1961 purporting to be an exposé of Soviet spies at work in England and America, 'with documented facts straight from the Soviet Secret Service files'.[43] The German-educated author, Josef Heisler, was a graduate of Berlin University and a Czech journalist on a Communist newspaper in Prague, and a member of the Party's Central Committee who went to Moscow in 1934 to spend four years at the Lenin School, and work on the evening paper *Vecherniaya Moskva*. In 1939, as Czechoslovakia was occupied, Heisler fled to London and later, having anglicised his name to Joe Bernard Hutton, served as press attaché in Jan Masaryk's Czech government-in-exile. As a Communist convert, Hutton was apparently well-placed to write about espionage and subversion, but in *School for Spies* he gave a detailed description of five KGB training schools in the Soviet Union, concentrating on Gaczyna, 100 miles south-west of Kuibyshev, where illegals destined to work in the West spend ten years in a sealed-off area covering 425 square miles in which western towns had been faithfully reconstructed with a 'true replica of streets, buildings, cinemas, restaurants and snack bars' so as to acquaint future agents with life in the West. Graduates from the decade-long course included 'Soviet Secret Service operators like Dr Geoffrey Noble, William Arthur Mortimer, Gordon Lonsdale, Reginald Kenneth Osborne and all the other Soviet spies in America, England, Australia, New Zealand, Canada, South Africa, Northern Ireland, Eire, India and other parts of the English-speaking world'.[44]

According to Hutton, there were other spy training centres at Prakhovka, seventy miles north-east of Minsk; at Stiepnaya 110 miles south of Chkalov; at Vostocznaya, 105 south-east of Khabarovsk; and at Novaya, ninety miles south-west of Tashkent. Agents destined to operate in the Soviet Bloc were trained at 'an institution known as

Soyuznaya', eighty-five miles southeast of Tula, and at Kytaiskaya, near Lake Baikal 'students of Asiatic origin' were taught to be spies.[45] In addition, there were special spy schools at Kuchino, near Moscow; at Dietskoye Selo, outside Leningrad; at Maiskoye, near Odessa; and Sigulda, near Riga.

What is curious about Hutton's list of Soviet illegals who supposedly operated in the West is that only Gordon Lonsdale is recognisable, and after his release from imprisonment in Britain in April 1964 he wrote his memoirs, *Spy*, which confirmed his real name as Konon Molody, but omitted to mention any training in Gaczyna. In Hutton's version, Lonsdale's true name was Vasili V. Pakhomov and he had undergone training at Gaczyna between December 1944 and September 1954. Not only did such a training facility never exist, three of the four agents listed by Hutton were equally fictitious. The author gave ostensible plausible case histories for Noble ('Mark B. Zagorsky'), Mortimer ('Yuri O. Karakov') and Osborne ('Gennadi M. Glazunov'), but each was bogus. Allegedly Dr Noble had swum ashore near Middlesbrough from a Soviet submarine in November 1952 and by February the following year, having rented a flat in London's Pimlico, he had established himself as 'one of the most active and important' agents in the country who collected 'valuable information on electronic research for secret weapons'.[46] According to Hutton, MI5 'received a tip-off from abroad' but twelve hours after they arrested Noble 'he was found hanged in his cell' at Gerald Road police station, 'before he could be questioned by Special Branch officers'.[47]

Glazunov's training at Gaczyna had begun in 1939, and in January 1950 he had been smuggled ashore off a Soviet ship in Australia as Reginald Osborne. Three years later, in September 1953 he arrived in London representing his 'Anglo-Australian trading company' but seven years later 'one of his informers warned him that Scotland Yard's Special Branch had him under observation and was planning an early arrest'.[48] Despite his training, and ten years undercover, Glazunov panicked and fled the country.

In Karakov's case, he had been assigned to Gaczyna in 1942 and adopted the identity of William Mortimer to work as a pianist in a Boston nightclub, and in July 1953 had moved to New York where he sang with a jazz band. Soon afterwards he had recruited a young U.S. Army officer from Alabama, attached to a 'secret weapons testing unit', and blackmailed him into supplying classified information. He also acquired sources 'working in well-guarded workshops in which prototypes for new secret devices for the Army, Air Force and Navy were being developed and produced; others he found were engaged on top-secret blueprints'. Between the summer of 1954 and the autumn 1957 he managed a nightclub, ran a photographic business in the Bronx and continued to recruit agents, among them Erzhika, the 'Hungarian-born fiancée of an American government official' and his fiancé Pamela, a 'personal secretary to a senior executive in a government department'. However, following the arrest of Rudolf Abel in June 1957, the unnamed army officer from Alabama became convinced he had come under FBI surveillance, and was shot dead. Similarly, Pamela took an overdose and because of the attention this incident drew to her private life, William Mortimer 'discreetly disappeared and was safely returned to Russia' in February 1961.

Scrutiny of all three cases show them to be imaginary. There is no record of any arrest of a Dr Noble in 1960, and none of a death in the cells at Gerald Road police station. The proposition that such an arrest, conducted at MI5's request, would not have been executed by Special Branch detectives, and that the prisoner would have been allowed to remain un-interviewed for twelve hours, simply beggars belief.

Another curiosity about Hutton's account of the KGB training school at Gaczyna is the way the story evolved over the next decade. For example, ten years later Hutton returned to the subject in *Women Spies*, but described Gaczyna as 'covering an area of some forty-two square miles' and again named Gordon Lonsdale as a graduate, together with Rita Elliott and Eileen Jenkins.[49] These women were actually Esfir G. Yuryna and Tanya M. Radyonska, and Hutton had mentioned them briefly in his earlier book. Trained as a high-wire artiste, Elliott had been smuggled into Australia in October 1955, after the mandatory decade of preparation at Gaczyna and, as 'one of the Soviet Secret Service's top agents, she managed to set up in a comparatively short time a widespread spy-ring'.[50] Her method of obtaining information from sources was dependent on hypnosis and drugs, and after five years she came to 'the attention of the Australian Counter-Intelligence'. Despite being under secret round-the-clock surveillance she 'managed to contact her informers, go-betweens, and other agents, and to dispose of all the incriminating equipment' she had used for her clandestine communications with Moscow. Finally, having 'discovered limpet microphones hidden in her home' she left the country in February 1961, ostensibly to fulfil engagements in India and Pakistan, and disappeared. According to Hutton's second version of her case history, Elliott 'met government officials and influential people who had first-hand knowledge of work in progress on the Woomera range and in research centres'.

As for Eileen Jenkins, not previously mentioned by Hutton, she was smuggled into England in May 1958 and found lodgings in King's

Cross before emigrating to Canada in March 1959. There she worked in a Montreal bakery for six weeks, and then moved to Ottawa where she found a job in a lingerie shop and 'successfully established herself as a master spy'. She 'not only operated an espionage set-up, but maintained a terror group, which kidnapped and murdered'. One of her victims was 'a Slovak immigrant working as a draughtsman in an aircraft design company' who was abducted off the street when he refused to cooperate, drugged and smuggled aboard a ship bound for Russia.[51]

At Christmas 1959 she met 'a police official' buying a gift for his mother in her shop who was well informed about the GRU defector Igor Gouzenko, and became his fiancé. He apparently described how Gouzenko had stolen a quantity of incriminating documents from the embassy's *referentura*, and these had been sufficient to put 'a dozen diplomat spies behind bars'. However, having concluded that her lover either did 'not know or is too careful to divulge Western counter-intelligence methods', she received orders to leave Canada and was redeployed to another English-speaking country.

Neither of these two stories bear any scrutiny whatever. The Australian Security Intelligence Organization (ASIO) has no record of any circus performer who was suspected of being a Soviet master-spy, and the proposition that Eileen Jenkins had 'first heard about Igor Gouzenko' from her Canadian fiancé suggests that her ten years at Gaczyna had been far from complete, as Gouzenko had defected more than fourteen years earlier, and all the counter-intelligence details of the case had been included in the Royal Commission Report, published in March 1947.

Hutton not only invented most of the case histories to which he referred, but he adopted the same approach with *Women Spies*, published ten years later, which was a catalogue of incidents of female espionage. He returned to a slightly embellished version of the Eileen Jenkins case, and revealed that during his research he had been told of Anne, a clairvoyant with 'a good working knowledge of German' who had been employed by British intelligence during the Second World War to 'mind-travel' to 'Nazi headquarters in Berlin'. There she had 'picked up a certain amount of information about military movements' and 'the information she brought back to British secret service headquarters was treated as respectfully as information provided by other spies. British political and military strategy was influenced and helped by Anne's reports'.[52]

This splendidly fanciful tale could be written off as an example of the author being hoaxed, but he insisted that he was 'able to trace Anne and meet her unofficially' to test the story and confirm the old lady's paranormal powers.

That Hutton made up this episode, together with numerous others in *Women Spies* can be seen by his curious claim that British and American intelligence agencies spy against each other. If there is ever one single certainty in the intelligence profession, it is that the CIA and SIS do no engage in hostile operations, and do not recruit each other's nationals, except in a common cause. Thus Hutton's disclosure that 'one of the United States' spies who spied on Britain had the code name of 'Patricia' and she had been the manageress of a dry-cleaning establishment in London's West End, and was thus well placed in the heart of Britain's metropolis and within a stone's throw of Whitehall where all important political and military decisions are made' deserves to be treated with scepticism. Patricia 'was efficient and over a period of many months her network of informers and agents ferreted out every detail of the specific subject that interested U.S. Intelligence Headquarters.' According to Hutton, this was not an isolated event, and that the duplicity had been reciprocated. 'The British Secret Service is equally capable of treachery towards their friends across the Atlantic' and he revealed that an American woman named Gene had been carefully cultivated and recruited by a 'young man who was, of course, a British Secret Service agent'. She supplied him with 'classified information from Washington's files' and when she returned home she 'established a spy web of agents and informers and, over a period of years, supplied London with much secret information about the United States. What particularly interested Gene's superiors in London was not what was entered in official inter-governmental and inter-military communications but what was omitted from those communications, and also the behind-the-scenes reasons for these omissions'.[53]

Quite why Hutton should have persisted with such nonsense is hard to fathom, but he was to return to the same theme in 1972 with *The Subverters*, in which he again referred to Gaczyna, 'the best known of the Soviet Ace spy schools', and also mentioned Dietskoye Selo, Maiskoye, Sigulda, Prakhova, Stiepnaya and Kuchino, although none actually existed. By 1972 the West had received numerous KGB defectors, among them Oleg Lyalin, Yuri Nosenko, Reino Hayhanen and Anatoli Golitsyn, so much was known about the KGB's training procedures. Furthermore, other defectors, including Piotr Deriabin and Yuri Rastvorov had published accounts of their experiences, but none had ever mentioned Hutton's network of training facilities. We now know, with the benefit of information from more recent sources, such as Oleg Kalugin, Vassili Mitrokhin, Viktor Sheymov, Vladimir Kuzichkin and Oleg Gordievsky, that these places did not exist outside Hutton's imagination, so why did the author persist in peddling a tale he must have known to be false? Hutton's determination to mislead even extended to his reference to his own defector source, 'Lieutenant-Colonel Burlitsky', who was probably Grigori Burlutsky, a former border guard who slipped over to the West in southern Turkestan in June 1953, a curious choice to make in preference to the others cited above, as he had no knowledge of Soviet foreign intelligence operations, as he made clear in the only interview he granted, to *Life* in July 1954 in which he described his role in the second battalion of the 68th Border Guard Division. Indeed, although Burlutsky had attended two schools for the Border Guards, he knew nothing of any NKVD training facilities, and had not taken any courses at one. After working on a collective farm Burlutsky had been a student at a technical zoological institute and had used his connections as a Komsomol member to join the cadet school for the Border Guards. His first assignment, in 1941, had been to the Romanian border, but he was later transferred to the Ukraine where he had fought the Germans. He also saw service in the North Caucasus, but his experience in the Chechen-Inguish Republic, forcing the removal of the entire population to the Soviet Far East as a punishment for having collaborated with the Nazis, and his participation in the deportation to Siberia of the Crimean Tartars, left him disenchanted with Communism and determined to escape to the West. The opportunity did not arise when he was posted to East Prussia and then Lithuania, but after he had graduated from the senior Border Guard school at Babushkin he was able to choose an assignment where he could slip over the border to freedom. While Burlutsky proved to be an articulate witness to Stalin's atrocities, he really had no knowledge of the NKVD's training schools, and one is left wondering why Hutton chose this particular defector to support his argument.

Hutton was a prolific writer on the subject of espionage and during his lifetime few doubts were raised about the authenticity of his information, but with the passage of time it has been possible to double-check many of his assertions, and in particular examine the basis of three of his books, *Frogman Spy*, *Commander Crabb is Alive* and *The Fake Defector*. It is certainly unusual for an author to write a second book on an identical topic, even after a lapse of eight years, but when Hutton first investigated the mystery of Lionel Crabb's disappearance he had relied upon a Russian document which revealed the truth, or so he said, in no fewer than three books.

Known as 'Buster' Crabb after the pre-war Hollywood movie star, Lionel was quite a character, instantly recognisable by his monocle, his pork-pie hat, the whiskers on his cheeks and his habit of carrying a Spanish swordstick. He had worked as a mine clearance expert in the waters around Gibraltar during the war, and he had pioneered and perfected many of the techniques now associated with the sport of Scuba diving. However, Crabb's role had been to inspect the hulls of Allied merchantmen and remove any limpet charges placed by underwater saboteurs, usually Italians working from Spain, and his exploits had led to the award of an OBE and the George Medal. Crabb ended the war in Venice, clearing the port of explosives and obstacles, and later he was to be attached to the Admiralty Research Laboratories at Teddington, and participated in dives on the wrecks of HMS *Truculent*, the submarine lost in the Thames estuary in January 1950, and on HMS *Affray*, four years later in the English Channel.

A heavy smoker and drinker, Crabb was a weak swimmer. Paradoxically, he was universally recognised as an exceptional diver, and in the post-war era, after his official retirement from the Royal Navy in April 1955, he had been employed by SIS to undertake some particularly sensitive and hazardous operations, usually to inspect the sonar equipment and propulsion systems of Soviet warships, such as the *Sverdlov*, which had visited Portsmouth in October 1955. It was on just such a mission, in April 1956, under the Soviet cruiser *Ordzhonikdze* while the warship was on a goodwill visit to Portsmouth, that he disappeared, and generated one of the most enduring mysteries of post-war espionage.

Almost all the events of 19 April are shrouded in secrecy because Crabb's mission ended not just in disaster for himself, but led to a major domestic political scandal, an internal enquiry into SIS's activities headed by the former Cabinet Secretary, Sir Edward Bridges, and an international crisis because the cruiser had been carrying the Soviet premier, Nikita Khrushchev and Marshal Bulganin, to England on an official visit. The Prime Minister, Sir Anthony Eden, thought he had banned any potentially embarrassing clandestine operations for the duration of the visit, but through a set of bizarre circumstances SIS's Foreign Office Advisor, (Sir) Michael Williams, inadvertently gave permission to the head of SIS's London station, Nicholas Elliott, to conduct an underwater inspection of the *Ordzhonikdze*'s hull, a mission requested by the Admiralty. Williams should never have sanctioned the operation, which was in defiance of a temporary ban placed on clandestine operations by the Prime Minister but, moments before Elliott telephoned him for his official consent, he had received a call to inform him that his father had just died. Distracted by this news, Williams had allowed Elliott to proceed, and thereby set in train an extraordinary sequence of events that were to become a *cause celebre*. Having been given the go-ahead, Elliott authorised Ted Davies, a Welsh RNVR officer and the head of SIS's naval section, to hire Crabb and prepare for their assignment.

Davies escorted the forty-six year-old Crabb to Portsmouth the day before the target ships arrived, and they both checked into the Sallyport Hotel, registering under their own names. During the course of the next day, however, Crabb suffered a minor heart attack, but insisted on being allowed to continue with his mission, and Davies appears to have acquiesced. Early on the morning of 19 April they had taken Crabb's equipment to the Gosport ferry slip and the experienced diver had donned his gear and swum towards the cruiser and one of its escorts, the destroyer *Smotriashchin*. A few minutes later he had returned to adjust the weights on his belt, and then disappeared from view, not to be seen again until a headless, handless body dressed in the frogman's distinctive, Italian-made two-part rubber dry-suit, was recovered from the entrance to Chichester Harbour twelve miles away, in June the following year. The Soviets had registered a formal diplomatic protest when a sentry spotted a diver on the surface between the two Soviet warships, and this had made the matter public, forcing the Admiralty to acknowledge that Crabb had gone missing, allegedly three miles away in Stokes Bay while testing classified equipment, and Sir Anthony Eden to admit to the House of Commons on 9 May that 'what was done was done without the authority or the knowledge of Her Majesty's Ministers. Appropriate disciplinary steps are being taken'. He declined to make any further statement, insisting it was not in the national interest to do so, thus fuelling a frenzy of speculation. Behind the scenes, Eden was furious and demanded the resignation of SIS's Chief, Sir John Sinclair, who was anyway ready to retire. The other principal victim was Ted Davies who was sacked, leaving him to complain that he had been made a scapegoat.

Within a couple of months, a German newspaper, *Bild Zeitung*, reported that Crabb had been seen at Lefortovo prison in Moscow, and in June the following year veteran journalist Chapman Pincher revealed in the *Daily Express* that Crabb had perished while on a mission for the 'United States Intelligence Service'. Meanwhile one of Crabb's friends, the journalist Marshall Pugh, wrote *Frogman: Commander Crabb's Story*, which gave a factual account of Crabb's adventures as a diver, but the author restricted himself to only the facts as he had established them, and declined to indulge in any speculation that dominated the press.

Had Crabb been abducted by the Soviets? Did he drown under the warships? Was it really his body that was found months later in

Chichester? Who was his mysterious companion whom the police had sought to protect? Were the Americans behind the operation? The mystery deepened and, in the absence of any official comment, Joe Hutton revealed in 1960 that he had acquired a copy of a secret dossier on the case from Moscow. It had been 'smuggled out from behind the Iron Curtain by secret agents' and had 'reached Britain in November 1959'.[54] Allegedly written by a Captain G.F. Styepanov, Hutton's document had been translated into German and disclosed that 'shore agent O2SD' had been warned in advance of the mission, and that Crabb had been intercepted, sedated for the voyage to Moscow, and interrogated. The dossier also included a lengthy transcription of Crabb's subsequent interviews at the Khimsky Naval Intelligence Station and, most sensationally of all, claimed that Crabb had agreed to join the Red Navy with the alias Lev Lvovich Korablov. Under that name he had served in the Baltic, in Odessa, and in September 1959 had been transferred to the Far East Command at Vladivostok. Bizarrely, support for Hutton came from a Labour Member of Parliament, Bernard Floud, who authenticated the dossier and stated that one of friends in MI6 had told him it was genuine.

Hutton pursued the story further in 1966 with *Commander Crabb is Alive*, in which he elaborated on the information contained in the alleged Soviet dossier, and confirmed that Crabb's companion was 'Matthew Smith' an American who had been controlled by a 'Mr X', the top Soviet spy in England. Mr X was 'a capable intelligence officer and a trusted War Office executive' who had been 'a close friend of Kim Philby'.

Through Philby, Mr X met Donald Duart Maclean and Guy Francis de Moncy Burgess. Their friendship matured and Mr X eventually became the 'fourth man' in the Burgess-Maclean-Philby set. Finally, the subversive quartet decided that there was room for a fifth man, Matthew Smith – ostensibly an American intelligence officer – who at Moscow Secret Service headquarters enjoyed the reputation of being an important double-agent.[55]

According to Hutton, Mr X and Smith had entrapped Crabb and then covered their tracks. Smith had succumbed to a serious illness, and when Mr X had finally come under suspicion he had fled the country 'and rewarded for his service by promotion to resident instructor at the unique Soviet school of Gaczyna, where master spies for the English-speaking world are trained'. Having written two books about Crabb, Hutton wrote a third in 1970, *The Fake Defector*, in which he asserted that the diver was still on active duty in Russia. The decomposed corpse recovered from Chichester harbour the following year, Hutton claimed, had been a substitute, dropped into the sea by a Soviet submarine.

It might be expected that for Hutton to return to the same subject for a third time he must have been prompted by yet more sensational information, but in fact *The Fake Defector* contained almost the identical text as *Commander Crabb is Alive*, written two years earlier. A comparative analysis of the two titles shows that seventeen chapters of the earlier book are reproduced, word for word, in the later volume, which also contained a large extract from *Frogman Spy*. In fact, careful study shows that in this third book contains just ten pages of entirely new text, but they seem significant because they deal in great detail with Hutton's sources, and he identifies them as 'Mr V.N.' who claimed to have met Crabb in Sevastopol in November 1967, and to have been asked to pass on a message from the diver to friends in England. Hutton concealed his source's name because to have done so 'could lead to most serious Russian Secret Police retaliations', but instead reproduced what he described as a transcript of a recording of his interview with him. He also examined his passport to confirm that his source had been in the Soviet Union.

Hutton's second source, not previously mentioned, was 'Mr X, an Iron Curtain executive' who had enjoyed 'extensive dealings with his Russian counterpart – a top official in the Soviet Foreign Ministry's Department of Information'.[56] Once again, Hutton insisted that 'his identity cannot be disclosed for fear of Secret Police reprisals' but all he had to offer was the assertion that during a meeting with a Soviet official he had raised the topic of Commander Crabb, and that the official had neither confirmed nor denied that Crabb was in the Soviet Union. These supposed witnesses are very unsatisfactory because neither clarify Hutton's central theory, that the Russians 'tricked Crabb into carrying out the underwater spying mission'.[57] This, of course, was a repetition of the author's theory which he had first put forward in *Frogman Spy*, but this time there was some embroidery. Hutton now claimed that the British government knew that Crabb was working for the Soviet navy, and that a secret agreement had been reached, during the July 1969 spy-swap of the lecturer Gerald Brooke for the Soviet spies Peter and Helen Kroger, not to put Crabb on public display in Moscow.

Moscow warned that if Britain stubbornly refused to barter the Krogers, Commander Crabb would be 'exhibited' in Moscow and made available for questioning by Western journalists. Britain was told Commander Crabb would be introduced as 'Red Navy Kapitan Krab'. He would state he *defected* to the Soviet Union. He would name British Naval, Government and Intelligence officers who had sent him on his spying mission in Portsmouth Harbour, and he would expose '*other matters*' that would seriously embarrass Britain at home and abroad.[58]

But could any of this really be true? Hutton's theory was that the Soviets had been so anxious to free Peter and Helen Kroger from prison that they had used the threat of exposing Crabb as a defector to coerce the British into accepting their proposals for a swap. Strangely, although Hutton warmed to this interesting idea in *The Fake Defector*, the precise chronology of events serve to undermine its validity. The Krogers had been arrested in January 1961 and sentenced to twenty years' imprisonment in March, so they had been incarcerated for eight and a half years before they were exchanged for Brooke in July 1969. If it were true that the knowledge the Krogers held was absolutely vital for the KGB, which had been desperate to obtain their release, why the delay? Hutton claimed that only the Krogers 'know the whereabouts of the many Soviet agents who went underground immediately Lonsdale and the Krogers were arrested. A complete spy network is ready and waiting in Britain to be hooked up to the Soviet Union. But contact can only be made through the Krogers.'[59]

But can this really make sense? If the KGB really had seized Crabb in 1956, and had regarded him as a useful pawn, why had they not used his value as a bargaining chip much earlier? Konon Molody, the KGB's illegal *rezident* in England, had been caught with the Krogers in January 1961, and had been freed in an exchange, for the SIS courier Greville Wynne, in April 1964. Could it really be true that the Krogers possessed valuable information that was unknown to Lonsdale? And if so, why had it not been the Krogers who had been selected for the earlier, 1964 spy-swap?

One further curious contradiction lies is the role of Hutton's other 'Mr X', the person he had described as 'the 'fourth man' in the Burgess-Maclean-Philby set. Either Hutton believed Crabb had been the victim of an elaborate plot hatched by the Soviets, and supervised by 'the fourth man', or Crabb had been the hapless participant in a mission that would embarrass the British government, but it could hardly be both. With the benefit of time, and the Prime Minister's disclosure in November 1979 that Anthony Blunt had been 'the fourth man', Hutton's theory appears even more strange.

Undoubtedly the circumstances of Crabb's disappearance served to encourage the speculation, as did a rather clumsy attempt by the head of the Portsmouth CID, Detective Superintendent Stanley Lamport, to confiscate the pages of the hotel register where Davies (or 'Smith') and Crabb had signed in. Conspiracy theories abounded, exacerbated by a decision to seal the relevant Cabinet papers for a hundred years, but no insider revealed the truth until Peter Wright recalled the episode in his notorious memoirs, *SpyCatcher*. In Wright's version, Crabb had been sent on an SIS operation and perished in an accident, leaving MI5 to try and cover up what had happened by persuading the Portsmouth CID to sanitize the incriminating hotel register which contained the real names of the two key participants. This evidence is significant because if there was no 'Matthew Smith', and if Crabb's SIS companion, Ted Davies, had used an alias, there would have been no need to have sent the hapless Superintendent Lamport, working 'for a higher authority' and citing the Official Secrets Act, to remove the evidence. The problem only arose if Davies had used his real name, and could be linked to the government, or at least to SIS. Lamport's clumsy intervention, organised by MI5 at SIS's request, was precisely because Davies was vulnerable to exposure. We also know, from *The Big Breach*, written by the SIS renegade Richard Tomlinson, that Davies remained bitter about his subsequent treatment by SIS and felt he had been a scapegoat, although Nicholas Elliott had narrowly escaped any disciplinary action following the enquiry conducted by Sir Edward Bridges. When Tomlinson underwent his induction training into SIS in December 1991, the case of Ted Davies was cited as an example of how an organisation can lose the support of a hitherto entirely loyal officer.

Elliott himself described these events in his 1993 autobiography *With My Little Eye* in which he explained he was breaking his silence 'to set the record straight and do justice to the reputation of a gallant officer who was, in his specialised field, not only a master of his art but a most engaging man of the highest integrity'. Elliott was particularly critical of the way Eden had handled the affair, which had enabled the Russians to make periodic capital out of this sad episode over the following thirty years or so. Stories have appeared with regularity in the press in many countries with the objective of discomforting MI6 and the British government, to the effect that the unfortunate man had been captured by the Russians as a result of the incompetence with which the operation was carried out and that he was now in Russia. It has been a typical example of Soviet disinformation.[60]

All of this serves to confirm that the fiasco was one of SIS's own making, and had no CIA participation. However, it also casts further doubt on Hutton's extraordinary claims and raises the spectre that he may, unwittingly or otherwise, acted as a conduit for a Soviet disinformation exercise. Indeed, shortly before his death in 1977, Hutton was still insisting that he was in touch with his original contacts who had supplied him with the Crabb dossier, and for the previous three years he had peddled the line that Crabb was due to be released from his naval service in the Soviet Union in August 1976, and then would be free to settle in Italy. As the date of his retirement approached, Hutton announced that Crabb, alias Korablov, had been taken ill in Dresden, diagnosed as having cancer, and then had been transferred in September 1977 to a sanatorium in the Czech resort of Karlovy Vary, where he had died.

Since Hutton's death the speculation about Crabb's demise has been pursued in yet another book, also called *Frogman Spy*, by Michael Welham and published in 1990, the year in which a former head of Soviet naval intelligence, Joseph Zverkin, emerged from his new home in Haifa and made a startling disclosure: Zverkin claimed that in 1956 he had been living in England under a German alias and had heard from a reliable source that a sentry aboard one of the warships had spotted a frogman in the water and, from a range of just twenty metres, had shot him in the head with his rifle. This story sounds highly improbable as a shot early in the morning in Portsmouth Harbour would have been heard for miles, but the claim illustrates the longevity of the continuing interest in Crabb's fate.

Two further complexities to compound the puzzle further is the revelation made by Peter Wright that the MP who authenticated Hutton's claims, Bernard Floud, himself had been a Soviet spy before the Second World War. When eventually he was interrogated by MI5 in October 1967, he committed suicide, leaving his motives for authenticating Hutton's claims unexplained. To enhance Floud's status, the author had stated that 'he knew Mr Floud had been an intelligence officer for some ten years', but in fact Floud had spent only two years in the Intelligence Corps before joining the Ministry of Information in 1942. Why did Hutton exaggerate Floud's experience in intelligence, and why did Floud intervene in what Nicholas Elliott believed to be a classic exercise in Soviet disinformation? Whatever else, it was completely untrue that SIS had acquired an identical copy of Hutton's secret dossier on Crabb, and certainly no SIS officer had made such an assertion to Floud, so why did he lend his weight to Hutton's claim? The implications are labyrinthine, because either Hutton knew his dossier was a forgery, in which case Floud's intervention is open to several interpretations, including collusion with Hutton, or if the author was an unconscious conduit for Soviet disinformation, why did Floud make up his tale unless he had been acting under Soviet direction?

The other curious coincidence was the contemporaneous existence of yet another (as yet undiscovered) Soviet spy based at the Admiralty Research Laboratory, Dr Alister Watson. When he was questioned by MI5 he admitted, according to Peter Wright's account of his interrogation, to having met known Soviet intelligence officers who operated under diplomatic cover from the embassy, but denied ever having passed them any classified information. Whether the Soviets were tipped off in advance to SIS's intention to conduct a clandestine inspection of the *Ordzhonikdze*'s hull remains uncertain, but within SIS there was never any doubt that Crabb had died in an accident, and that it had been his body that had been buried at Milton cemetery, in the grave bearing his name. On his last dive he had been wearing oxygen breathing equipment, designed for use in combat, which released no tell-tale bubbles and was entirely safe up to depths of thirty-three feet, but any deeper and the oxygen became toxic. It was considered highly likely that Crabb may have swum deeper to clear a hull, and then found himself in difficulties and was swept away by the tide to drown. Whatever the precise circumstances of his loss, the Crabb affair became a major political and diplomatic embarrassment, but one can be certain from Harold Macmillan's diaries, in which he commented that 'the PM's order had either been overridden, evaded or merely not passed down the line'[61] that the decision to proceed with the operation had been SIS's, and had not been engineered by any Soviet spy, let alone Hutton's 'fourth man'.

Nevertheless, not all of Hutton's claims were entirely groundless, for a Soviet defector, Anatoli Golitsyn, had stated in December 1961 that the KGB had been given notice of SIS's intentions. If there were to be considerable doubts about Golitsyn's reliability, for he was to be accused of embroidering information to make himself more attractive to his CIA handlers, there was never any question about Hutton's role as a fabricator.

But why did Hutton seem to prefer invention to authenticity? The answer, alas, is hard to fathom because, having lived in Worthing, on the south coast of England with his wife, daughter and two sons, he died in 1977, leaving no explanation, his legacy being the single largest collection of completely fabricated books on the subject of intelligence. Evidently Hutton's fascination with the world of espionage and intelligence had an unfortunate impact on his family, for his son was convicted of large-scale money-laundering and drug smuggling in 1990, and his counsel, Lord Carlile QC, claimed in the defence of his client, a former street trader, that Alan Hutton had been adversely influenced by his father's career.

Chapter 6

Greville Wynne's GRU Defector

One of the consequences of the end of the Cold War has been a greater willingness, on both sides, to discuss what really happened during the era of superpower confrontation. Some of the results have been quite astonishing, with the KGB's former Chief of Counterintelligence, General Oleg Kalugin, giving evidence under subpoena in Florida, at the trial in June 2001 of Colonel Trofimoff, a long-term Soviet asset who had betrayed thousands of U.S. military intelligence secrets from his post in West Germany. Originally identified as a spy by the KGB defector Vassili Mitrokhin in 1992, the FBI conducted an elaborate sting operation to persuade Trofimoff to boast of his espionage, and recorded some forty hours of videotape in which the retiree recalled his exploits, thereby compromising himself completely.[1]

Although technically, Kalugin was never a defector, and Vassili Mitrokhin most definitely was, there remains an element of uncertainty about the precise numbers of those who chose to switch sides during the Cold War. Within the professional intelligence community there is an agreed definition of a defector, as an individual who opts to join the adversary. This is a physical action, thus excluding some famous spies, such as Colonel Oleg Penkovsky and General Dmitri Polyakov of the GRU, from the definition as neither was able to leave the Soviet Union and make good their escape, even after years of contact and collaboration with the CIA.

The true defector is Anatoli Golitsyn, who simply turned up unannounced at the home of the CIA chief of station in Helsinki in December 1961, or even Oleg Gordievsky, who was exfiltrated from Moscow in 1985 after he had fallen under suspicion as a spy run by the British SIS. From the end of the Second World War in 1945, and the

95

disintegration of the Soviet Union in 1991, there have been a total of thirty-eight defectors from the KGB, and eleven from the GRU. Not all the cases have been well documented, or even disclosed, but of that combined total nineteen have published books describing their experiences. Some, like Viktor Sheymov, initially concealed their disappearance and remained silent about their espionage, presumably for operational reasons, but even some of these undeclared defectors eventually surfaced, and Sheymov himself emerged to write an autobiography, *Tower of Secrets*.[2] Other defectors, such as Vitali Yurchenko, found the experience too hard and re-defected, making the hazardous return journey to Moscow.

Thus by strict definition, those spies recruited while overseas who remained in their service, and for one reason or another failed to leave the Soviet Union, cannot be described as defectors in the true sense of the word, and therefore there is no such person as the individual occasionally described as the 'defector in place'. In a person who is described as a defector, the meaning is clear, and a physical departure to the West has taken place. There are examples of handlers who urged their agents to escape, but they declined, just as there are examples of 'walk-ins' who have attempted to negotiate their 'meal-ticket' for resettlement in the West, and have been persuaded that they must indulge in some espionage to prove their worth before they can be accepted.

Motives for the phenomenon of defection vary considerably, although most claim ideological reasons at the time. In reality the motives divide into several categories, including a simple economic impulse, being the desire to improve a family's standard of living. Most likely this is manifested at the end of an overseas tour, when a return to Moscow is imminent. With Igor Gouzenko, his defection in Ottawa in 1945 with his wife and children was unrehearsed, and he made his claim for political asylum without any advance warning. For Vladimir and Evdokia Petrov, their recall had been long delayed, and his defection had been planned in advance with considerable care. In contrast, when Oleg Lyalin pleaded to be allowed to stay in London in 1971, following his arrest on drink-driving charges, he had been cooperating for the several past months with the Security Service, supplying high-grade information from within the local KGB *rezidentura*, and had been allowed to remain. These cases are all relatively straightforward, to the extent that such an adjective can ever be applied to such complex individuals, but none has been more baffling than that of Sergei Kuznov, the central figure in a book written by an SIS courier, Greville Wynne, a forty-three-year old engineer and foreign trade negotiator who had been arrested in Budapest in

November 1962 and tried in Moscow in May the following year, together with his fellow conspirator, Colonel Oleg V. Penkovsky. After their convictions Wynne had been sentenced to eight years' imprisonment, five of which were to be spent in a labour camp, and Penkovsky had been executed by a firing squad.

Wynne is probably best known in this role, as the vital link between Penkovsky, who was executed immediately after his trial in May 1963, and his British and American controllers based in London, but after his release, in April 1965, he revealed that quite apart from Penkovsky, he had also been involved in another case of GRU espionage.

Wynne himself died on 27 February 1990 and during his lifetime had exercised what amounted to proprietorial rights over almost anything to do with Penkovsky. In some respects, this was quite understandable. His prison ordeal in the Soviet Union had been devastating, and upon his return to England he had undergone a complete nervous breakdown. He had divorced his wife Sheila, virtually disowned his only son, Andrew, and had developed an acute alcohol problem which sometimes made him violent. The episode for which he became so well-known dominated him entirely, and none of his subsequent business ventures ever amounted to the successes he claimed them to be. His second marriage to a Dutch girl, Hermione Van Buren, in 1980. ended 'because of his drunken rages' caused by his abuse of alcohol which, she claimed in a newspaper interview, had 'changed his personality.'[3] He moved from the Canaries to Malta, Marbella and finally to Majorca, and became a well-known figure in the bars frequented by the expatriate community in Palma. 'Wynne's drink problem started in Lanzarote where whisky was cheaper than a glass of mineral water' recalled Hermione.[4] Wynne had been employed to sell villas at a development in the grounds of the San Antonio Hotel but his efforts ended in failure. Perhaps because of his inability to sustain relationships, Wynne became increasingly litigious and brought numerous legal actions against almost anyone who wrote about him. He variously sued or threatened to sue the BBC, the *Sunday Telegraph* and Sir Fitzroy Maclean, but none of his cases ever met with success in court.

In addition to *The Man From Moscow,* and the sequel that was published in 1981, *The Man From Odessa*, written with Bob Latona, he gave numerous newspaper interviews and was an eager commentator on events relating to the Cold War. According to his own account, Wynne first came into contact with British intelligence in 1938, just prior to the Second World War, when he accidentally discovered a German spy using a clandestine transmitter in the Nottingham factory where they were both working. Having denounced the Nazi agent Wynne was selected for an undercover security role acting as an *agent provocateur*, identifying potentially disloyal Fascist sympathisers. Although posing as an ordinary soldier, Wynne allegedly ended the war with the rank of major and then went into business on his own, first as a property developer and club owner, and then as a representative abroad of several leading British engineering companies.

Wynne's first book included an intriguing reference to Odessa, and a visit he had made there 'about five years ago' which would have placed him there in 1957. Further details were to follow in *The Man from Odessa* in which Wynne revealed that before his involvement with Penkovsky he had undertaken an earlier mission for his SIS contact whom he only referred to as 'James'. This dangerous operation had occurred in 1959 and had enabled a Soviet GRU officer, known to Wynne as Sergei Kuznov, to defect to the West with vital information. Indeed, Wynne's second book was to also to make new disclosures about the celebrated Penkovsky case. Apparently Wynne had accompanied Penkovsky on a secret visit to Washington where they had been received by President Kennedy.

Wynne's remarkable claims, which formed the basis of a BBC Television drama documentary in 1983, were only challenged in 1988 when they became the subject of libel proceedings following some very trenchant criticism. What emerged during the lengthy litigation was to cast doubt on practically every aspect of Wynne's bizarre life and expose his memoirs as sheer fiction. The first contradiction in Wynne's life concerns the way in which he says he was originally recruited into British intelligence. His account describes how, in November 1938, he accidentally discovered a German spy operating an illicit wireless from within the factory at Beeston, Nottingham, where they both worked. At the time Wynne had been an engineering apprentice at the Ericsson Telephone Company and had returned to a storehouse after hours to recover some tools he had forgotten, when he stumbled upon the Nazi agent. This episode is important because it is the foundation of Wynne's clandestine career as an undercover agent. According to his story, the spy was in an underground cellar, and Wynne heard 'a series of staccato-like phrases in German'[5]. When he looked more closely, he could see a transmitter and an aerial, and this is what he reported to the authorities and subsequently led to his recruitment.

There are two immediate difficulties with Wynne's story. Firstly, there is no record of any espionage case even remotely resembling that described by Wynne. In 1938 there was a single example of a German spy for the *Abwehr* being caught in Britain, but none of the details concerning Mrs Jessie Jordan, who was arrested in Dundee, coincide with Wynne's. Furthermore, it was learned after the war that even Mrs Jordan's case had been unusual because the Nazi government had placed a ban on *Abwehr* activity in England in order to avoid provoking the British authorities. The second problem relates to the technical feasibility of a small portable transmitter, operating underground, being able to transmit a voice channel over the distance to Germany. Indeed, even with an antenna above ground level, no equipment would have had such a range.

Although Wynne's military record makes no mention of any service other than as a member of an anti-aircraft battery with the rank of private, he invented for himself an alternative undercover career as an *agent provocateur*, testing the loyalty of suspect Communists and Fascists. On the issue of rank, Wynne always insisted that he 'finished up at the end of World War II a major'. This is not borne out by the Army List which catalogues comprehensively the progress of all those holding a commission. Wynne's name appears nowhere in it. That Wynne manifested some distinctly Leftist politics while still in the Army is demonstrated by his authorship of an undated four-page pamphlet calling for a post-war Socialist administration. Entitled *After the War - What Then Soldier?* it denounced capitalism and the government in strident terms and demanded a new order to replace the system that had been responsible for the slump after the Great War:

> In those days, like at the present time, there were among our Government and leading statesmen many false prophets, men who planned large profits for themselves rather than for the need of ordinary people. The great landlords and directors of industrial combines through their false prophets and vested interests gained a majority in the House of Commons, and they governed our country. Through their Tory policy and money invested interests we saw in our country between the Great Wars millions of unemployed, millions of money held from circulation, factory and industrial areas in a criminal state of depression, mines standing idle, fields uncultivated, raw materials unused. Yet all this time millions of our people were in want of the bare necessities of life, and the great industrial combines still continued to manufacture luxury at a profit for the rich ... The past twenty-five years is sufficient proof that the old system has failed; there is something wrong about any system which allows millions of its people to exist permanently upon the verge of starvation amidst plenty.

That Wynne should have put his name to a leaflet espousing doctrinaire Marxism is remarkable, but the document's aims were clear:

The majority of poor people between the Wars were without sufficient of the bare necessities of life. Many were unemployed, many were underpaid, yet industries were not producing sufficient commodities to supply the needs of ordinary people. Our country was still wealthy yet raw material lay unused. Mines were idle, fields lay uncultivated. All this takes place when the resources of the country are owned by a few rich people. They own the land where the raw material is found. They own the goods produced in the country, and they use their rights, as owners, to make themselves rich. The ordinary people who have no share in owning the land and its industries, but only work for wages, have no control over what happens to the things they produce. This system is known as capitalism and it is the system which we have been living under for twenty-five years. Under capitalism the interest and profits of a few people are considered far more important than the interests and living conditions of the majority of people. The fact that this system leads to waste and inefficiency has already been proved; for instance, it is necessary under capitalism to have unemployed in order to hold a reserve of labour and thus keep the wages of the worker at a low level for with cheap labour higher profits can be gained.

Wynne concluded his pamphlet with a direct appeal to soldiers which appears to border on incitement:

You, Soldier, are you content to let your country fall back and be run on the old system, back to 1939 Capitalism, or will you take up the fight now and do all you can to build a real land fit for heroes to live in? Is it right that our soldiers are underpaid and their dependants suffering in poverty? The magnificent achievements brought about by Socialism in Soviet Russia should be all the proof that is needed to the thinking mind as to – WILL IT WORK.[6]

Whether this document was truly inspired by the security authorities with whom he claimed to be in touch is difficult to ascertain but, having signed it 'yours fraternally in Socialism, Greville M. Wynne, Ystrad Mynach, Cardiff', there could be no doubt about the identity of its author. The text refers to the forthcoming General Election, which suggests that it was distributed before the 1945 polls, but it also asks:

Is it right that the present Government, after nearly five years of war, does not tell our Soldiers what sort of country is being planned for them? Is it right that our soldiers are denied political freedom in their own country for which they are fighting?

This passage implies that it was written before September 1944 when, according to Wynne's account in *The Man From Odessa*, he was stationed in northern Europe in a vehicle repair unit, having reached France 'ten days after D-Day' and made it in September 1944 'as far as the outskirts of Brussels.'[7]

Like so many of Wynne's assertions, this contradiction is unexplained. Certainly many of his other claims do not appear credible. For example, Wynne recalls a tragic love affair he conducted with a beautiful girl named Vicki, 'the first and only time' he had ever been in love. 'With her high cheekbones, lustrous ash-brown hair and an ineffable air of chic, so charmingly French ... and exotic' he recalled. They saw each other regularly over a period of months, and Wynne learned that Vicki was a wireless instructor and a British Army lieutenant, working as a liaison officer with the Free French. Their relationship came to a sudden end when Vicki disappeared and Wynne subsequently discovered that she had been captured by the Nazis in France. Apparently she had been dropped in and pulled out of occupied territory 'several times' and had been teaching the French Maquis when she had been caught.[8]

Although Wynne gave few details about Vicki, apart from the fact that she wore an Army uniform and had spent a good deal of her childhood in France, and worked at an office in Whitehall, there is good reason to doubt she ever existed. The principal organization that employed women agents in France was Special Operations Executive, and the personnel files of all fifty of those who were sent on missions into France have been carefully preserved. What makes Wynne's story so odd is that if Vicki had been French, and he mentions that her mother had been French and she 'had spent a good part of her childhood in France', she would probably have been in a branch known as RF Section, yet none of its women agents bear even the slightest resemblance to 'Vicki'. A study of SOE's archives reveals that none of the British women agents sent to France held Army ranks. Twenty-four were nominally members of the First Aid Nursing Yeomanry (FANY) and fourteen held commissions in the Womens Auxiliary Air Force. Nor were any women wireless instructors sent into enemy territory. For security reasons, all training was conducted in England.

SOE agents deployed in France worked for one of two separate sections. F Section did recruit British nationals, but of the three women sent on more than one mission to France, and were captured, Lise de Baissac and Virginia Hall survived. Only Violette Szabo was executed, and she was emphatically not Wynne's 'Vicki'. She had been a FANY, and a courier, not a wireless operator. Furthermore, she had never been employed, as Vicki had been, as a liaison officer with the Free French. SOE's F Section had been created specifically to operate in isolation from the Free French. As for RF Section, which did liaise closely with de Gaulle's forces, it only employed French women, and none of its eleven female agents were ever captured. Thus it would certainly seem as though Vicki was nothing more than Wynne's invention. One possible explanation is that he had fantasized a relationship with 'Vicki' having seen *Carve Her Name With Pride*, a movie loosely based on Violette Szabo's experiences in the field. This may be the reason why Wynne omits any date regarding his affair with Vicki and says vaguely that it lasted months, when Wynne was 'in London between postings.'[9]

Attempts to verify Wynne's claims concerning his relationship with the Security Service, under whose instructions he alleged he had operated during the war, meet with failure because of the erroneous information Wynne has propagated about 'Captain James', his case officer. This is the individual who supposedly recruited Wynne in 1940 and supervised him while he allegedly undertook three different types of enquiries for the Security Service. As well as undercover surveillance of Fascist sympathisers, he also monitored Communist subversives in the Army and investigated the activities of suspect Czech and Polish exiles. Perhaps surprisingly, his admission to being 'hopeless' at languages apparently did not undermine his effectiveness in the latter task. As for 'James', Wynne vouchsafed the following about him: that he was 'a good ten years older than I', that he was a 'Sandhurst man', had been 'educated at Trinity College, Cambridge', had been 'parachuted into Yugoslavia to make contact with Tito's partisans' and finally, is 'now approaching eighty is retired and farming in Sussex.'[10]

In reality Wynne was run by Dickie Franks whose career coincided with only some of the claims made for him. Franks was never in the Security Service, but as an intelligence officer recruited into SOE in Cairo he did jump into Serbia in 1944, and in 1981 (when *The Man From Odessa* was published), aged sixty, was still the Chief of the Secret Intelligence Service. He had been educated at Queen's College Oxford, had not gone to Sandhurst, and his home was in Aldeburgh, Suffolk.

Wynne says that James made contact with him again in 1959 in anticipation of a secret mission to Odessa where he was to assist in the exfiltration of an officer who 'held a high position in the GRU.'[11] Since this is the central issue in Wynne's second book it is worth examining what he says took place in some detail. According to his version he acquired a visa to visit Odessa from a senior commercial attaché at the Soviet Trade delegation in Highgate named Pavlov. Once at the port he had been introduced to the man he was to know as Major Sergei Kuznov. Having made successful contact, Wynne received an important package from him which he hid on the *Uzbekistan*, a Russian liner on which he was scheduled to travel to Varna. However, the original plan for Kuznov's escape had called for Wynne to act as a decoy and distract certain guards away from the area in the port where Kuznov was to be. In the event Wynne fell off the *Uzbekistan* at the vital moment and broke his leg. Nevertheless, Kuznov had managed to escape, and his package had later been retrieved from the *Uzbekistan*. Once in the West, Kuznov had supplied a wealth of information and eventually had retired under a new identity to the United States where he was rewarded with a consultancy post in the Pentagon.[12]

There are, characteristically, more than a few problems with Wynne's account, bearing in mind that *The Man From Odessa* was set in 1959. Starting at the beginning, there was no-one named Pavlov at the Soviet Trade Delegation in 1959. The record shows that Anatoli G. Pavlov did not arrive in London until 1961. Nor was the *Uzbekistan*, which Wynne described as 'a fairly new ship', launched until 1962 – two years *after* these adventures. Further research casts doubt on other aspects of Wynne's story.

The key figure in the book is Sergei Kuznov, and there are three fundamental problems concerning him. First there is the question of whether he ever existed, for there is no record of any GRU officer defecting to the West in 1959. In fact, as we shall see. there were no defections from that organization between 1948 and 1971. Secondly, the way in which Wynne says he made contact with Kuznov is, upon analysis, impossible, and thirdly, there is the information Kuznov is alleged to have conveyed to the West, which entirely contradicts what the history books tell us.

Over the years there has been much research undertaken into the phenomena of political defection and, as might be expected, the world's counter-intelligence agencies have devoted much of their resources to this most valued method of acquiring data on their opponents. There are no less than three basic sources of non-classified information regarding Soviet intelligence defectors: an arrest list of suspects covering the period May 1945 to April 1969 maintained by the KGB but released by *Possev*, a Russian emigré newspaper; a comprehensive list of GRU and KGB post-war defectors accurate until April 1988, published in *Games of Intelligence*; and the memoirs of the defectors themselves. Of the fifty Soviet intelligence officers who defected during the post-war era, no less than twenty-six have either released their own autobiographies or cooperated with writers who have published accounts of their lives while in the Soviet service. That so many should have done so is hardly surprising. There are relatively few opportunities for a Soviet intelligence defector to make a living in the West, and a book collaboration is an easy and safe way to capitalise on their experiences. There are also numerous references in the burgeoning open literature to the minority of individual cases which did not go into print.

Uniquely, there is absolutely no reference to Sergei Kuznov, or any GRU officer resembling him, in any of the literature. Indeed, only two Soviet intelligence officers defected to the West in 1959. One was operating under diplomatic cover in Rangoon, the other was an 'illegal' in the United States, and both were KGB officers, not GRU. If Kuznov was truly a GRU officer who had successfully defected one would certainly have expected his name to appear on the KGB's arrest list, which has been the subject of intensive analysis by Professor Vladimir Krasnov, or at least be mentioned by subsequent GRU or KGB defectors. Significantly, none have. In fact, of the hundreds of books published on Soviet and American clandestine operations since 1959, not one has referred even obliquely to Sergei Kuznov. Vladimir B. Rezun, who defected from the GRU in 1978, and subsequently wrote (under the pseudonym Viktor Suvorov) the standard textbook on his former service, *The Aquarium*, has confirmed that he has never heard of Kuznov. This is surprising, if Kuznov ever really existed, because until Rezun sought political asylum at the British Embassy in Geneva only seven GRU members had defected to the West, and the cases of each were well known.

As previously mentioned, obtaining employment for defectors is a specialist field, and Wynne mentions that Kuznov was rewarded with a consultancy post 'at the Soviet desk in the Pentagon'. Curiously, none of the CIA counter-intelligence experts who were serving at this time have any recollection of such an individual. Nor does the Jamestown Foundation, an organization specifically dedicated to the task of placing Soviet defectors in suitable employment. According to Wynne, his initial contact with Kuznov was set up in January 1959 when he was first shown his photograph in preparation for their meeting in Odessa, which took place shortly before Easter of that year. Now Wynne insisted at the outset that 'Major Sergei Kuznov' was not the true name of the man from Odessa. It was merely the name by which he was referred to by SIS in Wynne's presence. He explains that he was never told Kuznov's real name in case he 'was arrested and interrogated' by the Soviet authorities.[13] All of this makes perfect sense, yet in *The Man From Odessa* Wynne describes how he was first introduced to Kuznov by two fellow Britons in the Savoy Hotel in Odessa:

> We ... had a round of introductions and warm handshakes. When I
> was presented to Kuznov, he hesitated a moment when I told him my
> name.[14]

The issue of Kuznov's name is important because the agreed recognition
signal to be made when the two men met was to be what would appear
to the bystander as a slight confusion over Greville Wynne's own first
name. Kuznov was to mistake it for Gabriel, and Wynne was to correct
him. 'This was the recognition signal that had been decided on back in
London', Wynne says.[15] But if this introduction took place in the way
Wynne later described, *he must have learned Kuznov's real name.*

There must be some scepticism attached to Wynne's insistence that it
was security considerations that prevented him from learning Kuznov's
real name. Certainly before the exfiltration had been accomplished
security had been a low priority, for even if he had not been informed of
the GRU officer's name, he knew plenty about him, and more than
enough for the Soviet authorities to identify him if they extracted the
information from him. Wynne confirms that he had been issued with
photographs of him, which he had been allowed to keep, and had been
informed that Kuznov 'had been a member of the Soviet Commission in
Vienna after the war, which is where he had first made contact with
MI6.'[16] Furthermore, Wynne was supposedly told that Kuznov's parents
lived in Odessa. Worse still, Wynne was in possession of all this vital
data, weeks before the operation was undertaken, and during a period
that he made two visits to the Soviet Union and several trips to Romania,
Hungary, Poland and Czechoslovakia! If this were all true, one wonders
how SIS ever expected to pull off the exfiltration successfully.

Credibility is stretched even further when Wynne explains that one
of the reasons why Kuznov is to be brought to the West is because he has
fallen under suspicion. His security clearance had been withdrawn, yet
SIS had somehow managed to pass him photographs of Wynne so he
might recognise his contact. Once Wynne had made contact with
Kuznov, and handed over a gold ingot 'to pay off' his helpers,[17] the
scheme devised by Kuznov called for Wynne to operate as a decoy. The
plan itself seems unnecessarily complex and risky, considering Kuznov
was supposedly already under suspicion. It required 'a lifelong friend'
of Kuznov's to drug a colleague, take control of a pilot vessel in Odessa
harbour, collect Kuznov from 'a deserted loading facility' and then put
him aboard a foreign cargo vessel that was scheduled to leave the port
shortly before midnight.[18]

Wynne's role as decoy was to fall off the *Uzbekistan* at exactly that
moment, thereby creating a diversion that would allow Kuznov to

escape. What is not explained about this elaborate plan is quite why Wynne should have been needed at all. SIS apparently had the means to deliver a set of photographs to the enterprising Kuznov, so why not a gold ingot too? So was it really necessary to have Wynne travel out from England to fall off a ship when, according to his own account, SIS already had people in the area? Wynne says (twice) that SIS had made arrangements to place some sand on the dockside to break Wynne's fall.

One of the most interesting aspects of the Kuznov story is the question of his value to the West as a source of information. Undoubtedly, if he really had been haemorrhaging secrets since the Soviet occupation of Vienna, he must have been responsible for a very great deal of valuable data and he would have been by far the West's most successful Soviet source. In contrast, Oleg Penkovsky survived just eighteen months as an agent, and the only other GRU officer known to have spied for the West during that period was Major Piotr S. Popov who had been recruited in 1953 and was arrested and executed in 1959. Thus if Kuznov had really existed, he would have attained something approaching celebrity status within the intelligence community and, until Dmitri F. Polyakov of the GRU was revealed to have been a long term CIA source dating back to 1961, would have been the most successful spy ever run by the West in the Soviet Union.

Considering that in 1959 the CIA would have had at least ten years to test Kuznov's *bona-fides* as a reliable source of information, it is surprising that Wynne asserts that SIS anticipated difficulty in 'convincing the Americans that the stories Kuznov's been telling us are on the level.'[19] And despite his unequalled record as an agent in place, Wynne was only able to identify four specific items of intelligence Kuznov had vouchsafed to his SIS controllers. This itself is unusual, for a defector's 'meal-ticket' is his guarantee of continued support from his host country. The more secret his information, the greater the welcome he can expect to receive. But in Kuznov's case two items are laughably ridiculous, and the other two fail to stand up to examination: Details of 'the first factory in the Soviet Union to manufacture Wellington boots'[20] where all the initial production had apparently been allocated to the KGB so British agents 'were out on the streets clicking away with hidden cameras at anyone wearing the tell-tale gum boots.' The second was almost as preposterous: details of the production of defective trilby hats which had been delivered to 'Party officials and government functionaries.' This information was especially valued, claimed Wynne, because it 'enabled MI6 to extend their list of known or suspected Soviet agents'.[21]

Whilst it would be hard to take the above seriously, and scarcely justifies a decade of investment in Kuznov, two further items would appear to be more plausible: 'a list giving hundreds of names of Soviet agents from both the KGB and the GRU currently undergoing special training' and a 'photostat' of a plan 'with Khrushchev's signature on it' to build a wall across Berlin.[22] As to the first, it is quite true that a list of GRU personnel deployed under diplomatic cover in the West was circulated to intelligence and security agencies in the early 1960s, but the information it contained is usually attributed to another, better documented GRU source, Colonel Oleg Penkovsky. The material was codenamed RUPEE, but was not received by counter-intelligence staffs until 1961 at the earliest, which implies that if its true provenance was Kuznov, as alleged by Wynne, then SIS must have suppressed it for two years before distributing it. This seems very strange behaviour, given the data's limited shelf-life. Turning to the claim relating to the Berlin Wall, which really amounts to saying that the West had more than twenty-eight months' warning of Khrushchev's intention to build the Berlin Wall. This is indeed a grave charge, but it is entirely unsubstantiated. All contemporary accounts of this episode concur on one central point: that the Soviet and East German authorities took elaborate measures to conceal their intentions, and the construction work initiated in August 1961 took the American, French and British intelligence agencies completely by surprise.

Although not mentioned in the context of Kuznov's meal-ticket, Wynne states that the GRU man had 'given advance warning of the Russian plan to station their short and medium-range missiles on the Caribbean island where Castro had come to power just three months earlier.'[23] This, upon examination, seems quite unlikely. Of course, in April 1959 Castro had not yet declared himself a Marxist or committed his country to the Eastern Bloc, and we now know that Khrushchev's decision to deploy MRBMs and IRBMs (but never SRBMs) was not taken until very late in 1961. But even if Khrushchev had exercised breath-taking foresight and drawn up a plan as early as 1959, one wonders how a GRU major, whose security clearance had been withdrawn, could have acquired it.

Some of this documentary material was, so Wynne tells us, entrusted to him in the form of a package. This 'most vital information' had to be delivered to SIS 'with all possible speed' because it contained the 'evidence to convince the politicians' that the Eastern and Western zones of Berlin were to be divided by a wall.[24] Wynne took the package and apparently followed Kuznov's meticulous instructions about exactly where on the *Uzbekistan* it should be concealed. However, because of the injuries he sustained in the fall from the ship, Wynne says that he was unable to recover the package from its hiding place until August

1959 when the *Uzbekistan* called in to a Bulgarian port. Wynne then travelled to Vienna via Sofia and Budapest with Kuznov's documents still in his 'breast pocket'.[25]

Quite apart from the most obvious problem in Wynne's account, namely that the *Uzbekistan* was still under construction in a Leningrad shipyard while these events were supposed to have taken place, there is no explanation as to why Kuznov could not have carried them to the West himself. Nor, indeed, is there any obvious reason why SIS should have waited four months before recovering the package from the ship. Given the many absurdities in Wynne's tale about Kuznov, one is bound to conclude that this individual never existed outside Wynne's imagination. In fact, a slip by Wynne supports such a conclusion. While discussing the obstacles to making a recruitment pitch to Oleg Penkovsky after he had allegedly first been spotted in Ankara in 1955, Wynne inadvertently remarked that 'no regular British agent existed in the Soviet Union who was in the sort of position that might cross or have any connection with Penkovsky's career as an army officer'.[26] Now this is an astonishing admission to have made if, when he made it in 1967 in *The Man From Moscow*, he knew about Kuznov. Based on what Wynne has said about Kuznov, describing his age ('in his late forties') and his 'high position' in the GRU, he would have been the ideal person to service Penkovsky as they were both of roughly the same age and rank in the same organization. The reality, of course, is that Kuznov was an invention, and had been dreamed up long after *The Man From Moscow* had been published. One is therefore left wondering about the validity of some of his other more extraordinary claims. Two in particular seem rather unlikely, and the first concerns Oleg Penkovsky himself.

Although he made no mention of it in *The Man From Moscow*, Wynne claimed in his later book that he had accompanied Oleg Penkovsky on a secret visit to the White House during the latter's second visit to London, which took place during the summer of 1961. Wynne's sensational disclosure revealed that both men had been flown to Washington DC where they had been received by the President who had taken the opportunity to thank them for their vital undercover work. This was an extraordinary breach of the protocol which keeps heads of government (and heads of state) aloof from the sordid business of espionage and was a key incident in Wynne's book. Indeed, the episode was accepted as true by the BBC researchers who never questioned it and faithfully reconstructed it when the BBC filmed its television series *Wynne and Penkovsky*. In fact, the truth is that Wynne duped his readers and the BBC, for no such visit ever took place.

Although Wynne was always characteristically vague about exactly when the visit took place, he inadvertently left just enough information in the text to pin it down. He mentioned that the journey to America had taken place 'in eighteen hours' when Penkovsky had been smuggled out of his London hotel, SIS having taken care to avoid alerting the other members of the Soviet delegation. The exact day can be identified because Wynne states elsewhere that the secret trip immediately followed the weekend that Penkovsky had seen the Queen at a polo match at Windsor. From this single slender clue, it has been possible to narrow down the exact date upon which Penkovsky is alleged to have been received by President Kennedy.

Penkovsky's second visit to London took place between Tuesday 18 July and Thursday 10 August, a total of twenty-four days which spanned three separate weekends. According to Buckingham Palace, which keeps a record of all the Queen's movements, she was at Cowes on 29/30 July 1961, Scotland on 5/6 August, and at Windsor on 22/23 July. On Sunday 23 July 1961 she had watched Prince Philip umpire the Captains and Subalterns Final at the Guards Polo Club, and this was the only time Penkovsky could have seen her in the flesh, as Wynne described. Accordingly, 'twenty-four hours later' would have had the secret flight to America occurring on the evening of Monday 24 July 1961.

Wynne asserts that the entire journey, from London to Washington and back was accomplished in 'eighteen hours' and recalls that they were flown in a 'military jet liner'.[27] Having landed at an unnamed air force base they had been whisked to the White House for a short reception, and then flown home in time for Penkovsky to be restored to his hotel without his Soviet colleagues having noticed his absence.

When it was pointed out to Wynne during litigation in 1989, that it had been a physical impossibility to have undertaken such a journey in 1961 in the time claimed, Wynne conceded having made a slight error and provided further details of the trip which he suggested proved the authenticity of his claims. His revised itinerary included a car journey to Manchester, a further ride to an RAF airfield, and then a transatlantic flight. Significantly, he failed to alter the other details, such as the 'military jet liner'. In fact, in 1961, the United States Air Force possessed only one such plane, and that was President Kennedy's personal Boeing 707, which was actually deployed elsewhere. And the additional details supplied by Wynne actually lengthened the journey's duration and made it even more improbable than ever.

Research in Washington and the Kennedy Archive in Boston confirmed that neither Wynne nor Penkovsky ever visited the President.

The recently declassified visitors log for the period Wynne said he had been in Washington shows that Kennedy had constantly been in the company of others, and that his time was fully accounted for on a minute by minute basis. This was further confirmed by his personal secretary, Mrs Lincoln, who swore an affidavit insisting that Wynne was mistaken. Indeed, she was supported in this view by the then Deputy Director for Plans, Dick Helms, Penkovsky's CIA case officer, George Kisevalter, and the CIA's distinguished counsel, Walter Pforzheimer, who had briefed Congress on the case. All swore that Penkovsky never came to America in July 1961 – or at any other time. Their recollection was supported by nine other CIA officers who had a knowledge of the case.

That Wynne could have expected to get away with such a blatant invention says much about the man, and further research into his claims in regard to Penkovsky show that not only did he exaggerate his own role in the case, but made numerous claims on behalf of the GRU colonel that are themselves completely unsustainable. Some, indeed, have a marked resemblance to previous claims made on behalf of the imaginary Kuznov. For example, Wynne says that Penkovsky 'named the day – 12th August' that the Berlin Wall was to be erected.[28] This is particularly odd, considering that Wynne states elsewhere that work on the wall had begun 'just days after Alex returned with his delegation to Moscow'.[29] In fact Penkovsky did not leave London until 10 August, and Berlin had been divided on 6 August – while Penkovsky had still been in London. Wynne also tried to turn this incident into a matter of political controversy by charging that the United States administration had 'wanted the Berlin Wall' to be constructed, for its own obscure motives, and had 'cynically overruled' British demands to prevent the wall from being completed.[30] There is no evidence to suggest that any such inter-Allied dispute ever took place.

Study of Wynne's claims in the light of his tendency to invention reveals that much of what he wrote about Penkovsky was completely untrue. He did not supply him with a 'long range transmitter' and there are several instances of Wynne exaggerating Penkovsky's access to Soviet secrets.[31] It seems improbable that Penkovsky told the West of the 'location of hidden rocket sites' in the Soviet Union.[32] If he did, it was not because, as Wynne claimed, that the indiscreet Marshal Varentsov was 'Penkovsky's father-in-law'.[33] Quite simply, he wasn't. Penkovsky's wife's maiden name had been Vera Gapanova. Nor is it likely that Penkovsky obtained 'official minutes of the Central Committee meetings at which the Soviet Premier admitted his country's vulnerability'.[34] Not even Penkovsky himself ever claimed to have

110

enjoyed access to sensitive political intelligence. Nor, apparently, was this kind of material ever made available to President Kennedy, judging by his private correspondence with Khrushchev that was subsequently published by Robert Kennedy in *Thirteen Days*.

Nor are all the inventions restricted to *The Man From Odessa* – Wynne's first book has its own share of dubious material, and one incident in particular is worth highlighting. Wynne recalled an episode in which Penkovsky, while in London, had been reunited with an army colleague whom he believed dead. Actually, he had defected, and the Soviet authorities had faked his funeral to conceal his escape to the West. Indeed, a week after this emotional meeting, another was arranged at which Penkovsky was reunited with no less than 'twenty men, all Russians, whom he had known long ago',[35] old friends whom he had also believed to be dead. Whilst such a grotesque breach of security would have been unthinkable, exposing an agent currently in place to twenty-one defectors, the incident was pursued further by Wynne in *The Man From Odessa*, in which he added further, even more ludicrous details. In the second account, Penkovsky's first Russian friend, formerly referred to as 'a Russian officer who had served with him, had been his friend' is promoted to 'a general in Alex's service.'[36] In fact, no GRU over the rank of major has ever defected to the West.

Wynne makes a trifling error in timing over the meeting with the twenty old friends, 'all former top Soviet officials' saying in his first account that it took place 'less than a week' after being reunited with his friend.[37] In *The Man From Odessa* the meeting happened instantly, when his friend 'took Alex by the arm like a little child and led him into the next room. There were twenty others like him'.[38] The BBC swallowed the latter version whole and apparently failed to notice another interesting discrepancy: while elaborating on the drama of the second account, Wynne included Sergei Kuznov as one of the twenty old friends of Penkovsky who had defected! Thus Wynne had alleged, albeit indirectly, that Kuznov and Penkovsky had known each other.

There can be little doubt that Wynne was a shrewd opportunist who sought to capitalize on his brief but harrowing experience as Penkovsky's courier. It will be recalled that when Wynne's second book was published in 1981 one of the topical issues of the day was Soviet penetration of the British Security Service. Wynne latched onto this subject by suggesting that Penkovsky had warned SIS in 'April 1961' that 'the KGB have placed one of their agents at the very highest level of MI5'.[39] This proposition is scarcely credible since it is now known that the first allegations of a Soviet mole inside MI5 were not made until 1963, a good two years later. By straying into this uncharted territory Wynne quickly found himself in difficulties. Having fabricated Penkovsky's warning about a Soviet spy in MI5 it was logical for Penkovsky to insist that MI5 should be excluded from any involvement in his case. Wynne gave 'a personal guarantee that MI5 would not be brought in' and that Penkovsky was being handled by SIS – but omitted to mention that (if his own tales were true) he and 'James' had both previously worked for MI5 during the war. In fact, as is confirmed by Peter Wright, MI5 had been indoctrinated into the case at an early stage and had played a key role in taking counter-surveillance measures throughout Penkovsky's two visits to London.[40] Wynne's clumsy attempt to draw on the controversy then surrounding the loyalty of the late Sir Roger Hollis goes awry when he makes a series of fundamental errors, mistakenly referring to him as an 'MI6 mole' when Hollis had never worked for SIS, and suggesting that in 1961 Hollis had been 'the acting director' of that organization.[41] In reality, of course, Hollis was Director-General of the Security Service in 1961, a post he had held since 1956.

Apart from Wynne's two accounts of his dealings with Penkovsky, there are two other published sources which give some insight to their case. One is the transcript of their four-day trial in Moscow in May 1963, and the other is a little known English language booklet entitled *Penkovsky: Facts and Fancy*, published by Novosti. Much of the latter is devoted to denigrating Penkovsky and ridiculing the idea that he might have been an ideologically-motivated spy, but by far the most interesting material concerns Wynne, and in particular the transcript of his interrogation by Nikolai Chistiakov and Aleksandr Zagvozdin of the KGB on 22 November 1962, in which Wynne offered to work for the KGB for a period of two years after his release. Of course this may have been a convenient ploy to facilitate an escape from his predicament or it might have been more serious, one cannot tell, but the reference to 'King' in the transcript is intriguing, for this was the name of one of the SIS officers who had handled Wynne.

SIS had run Penkovsky at four levels. The then Chief, Sir Dick White, had been introduced to Penkovsky during the latter's second visit to London. During his trial Penkovsky disclosed that White had been referred to simply as 'RAJ'. The operation itself had been supervised by Oliver St John, a veteran SIS officer who had once run a network of agents in Cairo, leaving two case officers to deal with Penkovsky and Wynne separately. They were Harold Shergold, who never met Wynne, and Dickie Franks who was transferred to Bonn from SIS headquarters as soon as Wynne had been arrested. In addition, there were two other senior officers indoctrinated into the case: Harry Stokes, then the

Deputy Head of Station in Washington to (Sir) Maurice Oldfield, who liaised closely with the CIA, and Herbert J. Collins, Shergold's controller. The latter's London flat, at 52 Coleherne Court, had been used to entertain Penkovsky in London, and had been the venue for Dick White's meeting with him. While giving evidence at his trial Wynne could say very little about the involvement of the CIA as precautions had been taken to prevent him from learning the identities of Penkovsky's two American case officers, George Kisevalter and Joe Bulik. However, Wynne had identified various SIS personnel, including Ruari Chisholm who had run SIS's station in Moscow until July 1962 and his wife, Janet, who had held regular meetings with Penkovsky in December 1961 and January 1962. The clandestine role of this pair, of course, had already been disclosed to the KGB by Chisholm's former colleague in Berlin, George Blake. Indeed, Blake had admitted to SIS in April 1961 that he had compromised Chisholm, which makes one wonder about the wisdom of the decision to allow him and his wife to maintain contact with Penkovsky eight months later. Wynne had also named three people as having pressured him into what he had presented as his reluctant collaboration with SIS: a security officer named Hartley, a Foreign Office official named Ackroyd, and his subordinate, Mr King. What makes Wynne's statement so intriguing is that when Wynne and John Gilbert came to write *The Man From Moscow*, they changed King's name to 'Robbins'.[42] The name Robbins appears nowhere in the trial transcript, and King is repeatedly identified as one of Wynne's SIS handlers. Yet in *The Man From Moscow* the authors have substituted 'Robbins' for King. The most reasonable explanation is that although 'Ackroyd' was a pseudonym, 'King' was an authentic name. In fact, the SIS officer who had assisted Franks had been Roger Andrew Ivan King who, according to recently declassified CIA files, had once come under suspicion for having illicit contacts with the GRU in 1940. This mystery has never been resolved.

Another area of speculation regarding the Wynne and Penkovsky case revolves around the exact date that Penkovsky was arrested. The official Soviet documents refer to Penkovsky having been taken into custody in Gorky Street at five minutes to two on the afternoon of Monday, 22 October 1962. Yet on this date Wynne was still in the West, for he crossed over from Vienna to Hungary on 31 October, only to be arrested there, in Budapest, at seven in the evening on Friday 2 November. Thus, by the time Wynne was arrested in Budapest, Penkovsky had been in the hands of the KGB for at least ten days.

On the day that Wynne was arrested, the KGB had conducted an experiment in Moscow to test the information extracted from

Penkovsky during his lengthy interrogation. Penkovsky had revealed his instructions on how to make contact with the CIA and had described the elaborate procedure they had adopted. It was tradecraft of the most classic variety. First, a signal had to be sent to two American diplomats at their homes. Shortly before nine in the morning they had telephoned 43-26-94 which had been answered by Alexis Davison, an assistant air attaché who also happened to be the U.S. embassy's Russian-speaking doctor. Without saying a word, the KGB had hung up and repeated the exercise with 42-36-87 which had been answered by Hugh Montgomery, who also lived in an apartment at 18 Kutuzovsky Prospekt.

In addition, a black mark had been placed on lamp-post number thirty-five on Kutuzovsky Prospekt. The American reaction to these signals had been for Davison to drive along Kutuzovsky Prospekt and, at the appropriate lamp-post, get out of his car to examine it. He then was seen to drive to the U.S. embassy. At 15.15 hours, later the same day, another American diplomat, Richard C. Jacob, was seized by the KGB while attempting to recover a small canister concealed behind a central heating radiator in the hallway of 5/6 Pushkin Street. Thus, having demonstrated that Penkovsky's confession was certainly true in as much as it referred to his means of communicating with the CIA via dead letter drops, the KGB arranged for Wynne's arrest.

It would certainly appear from the CIA's reaction that the first its Moscow Station knew that its star agent had been compromised came on 2 November, when Richard Jacob had been entrapped while attempting to retrieve Penkovsky's dead drop in Pushkin Street. Under these circumstances it would be understandable that there was insufficient time to warn Wynne in Budapest of the danger he was in. However, there is another bizarre side to the story, for it would seem that shortly before his arrest Penkovsky had sent a coded 'Doomsday message' to his new SIS case officer, Gervase Cowell, indicating that a Soviet nuclear strike on the West was imminent. At the time Penkovsky's behaviour had caused consternation among those indoctrinated into the case, but in retrospect it may have been his way of alerting SIS to the fact that he had either come under direct KGB control, or had merely detected hostile surveillance.

Penkovsky's last contact with the CIA had been in September when he had spotted his principal contact, Rodney Carlson, at a reception given by the U.S. ambassador for a group of visiting executives from the American electrical industry. On 6 September he had attended a film show of *A Taste of Honey* at the British embassy where he had been spotted by Gervase Cowell, his new British case officer, who had taken over from Rory Chisholm after the latter's return to London on 14 July 1962.

There are still many question marks hanging over the Wynne and Penkovsky case, and not a few of them have been placed there by Wynne himself. Some of those who worked with him on his overseas trips considered his consumption of alcohol to be a hazard to his regular business, quite apart from any espionage on the side, and he was a familiar figure to habitués of the British Club at the British Embassy who frequently saw him the worse for wear. The KGB's opinion of Wynne was also pretty low. Viktor Kutuzov, speaking on behalf of the organization, remarked: 'Wynne hated the British secret service agents who had ruined him, used him and discarded him like so much refuse. He wept and sobbed in front of the Interrogating Judge and in court, castigated himself, his rashness, his trust in those ruthless sharks from the Intelligence Service. Apparently this was why Wynne made to Soviet authorities some important revelation about a certain high ranking person in the British secret service, which with time may be made public. Wynne did not stop there. He cynically offered the Soviet authorities to perform espionage assignments against the West'.

Certainly Wynne's experience in the Soviet Union changed his life. Thereafter he was regarded as a pest by SIS and, to a lesser extent, by the CIA, which twice tried to accommodate him on visits to America. On neither occasion did Wynne take any interest in the business leads he was offered, but instead concentrated on drinking. He led a nomadic existence, working initially in Malta selling holiday apartments, a project that was abandoned in 1972, and then moving to the Canary Islands where a friend employed him to promote a villa development on Lanzarote. Finally, he bought an apartment in Palma de Majorca where he became a well-known member of the hard-drinking British expatriate community led by Lady Docker. It was here that he went into rose growing partnership, and later contracted cancer of the throat. His continued alcohol-induced abuse of his second wife that led to her estrangement, and she went to live in a windowless basement sauna at a property he had once owned in Lexham Gardens, south west London. In 1985, in an interview with Philippa Kennedy of the *Daily Express* she complained that she had been deserted by Wynne and said that he had 'missed the secrecy and tension of his other life'.

Shortly before his death Wynne had instituted a libel action which faltered when it emerged that a copy of Wynne's military record had been acquired from the Army, and that it showed Wynne had never received the commission he had claimed. Indeed, it also transpired that Wynne had a history of using a bogus military rank, and even elevated himself to the rank of lieutenant-colonel when applying for membership of the Naval Club in Mayfair, London.

The issue of Wynne's exact rank, combined with overwhelming evidence that he had fabricated every detail of the visit he and Penkovsky had supposedly made to Washington DC in 1961, was to force Wynne to abandon his action just two days before it was due to be tried in the High Court in London. This last-moment withdrawal, without payment of the damages demanded, his costs, or even a face-saving apology, was eloquent proof that Wynne had no intention of being exposed publicly as a Walter Mitty character.

The sad reality was that Wynne suffered from what might be termed a 'post-usefulness syndrome', a craving for attention from the media. This is a fairly familiar phenomena, particularly among ex-intelligence agents who have been unable to replace the excitement and adrenalin of their operational experience. He probably never really fully recovered from the physical and nervous breakdown he endured after his return to London from Moscow in 1964. As we have seen, *The Man From Odessa* was full of bizarre claims that could not be substantiated, and some must have been deliberately included to make the book controversial. He even suggested that the destruction of the Tupolov 144 supersonic jet which crashed so spectacularly at the Paris air show in June 1973, had been as a consequence of a scheme to plant deliberately falsified Concorde data on the Tupolev's Soviet designers. In a television interview to promote *The Man From Odessa* he even implied that he and Penkovsky had been granted a secret audience by the Queen. However, in a far more revealing radio programme, in which Wynne was analysed by a distinguished psychiatrist, Dr Antony Clare, he admitted that he had great difficulty in telling the truth from fiction. This perhaps was the single moment in Wynne's life when he was truly candid.

Chapter 7

Helga's 'Red Spy at Night'

According to her autobiography, *Red Spy at Night*, published in 1977, Helga Wannenmacher-Pohl was Polish, but of German extraction, whose family had fled from Daliatin, in Galicia, to Strehlen, near Breslau, in 1939, where she joined the Hitler Youth and worked in a military hospital. Her brother Jossi, a corporal in the Luftwaffe, coincidentally was posted back to Daliatin where he witnessed an atrocity, 'the shooting of many of our friends'. He then went into hiding, but was not court-martialed when he was returned to his unit because of the intervention of an influential friend.

At the end of the Second World War, aged seventeen, Helga moved again, fleeing the Soviets, to Güsten where, during the American occupation, she acquired Bob Kelly, an American sergeant, as a lover and then, under the Soviet occupation, was employed by the Red Army as an interpreter. However, a plan for her to marry Lieutenant Colonel Andrei Sidorv collapsed when he was recalled to Moscow in November 1946, apparently because he had applied for permission to wed a German. Dismayed at the prospect of having to work for Sidrov's odious deputy, Major Jatschuk, she found another job, at a hospital dispensary in Aisleben but was forced back when Jatschuk arrested her father.

Having resisted Jatschuk's unwelcome advances, and tipped off people scheduled for arrest so they could escape to the West, she was arrested on espionage charges, imprisoned at Magdeburg, interrogated at Potsdam, and sentenced in January 1946 to ten years' hard labour, to be served in a labour camp near Novosibirsk in Siberia. There, with the help of a doctor, Juri Stremilov, she managed to exchange identities with a dead prisoner and when she was discharged from hospital in March 1946, she started a new life as Jelena Pushkova, enrolling at Moscow University. While a student, she married Stremilov but this turned out to be a bigamous wedding when his wife, a veterinarian he had married in 1939, showed up, and the marriage was annulled. Then, unexpectedly, Andrei Sdiov, now promoted to a full colonel, tracked her down and married her in Gorki, taking her on a honeymoon to Lemburg. She then accompanied him to Kirovabad, a missile research establishment in the Caucasus, but in July 1949 Stremilov turned up unexpectedly, apparently in the hope that 'perhaps the KGB would leave me alone'.[1] Helga's reaction was that 'Those three letters terrified me as they did anyone in Russia at that time'.[2]

In September 1949 when her husband was away in Moscow, she attempted, though heavily pregnant, to reach the frontier with Iran, accompanied by Stremilov and a pair of German rocket engineers named Wilpert and Osten. As they attempted to cross the border, Stremilov was shot dead and she received a leg wound. The three survivors were caught and Helga was treated at a hospital in Baku, interrogated 'week after week',[3] flown to Moscow to be questioned at the Lubyanka, incarcerated in the notorious Butirka prison in solitary confinement 'for weeks'[4] and then sentenced to six years' hard labour. Although her husband was unaware of his wife's plan, he too was sentenced to a long term of imprisonment in Novaya Zemlya.

In March 1950, three months after the birth of her son Alik, Helga appealed her conviction before Nikolai Shvernik and Viktor Abakumov, won her release, and was granted a second floor apartment on Moscow's Gorky Embankment. Then she was recruited, reluctantly on her part, into the NKVD by Pavel Sudoplatov, who described her future duties as entertaining foreign visitors. 'They are looking for feminine charm and affection – which you will be able to offer them'. He went on to explain that 'KGB agents must trust nobody. Our work begins with searching waste-paper baskets and ends with … well, in your case, darling, it may end in somebody's bed. All in the interests of the Communist Party, you understand".[5] Helga was 'issued with the uniform of a lieutenant in the KGB' and a pistol, and then attended a party at the Kremlin where she was introduced to Stalin.

Helga attended a police college for six months, during which she performed a striptease for General Sudoplatov, and then was posted to Vienna to persuade an Austrian communist to provide the KGB with passports and other identification documents. For this assignment she was equipped with a Minox camera and a miniature transmitter, although she did not use either. One unanticipated result of her mission, was her introduction to a Lieutenant Charlie Rudford, but she reacted violently when Colonel Shalatov suggested that she compromise the U.S. Army officer with a camera hidden in her bedroom. Outraged, she hit Shalatov, but when the incident was reported to Sudoplatov, he took no action.

Having accomplished this task, she was sent in November 1950 to Vladivostok to investigate the disappearance of some military equipment but ended up penetrating a merchant seaman running a smuggling racket and arrested the ringleader. Upon her return to Moscow, Helga attended a New Year's Eve fancy dress ball at the Kremlin where she met Lavrenti Beria's son Semyon, whom she described as 'an excellent dancer'.[6] Then she was given an assignment in Paris to murder 'two men who were proving an embarrassment' using 'fountain-pens with lethal charges'.[7] One of the victims 'was a KGB officer',[8] but she warned him and they fled to Copenhagen. When the KGB learned of what she had done, through a listening device installed in her home, she was threatened with a court-martial, but narrowly escaped punishment by persuading Ivan Serov that, aged twenty-three, and having been in the KGB for only ten months, she had been poorly trained and had been ill-prepared for her mission.

Helga then had a brief affair with Semyon Beria, whom she accompanied to the Red Army Day Ball, where she met Stalin's son Vasili, and in March 1951 was posted to the Dzerzhinsky Military and Diplomatic Faculty before volunteering for a posting to Kazan to monitor the foreign students and supervise the prisoners at Zelenodolsk, where she bought a house for herself and her child.

During a visit back to Moscow by the KGB's head of personnel, Colonel Miranov, she was seduced by Viktor Abakumov who arranged for her to be reunited with her husband Andrei who was moved to Pertovka prison in Kazan in November and released the following month, after the intervention of Nikolai Shvernik. Reinstated in the army, he was given enough compensation to build a dacha on the banks of the Volga, a flat in Kazan, and a job on a local missile base. At this point Helga attempted to resign from the KGB, but was prevented from doing so by Abakumov, apparently his 'last official act'.[9]

When Stalin died in March 1953 disorder erupted across the Soviet Union and Helga played a role in restoring calm at the Pertovka prison, but in doing so she was injured in an attack by prisoners and suffered concussion, shock and 'a sort of nervous breakdown'.[10]

In May 1954, having graduated from the Kazan Institute, Helga attended a further course at the Dzerzhinsky Academy in June and, upon its completion in November, was posted to a counter-espionage unit at Potsdam, on the outskirts of Berlin. By May 1955 she had acquired 'a delightful house and garden'[11] with a friendly Russian maid in Karlshorst where, reunited with her mother and son Alik, she worked on attachment to the trade delegation at the Soviet embassy in the Unter den Linden. She attended the Leipzig Trade Fair and was expected 'to attend every official party where American agents might be expected.'[12] Posing as a Russian teacher, she participated in entrapment operations against American personnel, one of whom turned out to be a CIA officer named Smith who recruited her as an agent. However, instead of supplying him as intended with false information carefully fabricated by the KGB, she succeeded in passing him genuine material, 'a lsit of all the weapons in current use'.[13]

Evidently the CIA intended to run her as an agent in Moscow for she was given a Minox to copy documents, and the recognition system by which 'our man in Moscow will identify himself'.[14] However, instead of returning to Moscow Helga seized the opportunity to defect just when she was due to board the train with her son, and she was driven 'in silence' to CIA headquarters. On 16 June 1956, having identified herself to the CIA as a KGB captain, she and her son were flown from Tempelhof to West Germany, where she underwent a debriefing.

In Helga's tale, *Red Spy at Night*, she describes how she had been an athlete at a display attended by Adolf Hitler, shaken hands with Stalin in the Kremlin, performed a striptease for Pavel Sudoplatov and bedded both Semyon Beria and Viktor Abakumov. Although billed by her publishers as 'a true story of espionage and seduction behind the Iron Curtain' there must be considerable doubt about its authenticity. If the book is true, then it is the first by a KGB officer who was trained to seduce foreign visitors to the Soviet Union, and although there are plenty of references to real people, such as Viktor Abakumov, Ivan Serov and Pavel Sudoplatov, the story is really too improbable to be anything other than a work of fiction.

The most obvious problem is Helga's account of having joined the KGB in 1950, when the organisation was not created until 1954. However, setting that aside, her claimed experience was not only unusual, but would have been unique, especially for a foreign national. For a foreigner to be commissioned into any Soviet intelligence organisation as an officer, and a former member of the Hitler Youth at that, is incredible. So is the proposition that someone convicted of espionage should be even considered as a potential candidate. Even more bizarrely, Helga claimed to have been coerced into joining the KGB, which is ludicrous.

Helga's description of her training also raises some doubts. According to her, she attended a police college for six months in 1950, and then was sent on her first assignment to Vienna. Thereafter she was given several missions, and then in March 1951 was sent to 'the

Dzerzhinsky Military and Diplomatic Faculty' but left two months later in May 1951 when she had volunteered 'to work in the Ural Mountains'.[15]

A great deal is known in the West about the Soviet intelligence training structure because various defectors have given very detailed accounts of their experiences at the NKVD's High School, the MGB Higher Intelligence School at Balashikha, and the KGB School at 11 Kiselny Lane. Indeed, one defector in particular, Anatoli Golitsyn, who sought asylum in December 1961, spent much of the period mentioned by Helga at various different establishments so it is possible to compare Helga's version with the experience of not just Golitsyn, but the five NKVD officers who defected in 1954, being Yuri Rastvorov, Nikolai Khokhlov, Piotr Deriabin and Evdokia and Vladimir Petrov. Their testimony is that most post-war Soviet intelligence officers underwent a minimum of four years' training, and some underwent ten years. The three principal training establishments were Balashikha, the KGB School at Kiselny Lane, and some student places reserved for the KGB at the GRU's Military Diplomatic Academy. Quite simply, there was no such institution as the 'Dzerzhinsky Military and Diplomatic Faculty', which is fictional combination of the Dzerzhinsky Artillery Academy and GRU's Military Diplomatic Academy. Nor is it credible that Helga would have been posted to an operational post in Kazan, and been able to buy her own home in Zenelodolsk after, on her reckoning, just eight months of training.

Upon closer scrutiny, Helga's alleged KGB missions seem very doubtful, and this is especially true of her trip to Paris in February 1951, accompanied by Lieutenant Colonel Gorniak, to kill two unnamed men, one of whom was 'a KGB officer'.[16] Whilst it is not in dispute that the Soviets had both the will and the means to assassinate opponents, it seems odd that such a sensitive role should have been entrusted to an untrained neophyte with absolutely no preparation, especially when the Soviet intelligence monolith included an entire branch, the 13th Department, dedicated to similar tasks and staffed by personnel with plenty of wartime experience. The existence of the 13th Department would become known when one of its officers, Nikolai Khokhlov, defected in 1954, and his revelations would be expanded upon later by Bogdan Stashinsky who defected, also to the CIA, in 1961. With such a pool of talent to draw on, why was Helga sent to kill the duo? Helga offers no explanation, but her version is odd. Certainly no Soviet intelligence officer defected in 1951, from Copenhagen or anywhere else, so the fate of her targets is equally mysterious. Under normal circumstances any KGB officer who was proving a nuisance would be recalled from his *rezidentura* to Moscow, perhaps on a plausible pretext, but if her account is true then it is the only case of its kind during the entire period of the Cold War. Furthermore, in her account her companion, Gorniak, 'an ex-guerrilla leader and a ruthless and experienced agent'[17] invited one of their intended victims to dine with him 'because he needed some information'[18] and evidently the dinner took place, which suggests that the victim had no suspicion about Gorniak's plans.

There is something strange too about Helga's other mission, to Vladivostok in November 1950. According to her account she was ordered by General Sudoplatov to accompany Mikhail Tschernikov and 'trace a railway wagon loaded with submarine parts that had vanished without trace.'[19] Colonel Tschernikov was to 'pose as a naval engineer officer' and Helga was to 'mug up on ranks, naval jargon and so on' to play the role of his wife.[20] Unanswered, is precisely why such an investigation could not have been conducted by any of the various branches of Soviet intelligence already in Vladivostok, nor why her presence was needed at all. Nevertheless, the missing railway wagon was found, and Helga conducted an entirely separate investigation into a people-smuggling racket, for which she was awarded the Order of the Red Banner.

If the Vladivostock mission sounds strange, then what about Helga's assignment in Vienna where her objective was to persuade an already committed Communist to supply the Soviets with authentic Austrian identity documents? This was surely a task that could have been undertaken by the local *rezidentura*, as Helga herself pointed out, but the answer was that Colonel Minkovsky, the 'chief of the intelligence branch in Vienna', had to remain inconspicuous and therefore would supervise, but not participate in, the operation. As a result of information from Deriabin and Golitsyn, who both served in the Vienna *rezidentura*, much is known about the Soviet organisation in Vienna at this time but, according to them, there was never any Colonel Minkovsky there. The *rezidentura*, which had consisted of more than a hundred officers working under semi-transparent Soviet High Commission cover, had been headed by Yevgeni Kravtsov, who worked under the alias Kovalev. He had been the *rezident* in Latvia, Turkey and Switzerland and head of the German-Austrian Department. His deputy was Yevgeni Galuzin, an experienced former military counter-intelligence officer in East Germany, who supervised the *rezidentura*'s counter-intelligence work. Helga's supposed mission was to cultivate the manager of the passport office in Vienna, who was a Communist Party member, but given the very close relationship between the local

Party and the *rezidentura*, it seems odd that such a task would have been given to a neophyte from Moscow, especially when entrapment was not part of the plan.

One aspect of Helga's mission to Vienna coincides with fact, as it would later be discovered that the Soviets had indeed recruited an official in the Austrian passport office who had passed authentic identification details to the Soviets for the use of their illegal agents in the west.

Supposedly Helga was supplied with a pistol, a Minox camera and a miniature transmitter, and was accompanied by Major Okunin, to Vienna, posing as 'engineers going to Austria to buy machinery'.[21] To make her cover convincing, Helga attended 'a fortnight's course at the Railway Centre'[22] and then achieved her objective. But why the elaborate cover, and the unnecessary equipment? The inclusion of a Minox is also odd, for the Soviets had their own specialist cameras designed for the purpose of copying documents. Could Helga's version really be true?

With the seed of doubt sown by a close look at these episodes, other problems emerge with Helga's tale. Were fancy dress balls thrown at the Kremlin? Could a convicted German spy really have met Stalin socially within weeks of her release from prison? Would such an individual have been given her own apartment on the Gorki Embankment, and 'issued with a car and driver'? Could she have been decorated in the way she described, for having broken up an escape route run by a murderous merchant seaman to the United States from Vladivostok?

Helga's relationship with the CIA also sounds peculiar. In her version she says than in June 1956 she was deliberately deployed against two CIA officers in West Berlin, Smith and Mentor, with the intention of luring them into a trap in East Berlin. Posing as a teacher based in Karlshorst, her lure was an introduction to her husband, a missile expert, but she would not be present as she was to return to Moscow. Apparently entirely willing to accept this scenario, the two CIA officers had given Helga a Minox for her husband in case he had 'a chance to take a few photographs'[23] and had instructed her on contact with 'our man in Moscow'.[24] However, this does not really sound right, considering that in 1956 the CIA did not have a station in Moscow, and possessed not a single CIA officer in the city. As for the Minox, mere possession of such an expensive and incriminating piece of obvious espionage paraphernalia would place the owner in tremendous jeopardy the moment it was discovered, so such items were rarely offered to individual agents.

Although there is no single incident which points to *Red Spy at Night* being a fraud, the sheer accumulation of improbabilities makes the tale particularly hard to swallow, from the brother Jossi who deserted from the Luftwaffe but apparently suffered no consequences, to the idea that Helga had been sent to France to murder two men with 'fountain pens with lethal charges'.[25]

Since the publication of *Red Spy at Night* nobody has come forward to denounce it as a hoax, but on the other hand there has not been any endorsement from within the intelligence community. The author is not recognised as a legitimate Soviet intelligence defector, and her name does not appear on the KGB's arrest list published by *Possev*. But if she is a fraud, where did she acquire her information about some of the genuine personalities whom she mentions, such as Pavel Sudoplatov, Nikolai Shvernik and Viktor Abakumov? That is a conundrum that has yet to be resolved.

Chapter 8

The Vietnam Experience

The revelation in June 2001 by the *Boston Globe* that the distinguished American historian, Professor Joseph J. Ellis, had fabricated a glorious past for himself, engaged in combat during the Vietnam War with the 101st Airborne Division (at a time when he was teaching military history at the West Point military academy) shocked many of his admirers and those that knew him. The author of *Founding Brothers: The Revolutionary Generation* and a biography of Thomas Jefferson that won a Pulitzer Prize, had invented his harrowing tales of being on patrol near Mai Lai shortly before the 1968 massacre, and engaging in bitter fire-fights with the Viet Cong. In fact, Ellis had never served abroad as a soldier, and his military service, which had begun in 1965 when he had been commissioned, had been deferred for four years while he continued his university studies, at Yale.

Certainly he is not alone at having invented his personal involvement in that tragic conflict, which still haunts the American psyche, but why do so many seek to claim a role in what is now perceived as a deeply unpopular intervention in south-east Asia? Senator Tom Harkin often described having participated in air combat over Hanoi, but actually he had been employed ferrying Phantom jets to repair facilities in Japan. Such impostors are now cited as victims of 'pseudologic fantastica', most obviously manifested by Roni DeJoseph, a purported Marine veteran from New York, seen in a much published photograph, bemedaled, his head pressed against the Vietnam memorial wall in Washington DC. Subsequent enquiries showed that DeJoseph had never served in any of the American armed forces. Such claims are far from unusual. Those of the actor Brian Dennehy, one of the stars of *Rambo*, who told a *New York Times* reporter in 1989 about his experiences as a Green Beret, were disproved, as were those of a judge who falsely claimed a CIA background in Vietnam to obtain a judicial appointment, and those of an academic in Oklahoma who fantasised a career as a U.S. Navy SEAL.

The list of those suspected of having invented a role for themselves in the clandestine confrontation which spread into Laos and Cambodia is remarkable, and includes Lennox Gordon Cramer (*Slow Dance on the Killing Ground*); Frank Dux (*The Secret Man: An American Warrior's Uncensored Story*); Warner Smith (*Covert Warrior*) and Scott Barnes (*BOHICA*). Even a British author, Tom Abraham, who wrote *The Cage*, an account of his capture by the Vietcong while serving in the U.S. Army's 1st Cavalry Division during the Tet offensive, has prompted some criticism. Abraham claimed to have escaped from his harrowing captivity, and then to have been returned to his unit to complete his tour of tour duty before returning to the U.S. as an instructor. However, according to the U.S. Army, all escapees were repatriated immediately for lengthy debriefing, and apparently there is no official record of his capture or his subsequent escape. Not dissimilar questions were also raised about another soldier, Frank Dux, who also claimed to have undergone some unusual experiences in Vietnam.

Frank Dux enlisted in the U.S. Marine Corps in 1975, when he was aged eighteen, and volunteered for a Special Operations Group which was assigned to Laos, where he participated in Operation *Sanction*. He was one of the few to be able to survive a trek back into Thailand, and during the remainder of his military career was decorated with the Navy Cross, the Silver Star, the Bronze Star, the Distinguished Service Cross, the Navy Marine Corps medal, one purple heart, and the most coveted U.S. Medal of Honor. The latter was awarded in conditions of secrecy, following a clandestine mission, so remains unrecorded in any official documents.

Certainly Frank Dux is a living legend, and part of his life, as an international martial arts champion, has been used by scriptwriters as a basis of *Bloodsport*, an 1998 action thriller starring the Belgian movie actor Jean-Claude van Damme. However, it is Dux's autobiography, *The Secret Man*, which has attracted most controversy, for in it he described his background, and revealed his role in a series of deniable covert operations.

According to Dux, espionage had been in his blood for generations. His grandfather Alfred, later to be imprisoned by the Nazis, had been a spy, in 'the Austrian intelligence corps', and had fought with the Turks at Gallipoli, crossing into 'no-man's land separating Turkish and Anzac forces numerous times, impersonating a British lieutenant and daringly mingling with his enemies.'[1] He wounded General Birdwood, shot General Bridges, and killed his British aide-de-camp, Lieutenant B.W.

Onslow. His father Alfred had been smuggled from his home in Deutschkreutz to Palestine as a child, and at the age of fourteen was an accomplished car thief, and the driver of a bus to transport illegal Jewish immigrants at night. He 'stole police vehicles, mostly jeeps, for the Haganah and Mossad, the secret intelligence of the illegal Jewish defense forces.'[2]

In 1939 Alfred Dux joined the Jewish Brigade and the British used him 'as an instructor in the art of precision driving' although, due to his past, 'he limited his direct participation in intelligence work'. In 1942 'he was nearly apprehended in North Africa as a part of a group attempting to enlist the IRA in efforts to smuggle arms and munitions into Palestine.' Two years later Alfred was 'back in Austria as a clandestine member of the Avengers, a group composed of the Jewish Brigade operating paramilitary fashion and wreaking vengeance upon those who had destroyed their homes and families'. In 1945 Alfred was back in Palestine, 'smuggling the Jews out of internment camps on Crete and delivering them to' Tel Aviv. According to Dux, 'the British stepped up their efforts to disarm Jewish settlers and began rearming the Jordanians in hopes of a Jewish slaughter and an excuse for a British return'. During the 1947 War of Independence, 'Alfred and his Haganah comrades' 'convinced many Jordanians they possessed an atomic bomb' and later distinguished himself further by volunteering to drive medical supplies to Jerusalem.[3]

Dux's knowledge that he is 'the third known generation involved in espionage' sustained him through his childhood, which was spent in Canada when his family moved from Toronto to California in 1963, when he was aged seven. There he encountered an elderly gifted martial arts teacher, Takizo Tanaka, who also had a background in intelligence. In 1933 Tanaka had moved to England where his relative, Kunshinige Tanaka 'was head of Japanese intelligence. From that time Takizo began to use multiple aliases, adopting the name Senzo for his activities as a covert operative/strong-arm agent.[4]'

According to Dux's own official military file, he was on active duty from 15 June to his discharge on 23 October 1973, a total of just over four months, without any overseas service. He remained as a reserve private soldier until 1981, and in January 1978 was recommended for psychiatric therapy because of his tendency to exaggerate. His file shows no wounds, apart from a minor strain sustained in a fall while painting a vehicle in a motor pool in San Diego.

Nor does Dux's family history withstand much scrutiny, and certainly his story about his father's background in Palestine is inaccurate, not least because neither the Haganah nor Mossad existed before the Second World War, and the Jewish Brigade, which Alfred Dux is alleged to have joined in 1939, was not formed for another three years.

Inventing tales about Vietnam is by no means restricted to Americans, and a good example is Gayle Rivers, the pseudonym of the author of *The Specialist*, published in 1985, who claims to have served as a reservist with the South African Air Force, fought with the Anzac SAS in Vietnam, on secondment to U.S. Special Forces. Saying 'every incident in this book is true and the people are real', Rivers describes having joined F Troop of 21st SAS in 1975, a reserve unit attached to the territorial regiment, as opposed to 22nd SAS, the regular regiment, as a trooper, despite previously having held the rank of captain. His business at that time was supplying unspecified surveillance equipment, some of which was bought by the SAS, and he recalls that on one occasion he was asked to deliver a car with some of this equipment hidden in the boot to a car dealership in Belfast's Falls Road. For some reason the delivery was to take place after hours on a Saturday evening, but a Provisional IRA bomb wrecked the premises and left four SAS men stranded in the building for the rest of the weekend. Rivers' account of the deployment of the SAS between 1974 and 1976 is remarkable, and he asserts that after a couple of incidents in which SAS patrols strayed over the border into the Republic, the regiment was restricted to an intelligence-gathering role. Nevertheless, he,

> went on one patrol personally – and I was aware of several others – where a cold decision was taken to carry out an ambush, and take no prisoners. Once IRA terrorists were conclusively identified, they were engaged in a firefight and eliminated.[5]

Rivers mentions that during his weekend service in the territorials he 'would be buried under the turf' of 'bandit country' in South Armagh, hunting IRA terrorists in what they regarded as their safest strongholds. On one occasion, in October 1976, he was instructed to install audio and video equipment in a farm building in South Armagh, fifteen kilometres from the border, that had been identified by a local agent, a country doctor, as the meeting-place for an imminent IRA gathering. Ten IRA activists assembled in the barn while the SAS men, watching from foxholes dug into a hill overlooking the scene, monitored their activities. When it became clear that the doctor had fallen under suspicion, and was to be abducted by the IRA, the decision was taken at Hereford to extract the doctor but leave the IRA cell undisturbed. This was achieved by two SAS men who ambushed the car carrying the doctor, killing his two IRA kidnappers. Rivers then booby-trapped his equipment and, accompanied by an SAS sniper, made his way across the border to where his private plane was waiting on an airstrip in a country estate near Longford. The other four members of the SAS patrol intercepted and shot dead two members of the IRA who were returning to the Republic, and were flown by Rivers back to base at Hereford.

While still an SAS reservist, Rivers describes having been hired by the German *Bundeskriminalamt* in the spring of 1978, to hijack a suspected consignment of IRA weapons in transit in a German-registered TIR truck, ostensibly loaded with a cargo of food, between Colmar and the Channel ports. Assisted by a French mercenary, Rivers climbed about the moving tractor unit, shot two of the three IRA men on board with an Uzi sub-machinegun, and then seized control of the vehicle. They parked close to the frontier outside Mulhouse where they met an undercover team from the *Bundeskriminalamt* which escorted the truck through French customs, having removed the body of one dead IRA driver.

Although the objective of this particular operation was not the murder of a terrorist, Rivers claims to have been sent on such assignments by MI6 twice, one to Spain and then again to Greece, to interfere with IRA gun-running. In the first mission Rivers was sent to investigate Colin McGrath, an IRA bomb-maker living in Marbella after Belfast had got too hot for him, a wealthy Englishman who owned an ex-motor torpedo boat, and a woman who ran an IRA safe-house in Luton. According to Rivers, 'SIS (the Security and Intelligence Service)' believed his boat was being used to make radio contact with the cargo vessels going through the Strait of Gibraltar, passing on instructions about where to drop the weapons shipments, and identifying which of the ships were the carriers and which were the dummy-runs'.[6]

In Rivers' account he made an effort to befriend the boat's owner, chartering it for fishing trips, and hired him for an aerial photo shoot, arranging for him to take his craft three miles out to sea while he flew overhead. The night beforehand, however, he climbed aboard the boat, planted plastic explosives beside the long-range fuel tank, and detonated them by remote control, with help from a technician who had come in from London, as he headed for Tangier. The following day the pair returned to Malaga 'to hear the news of the tragedy. There never was any enquiry into the explosion' and 'the death of the IRA trio had done serious damage to the gun-running operation'.[7]

The success of this operation led to another, this time targeted against the Greek ship-owner who had been identified 'conclusively as the principal organizer of the arms-smuggling shipments from the eastern

Mediterranean to the Basque separatists ETA, and the IRA'.[8] Furthermore, his bodyguards had been responsible for the recent deaths of two Britons, in Paris and Athens. Rivers flew to Athens to meet the man on the pretext that he wished to charter a ship to carry a cargo of underwater diving gear from Beirut to San Sebastian, dropping a heavy hint that the equipment concealed illegal weapons. During an inspection of the vessel, moored of Piraeus, one of the bodyguards was killed by Rivers' companion, the French mercenary, who killed another later the same evening on a motor launch. The pair then abducted the Greek in his car, flew to the airport where he was shot twice in the back of the head, and then caught a flight to Geneva.

News of Rivers' reliability as a hitman apparently recommended him to the Spanish security authorities to whom he had supplied military equipment over several years, and had acted as a 'tactical adviser'. The Minister of the Interior, Juan José Roson, was keen to hire him to work against ETA targets and, sometime in 1979, he was put on a concealed payroll 'consulting on the maritime architecture of a new dock at Bilbao and advising a fabric company in Madrid'.[9] At a police safe-house in Madrid, Rivers was given a list of thirty ETA activists living in France and then, having recruited a Corsican gangster, set out on his first mission, the assassination of a man in Biarritz identified as the organisation's propaganda chief. In May 1980 he placed an explosive charge under the suspect's Renault and detonated it by remote control as his target and another ETA suspect climbed into the car. The propaganda chief was killed, and his companion was injured, losing both legs and an arm.

Impressed with what he had accomplished, the Spanish summoned Rivers to Madrid to discuss his next target, but he became involved in a gunfight in the street. Rivers' contact was attacked just outside his office, and Rivers was able to shoot dead one of the ETA gunmen.

Reinforced with another three Corsicans, Rivers returned to Bairritz and began stalking their next quarry, a senior ETA figure whom they eventually ran down with a stolen taxi. Then they placed ETA's leader, known as Zarra, under surveillance but he proved to be an experienced terrorist who rarely moved without a bodyguard. Rivers opted for a car-bomb rigged to detonate when Zarra's car moved, but in the event it was the bodyguard that was killed, with Zarra escaping with his life, but only narrowly.

Several more months of surveillance during 1980 established that Zarra was to attend a meeting at an isolated farmhouse outside Biarritz, and Rivers arranged to seize him and his deputy, and to kill all the others. The plan was for a group of ex-SAS men to surround and attack the farm while Rivers stopped the car in which the ETA leader was to travel. He would then be flown by helicopter to a freighter cruising in the Bay of Biscay for interrogation, and then delivered to a beach in Spain. In the event Rivers chartered a civilian-configured Gazelle helicopter in Paris and landed it in the path of the terrorists' Peugeot, raking it with machine-gun fire that killed two of the women passengers. Zarra and his wounded companion were thrown into the helicopter and flown to the ship where a team of Spanish interrogators tortured them. At the farmhouse, nine ETA terrorists, including two women were shot dead, while the attackers suffered two casualties. The following morning, one of the surviving terrorists on the ship was shot dead and his body, together with Zarra's, was dumped on a Spanish beach for the police to find. According to Rivers, an estimated 150 arrests had been made as a result of their confessions.

During the following year, 1981, Rivers says he was based in Southampton, apparently working at a local flying school run by a friend, but was arrested in Jersey when an acquaintance whom he had accompanied on a flight to Tangiers was found to be carrying drugs. However, after three weeks in custody, Rivers was released without charge and he returned to England unhindered. In 1982 he trained an Iraqi Special Forces unit and participated in a sabotage attack on three ships in the Iranian port of Khorramshahr. A German tanker, a Greek freighter and another ship, of Panamanian registration, were blown up, blocking much of the harbour and, most importantly, raising the Lloyds insurance rates in the Gulf. A year later, in November 1983, Rivers was hired by the CIA to lead a small team of U.S. Special Forces on a clandestine operation in Beirut, requiring the abduction of a senior Syrian intelligence officer and the destruction of a Druze militia headquarters. Although the Syrian was killed, the CIA apparently regarded the operation as a success.

In addition to his adventures experienced while working for MI6, Rivers claims that in 1976 he had been hired to train Iraqi paratroopers for combat against the Kurds and that 'on and off for more than three years' he had 'led missions against the Iranians'.[10] Before that, in 1975, he had earned the wrath of Mossad by working on a defence sales contract involving the purchase by Egypt of some French Mirage jet fighters. Rivers narrowly escaped from an aircraft sabotaged by the Israelis, and then was forced to shoot an assassin sent to kill him in Cairo.

For a man who cheerfully acknowledges his participation in the violent deaths of more than a dozen people, it is a little surprising that Rivers has only attracted the attention of the police over a small quantity of cannabis, even if, as he says, some of the murders had been sanctioned by MI6. But could any of this really be true? Does the Secret Intelligence Service really indulge in contract killings? According to Rivers, such events are quite routine, and there can be no doubt that his orders came from MI6 which preferred to employ him, as a matter of policy, as a 'deniable person', the implication being that in the event of something going wrong, there would be no political blowback on the organisation. Although Rivers says he was then 'in the early to mid-1970s', working in Madrid, with a home in Marbella and his own plane at Malaga airport, he was approached over a lunch at the Athenaeum to handle the murder of the three IRA suspects by a civilian employee of the Ministry of Defence who held the rank of colonel in the reserve SAS. This individual, allegedly a familiar figure in Whitehall, the SAS mess in the Duke of York's barracks and the Special Forces Club, apparently acted as liaison between Whitehall and private contractors, so it is hard to fathom how he could have fulfilled any role as an intermediary.

So is it likely that MI6 would have wished to kill the three IRA gun-runners in Marbella who were apparently under the close scrutiny of the Spanish? According to the account given by Rivers, in a chapter unambiguously entitled 'MI6: Assignment to Assassinate', the Mediterranean smuggling route had been covered by men of the Special Boat Service and a small submarine, 'one of two that Naval Intelligence had been using in a major operation to track cargo vessels suspected of carrying IRA arms shipments'.[11] MI6 had established that the IRA bomber was on its 'most wanted list' and had already arranged one illicit consignment of weapons destined for Ireland. It was MI6 that delivered the remote-control equipment, and the technician to blow up the boat. Similarly, for the murder of the Greek ship-owner, Rivers describes his involvement with two MI6 officers. The first was 'one of MI6's Middle East operatives' who 'works for the British on a contract basis, but he chooses not to be an insider'. Apparently he had 'run agents for British Intelligence in Cyprus during the EOKA terrorist period before independence', while the second MI6 officer was 'a former Royal Green jackets major who had served with distinction in the regiment' then had become 'a director of a large defence company', and lived in a flat in St James's. A third MI6 officer, whom Rivers always met in pubs, was 'an experienced MI6 operative who would be reporting directly to a controller' and he worked closely with a fourth individual, 'who ran a shipping agency which British Intelligence used for a number of its freight-handling operations.' Thus, although the alleged purpose of employing Rivers was his isolation from MI6, bringing an element of plausible denial to the project, he was actually in touch with no less than five people who most certainly were very closely connected with the organisation. While it is hard to pin down the author to any specific dates, it would appear that these murders, of the IRA trio in Marbella and the Greek and his bodyguards in Athens, took place in the 1970s, prior to Rivers' acceptance by the SAS. As much as it is possible to check newspaper reports of such incidents over that long a period, no such events seem to have occurred.

However, Rivers' account of his participation in an SAS operation in Northern Ireland in October 1976 is rather easier to check, not least because the Provisional IRA have, for the purposes of the Northern Ireland peace process, developed a detailed chronology of the major incidents in which their active service units played a part, and there is a comprehensive list of their casualties. Whilst it is certainly true that various security and intelligence agencies maintained surveillance on suspect sites at the time Rivers describes, there was no one single episode in which two PIRA terrorists were shot dead in a car in South Armagh in the way portrayed, and nor is there any record of another two senior PIRA men being shot dead as they attempted to cross into the Republic from South Armagh, either in October 1976 or at any other time. Indeed, the proposition that a four-man SAS patrol would deliberately travel into Eire to fly out on a civilian aircraft is bizarre.

After his experiences in Northern Ireland Rivers claims to have been employed by the Spanish Minister of the Interior, Juan José Roson, to murder ETA suspects in France, beginning with the car-bombing of ETA's propaganda chief in Bairritz in May 1980. Altogether Rivers admits to his involvement in three assassinations, and in the major attack on the ETA conference at a farmhouse outside Bairritz, and the abduction of the ETA leader known as Zarra.

To understand these ostensibly bizarre events, one must grasp the nature of the so-called 'first dirty war' which was conducted between 1975 and 1981 against ETA. During that period no less than three organisations indulged in anti-ETA terrorism, being the *Anti-Terrismo ETA* (known as ATE), the *Acción Nacional Espanola* (ANE) and the main group, the *Batalión Vascol Espanol* (BVE), which is now known to have been sponsored by members of Spain's security apparatus. While little is known about ATE and ANE, much has been disclosed in recent years about the BVE and its notorious successor, the *Grupos Antiterroristas de Liberacion* (GAL) which sent death squads after ETA's leadership during the 'second dirty war' which occurred between 1983 and 1987.

The BVE came into existence shortly before the death of General Franco in November 1975, and targeted the men widely believed to have been responsible for the assassination in a Madrid street of Prime

Minister Luis Carrero Blanco in December 1973, an act that was to split ETA into two rival factions, and mark the beginning of a long and bloody conflict between terrorists operating on both sides of the French border, often with political refugee status in France which gave them immunity from extradition, and their frustrated opponents within the Spanish government. Another significant milestone in this dirty war was the shooting, in December 1980, in a café in Hendaye, which resulted in the death of two people, and injuries to nine others, including two ETA activists. The three gunmen left the scene in a car which immediately crossed the frontier into Spain, and into the custody of the Spanish police who thereafter refused to either prosecute them, or disclose their identities to the outraged French authorities. The Interior Minister responsible for shielding the suspects, and then ordering their release, was Juan José Roson, who insisted that they were police informers who had not committed the crime and were entitled to official protection. Incidentally, Roson's brother, General Luis Roson, was to be the target of an unsuccessful attack in November 1984 when his car was riddled with bullets in a Madrid street, wounding both himself and his driver.

It was in this environment of atrocities committed by both sides, in France and in Spain, that Rivers says he participated in the murders in Biarritz, and there can be no doubt, based on evidence offered in subsequent trials, that the BVE was officially sponsored and hired various mercenaries to carry out hits in France. The question is whether any of the incidents described by Rivers ever occurred in what is now a very well documented conflict, supported by official investigations, criminal trials and admissions of police collusion in the anti-ETA campaign. Careful scrutiny of the history of the conflict does not show there was any car bombing in Biarritz in May 1980, and nor did ETA suffer the loss of any 'propaganda chief' in that year. Indeed, the assault on the farmhouse and the abduction of Zarra is also completely untraceable, as is the supposed round-up of 150 ETA suspects following Zarra's alleged murder. Whilst it is true that the BVE was active in France during 1980, and ETA often used exotic codenames to conceal its membership, nothing occurred that comes even close to the events described by Rivers, and no ETA leader was either called Zarra or known by that *nom-de-guerre*. The terrible statistics of the period show that the BVE killed three ETA members in France in 1979, and a further nine in two random bombings and two rape-murders in Spain's Basque country in 1980, while ETA was responsible for seventeen murders. However, the BVE's only foray onto French territory took place in December, at the Hendayais Bar, and the well-publicised murders in Biarritz, in which three ETA men were killed and one was injured, did not occur until four years later, and were attributed to the GAL. In any event, none of these incidents resemble the events described by Rivers. The first was the death of Tomas Perez in June 1984 as he walked past a remotely-detonated bomb with a refugee priest Ramon Orbe, who was badly injured. Then there was the shooting in March 1985 of Xabier Perez, murdered by a lone gunman who escaped on a motor scooter as his victim filled his car with fuel at a petrol station, and in December of the same year Robert Caplanne was killed by the GAL in a case of mistaken identity. Caplanne was an innocent French electrician, but his murderers had incorrectly identified him as their true target, Enrique Villar. Of these three deaths, Tomas Perez was a known ETA leader (who had survived an earlier machine-gun attack on his car in 1976, which had wounded his wife), and Xabier Perez who was Domingo Iturbe's brother-in-law. No other incidents happened in or around Biarritz during either phase of the dirty wars, and none of these three sound like Rivers' handiwork. Accordingly, Rivers appears to have been wrong on both the dates and the circumstances of the BVE's activities, which makes it unlikely that he really had a hand in them. Whilst it is true there were other GAL killings in this latter period, for example of ETA's notorious Algerian-trained hitman Mikel Goikoetxea, in December 1983, who was shot by two gunmen outside his home in St Jean-de-Luz. Although Goikoetxea came from a long family tradition of ETA militancy he was, at the age of twenty-seven, by no means regarded as a leader.

Examination of the BVE's operations against ETA's leadership show that several senior figures were assassinated, but again, none of them come close to Rivers' story. For example, in July 1978, a car driven by Juan José Extabe, ETA's former leader, was machine-gunned by the BVE in St Jean-de-Luz, and his wife killed. In December ETA's leader Benaran Ordenana was blown to pieces in his booby-trapped car in the French Basque town of Angelet. Three weeks later José Pagoaga, widely believed to have planned Carrero's assassination five years earlier, was badly injured by another bomb; Domingo Iturbe survived two assassination attempts in 1979, and Tomas Alba, the deputy mayor of San Sebastian, was killed. However, there were no incidents of any significance concerning ETA's leadership in 1980, and certainly no abduction that led to a series of mass arrests as he recounts. In fact, the only episode comparable was the raids conducted by the French police in January 1984 in which forty ETA suspects were arrested.

Details of the two 'dirty wars' have emerged over recent years because of investigations conducted during the second half of the 1980s by magistrates in Portugal, France and Spain into the atrocities. The French prosecutions concentrated on individual hitmen, including Jean-Philippe Labade and Patrick de Carvalho, and prosecuted several mercenaries who admitted to having been hired to kill ETA targets, and implicated members of the *Guardia Civil* as their paymasters. In Spain Superintendent José Amedo of the Policia Nacional in Bilbao was implicated, as was his subordinate, Inspector Michel Dominguez, and they were later to testify against two other police superintendents in Bilbao, Julio Herro and Francisco Saiz, the police chief himself, Miguel Planchuelo, and his director of anti-terrorist intelligence, Francisco Alvarez.

As the searching enquiries continued, the evidence increasingly pointed to complicity at a high level in the Spanish Ministry of the Interior, the Director of State Security, Julián Sancristóbal, his deputy Rafael Vera and several members of their elite anti-terrorist unit were arrested in December 1984. General Enrique Rodriguez, the *Guardia Civil*'s senior anti-terrorist officer in San Sebastian, was convicted of two murders and sentenced to sixty years' imprisonment, and although convictions were obtained against José Barrionuevo in September 1998, Rosón's successor as Minister of the Interior between 1982 and 1988, it is curious that Rosón, the one minister named by Rivers, was never charged with any offence. In other words, Rivers appears to have identified one of the few individuals not directly implicated in the 'dirty wars', the controversies that were to plunge Spain into political turmoil for a decade. The links between the GAL and Spain's military intelligence service, CESID, the *Guardia Civil*, the *Policia Nacional* and the Socialist-run Ministry of the Interior, were explored in dozens of overlapping investigations, and while it is true that on occasions the authorities showed little enthusiasm to extradite fugitives, arrest suspects and pursue politically embarrassing leads, the carnage was considerable and at times threatened to destroy Felipe González' administration. Certainly one related scandal, CESID's tapping of King Juan Carlos's private telephone (among those of many other senior figures in the government) sent shock-waves across Madrid and led to many sudden resignations and dismissals. At one point Luis Roldán, the Director-General of the *Guardia Civil*, fled the country and had to be extradited from Laos and Thailand before he could be interrogated as a witness. However, in none of these cases did any of the events described by Rivers ever materialise, thus casting considerable doubt on his credibility.

Equally surprising is Rivers's alleged employment by the CIA in early November 1983 in the Lebanon to abduct a Syrian Army major, just six months after the destruction of the U.S. Embassy in Beirut. That catastrophic event, on 18 April 1983, goes unmentioned by Rivers, who says he joined a four-man American Special Forces team at a safe-house, a luxurious villa in the centre of the city owned by his agent, a successful international businessman and, after just a day of planning and surveillance, succeeded in 'taking out the whole of the Druze leadership in the area, and three top Syrians'.[12] Unexplained is why, with its own paramilitary Special Activities Division and the U.S. Army to call upon, the CIA required the services of a foreigner to lead American troops. Also, there is a tantalising reference to an entire 'private intelligence network – funded through me by the Americans' in Beirut, which, given the conditions then prevailing in the Lebanon, make the whole episode of very doubtful authenticity.

Rivers describes himself as a specialist who has undertaken 'snatch raids' in Vietnam, Mozambique, Iran and Northern Ireland, but offers little evidence in support. Such assertions as he does make, and the tales he had spun in *The Specialist*, fail to command any confidence and raise more questions than they answer.

Actually, Rivers is the pseudonym of a former logistics officer in the New Zealand Air Force, and the author of several novels with James Hudson, an American freelance journalist based in San Francisco, including *The Five Fingers*, and *The Tehran Contract*. In the former the authors describe a secret mission conducted in 1969 in southeast Asia to kill a group of senior North Vietnamese and Chinese staff officers, leaving some doubt in the mind of the reader about whether it actually happened. In fact, it did not, and nor did the dramatic evacuation of Iran's Jewish population, which was the subject of the second title. So did Rivers ever serve in F Troop of the SAS? Unfortunately, there is no such unit, although there was at that time a reserve squadron, designated R Squadron, which acted to replace battlefield casualties, but certainly never undertook the type of roles described by Rivers. So what about his claim to have served with the New Zealand SAS? This too is a curious claim because the unit's correct title is the First Ranger Squadron, which is not mentioned anywhere by Rivers.

There remains much mystery about the real identity of 'Gayle Rivers', for the person answering to that pseudonym is disabled and has a club foot, the kind of handicap that might be expected to preclude him from working with any Special Forces unit. Furthermore, there has always been speculation that *The Specialist* was actually written by George Greenfield, the literary agent who spent many years at Curtis Brown, the London-based firm which still represents Rivers.

Chapter 9

Tom Carew's 'Jihad'

In the weeks following the terrorist atrocity of 11 September 2001, when the World Trade Center in New York was destroyed by hijacked aircraft, one expert on Afghanistan was more widely quoted in newspapers and on television that almost anyone else. Tom Carew, the author of *Jihad! The Secret War in Afghanistan*, described himself as a former Special Air Service regiment soldier with experience of having fought with the *Mujahideen* against the Soviet occupation forces in 1984. He was constantly in demand, for he had first-hand knowledge of working alongside the tribesmen that subsequently had coalesced into the Taliban, the religious zealots that had ruled Kabul and much of the rest of the country following the collapse of the Northern Alliance, the coalition which had exercised power after the Soviet withdrawal in 1989.

According to *Jihad!*, co-authored with Adrian Weale, an experienced biographer with a military background in the Intelligence Corps, Tom Carew had joined the Royal Artillery in 1969, aged seventeen. After three years as a gunner, with parachute training and three tours in Belfast, he applied to go on the gruelling SAS selection course, and in February 1973 he joined a hundred and twenty other hopefuls in the Brecon Beacons to spend three weeks undergoing the Army's most rigorous physical tests. Only a handful passed through to join the 22nd SAS, and he 'spent the next six years in the SAS doing a wide range of tasks. These included a couple of tours in Oman on "Storm" and a long period helping to set up the Northern Ireland cell'.[1]

In the autumn of 1979, Carew 'was offered the opportunity to "sign off" and join a private military company' which was engaged in training special forces in Sri Lanka. However, by the following year he was back at Hereford and in May, accompanied by two men, attended an interview at Roebuck House, a government building in Stag Place,

Victoria, where the trio was asked by 'Sir William Lindsay-Hogg' to draw up a training programme for an unnamed group of guerrillas, somewhere in the Middle East. In an Author's Note, Carew states that 'for security reasons I have agreed the names of virtually all living members of the British special forces and intelligence communities' so the names of his companions, and Lindsay-Hogg, who was 'in his late forties or early fifties' and was to supervise a covert operation in Afghanistan codenamed *Faraday*, are not really relevant. Indeed, Carew was asked back to a second meeting, attended by a representative of the American Defence Intelligence Agency, and invited to fly to Pakistan for a reconnaissance mission into Afghanistan. As Carew explains, the Soviets had invaded Afghanistan, six months earlier, shortly before Christmas 1979, and his task was 'to find out what is going on' at Ber-Mel, near Kandahar, and at Wazir, close to Jellalabad.

A further briefing took place two days later, at lunchtime on Saturday, given by another Englishman and a new American, at which Carew was given his assignment: to reconnoitre an area inside Afghanistan that could be used for training, and 'to obtain various examples of Soviet military hardware, they were particularly interested in any bits I could get of the new MI-24 Hind helicopter, the AK-74 rifle, the AGS-17 grenade launcher, the RPG-18 anti-tank rocket and any NCB equipment I could locate'.[2] A few hours later, having been assured that he would only be away for 'a week or two', Carew was aboard a plane to Islamabad, via Amman, accompanied by Lindsay-Hogg who flew first class and, upon their arrival in Pakistan, caught an internal flight to Peshawar.

On their first day in Peshawar, having checked into the Khyber Intercontinental Hotel, Carew and Lindsay-Hogg visited Gulbuddin Hekmatyar, one of the leaders of the *Mujadideen*, who had his headquarters at Fackeyrabad and arranged for Carew to be escorted into Afghanistan on the following Wednesday. On that day they flew to Quetta, and early the next morning, Carew, equipped with $1,000, sandals and Afghan clothes, was driven in a journey lasting five hours, to the Afghan frontier in a battered Cherokee jeep by a pair of local tribesmen. They continued to drive for the entire day towards Shekzi and, 'late in the evening', arrived at a *Mujahideen* camp in the foothills of the Kushk-I-Rud. The following morning Carew set out towards Arghastan (or Arghistan) in a Gaz truck but soon encountered a group of wounded men that had been strafed by a pair of Soviet gunships. He helped with their evacuation and then found himself in the path of a pair of Soviet tanks. As night fell the ill-equipped *Mujahideen* prepared to make a stand against the Soviets, but by the next morning the tanks had moved off, towards Kandahar, leaving Carew to continue his mission on foot. After a further night camped in the open, Carew reached the Kabul to Kandahar road 'in mid-afternoon.' Here he was able to take some photographs, and then made the return journey to Quetta to report to Lindsay-Hogg.

Carew and Lindsay-Hogg both regarded this first mission as a disappointment that had accomplished next to nothing, but with Hekmatyar's assistance another was planned, involving a trek of more than 100 kilometres to six camps encircling Jellalabad, to be achieved in just seven days. On this occasion Carew insisted on taking a Bergen rucksack containing supplies, his boots and a webbing belt, and he set off with a pair of guides two days later, having argued with Lindsay-Hogg that he would be unable to complete his mission in the required period of one week. Carew has insisted that it would be more likely to take 'two and a half weeks, probably three, and maybe more.'[3] They drove through Parachinar and then collected an escort from the *Mujahideen*-run refugee camp at Mangel's Post. Accompanied by some thirty or forty *Mujahideen*, with mules to carry their supplies, Carew crossed into Afghanistan on foot and headed towards Khogiani. On this second mission Carew visited five *Mujahideen* camps, participated in an attack on a village in which he shot dead two Afghan Army infantrymen and a Soviet soldier armed with a new Kalashnikov assault rifle, was almost killed when a plan to destroy a road bridge went wrong, and succeeded in recovering a large piece of armour from the wreck of a downed Soviet Hind gunship. He was also able to recover a NCB kit from a dead Soviet soldier, survive an ambush in which many of his companions were killed by other *Mujahideen*, and witness sacks holding more than 1,000 kilos of smuggled opium being delivered to Pakistani military personnel at Parachinar.

Upon his return to Peshawar, Carew found that Lindsay-Hogg was away on a visit to Chitral, in the north of Pakistan, so he was debriefed by a beautiful, suntanned blonde, Kathy Blake, who was based in Islamabad, and with whom subsequently he had an affair. Three days later, Carew was back in Victoria to report on his mission to various intelligence officers, including a U.S. Marine colonel, before flying on with Lindsay-Hogg to Washington DC to attend further meetings at the Pentagon. Carew remained in the U.S. for only two days, and then took an early morning flight back to London. After three days of leave with his family in Hereford, Carew flew back to Pakistan with Lindsay-Hogg and an ex-SAS colleague, Paddy, who was 'in the process of leaving the Regiment' and with whom he had worked in Sri Lanka. Their objective was to return to the crashed Hind helicopter with cutting gear and recover more Soviet equipment. However, when they arrived in Peshawar, using the cover of aircraft ground crew, they learned that Hekmatyar was away, so they 'kicked their heels for the next couple of weeks' while Lindsay-Hogg 'was very busy fixing incoming weapon resupply flights', organising 'paper-trail-free refuelling for aircraft and Swiss-bank letters of credit for the Hezb [the Hezb-e-Islami Gulbuddin, an Afghan political party] to buy ammunition and weapons from Eastern Bloc countries, and bribe customs officials to let the weapons in'.[4]

When Hekmatyar returned, Carew, accompanied by Paddy, embarked on his third mission into Afghanistan, but this proved to be 'a huge waste of effort' and they were unable to walk over the Spin-Ghar as it had snowed, which involved a twenty kilometre detour on the way to Wazir. Once at the crash site, the two SAS removed the helicopter's rotors with disc-cutters and loaded them onto mules for the return journey, which took them on the high route, through the 'late November' snow. Their mission lasted twelve days, and apart from being detained briefly by the Pakistani military at Parachinar, it was uneventful.

Altogether Carew says he undertook six missions into Afghanistan, in between which he found time to have an affair with an SIS woman in Islamabad, but eventually he succumbed to a combination of malaria, hepatitis and jaundice, requiring twelve weeks in the Hereford General Hospital. Once discharged he re-joined the Army and 'went back to the training wing in March 1983 and from November the same year was back on training duty in Sri Lanka'. In April 1984 he was wounded in the knee by shrapnel from a mortar shell fired by Tamil Tigers, injuries requiring a stay at Stoke Mandeville. Finally, he 'resumed duty on a round that, during the late '80s and early '90s, took me to Namibia, Mozambique, Northern Ireland on several occasions', and to the United Arab Emirates at the start of the Gulf War. When he retired, it was after twenty-two years in the Army but even then he remained in contact with SIS, for Lindsay-Hogg's direct superior sent him, in November 1991, to Croatia on a reconnaissance assignment, although he remarks that 'much of what went on at that time remains highly classified'. Later he was to deliver large quantities of British Army uniforms to Split from Germany, and make a large purchase of weapons from a Syrian arms dealer living in Spain, apparently in contravention of the United Nations embargo then in force. He was also sent to Bosnia on a similar mission, but a plan for him to go to Kosovo was to be scrapped because of the political situation.

One curiosity about Carew's experiences after he left the Army, which are clearly of significance because he says he was operating on behalf of the British government, is his admitted involvement in wholly illegal activities, such as the acquisition of embargoed weapons for Croatia and Bosnia. Furthermore, Carew made a very unusual disclosure, revealing how, in 1981, he had collected a consignment of contraband from the U.S. Air Force base at Ramstein in Germany, having hijacked the cargo plane loaded with his illicit guns. This bizarre episode is described in detail, and highlighted on the dustjacket of the paperback, as his 'attempt to hijack an aircraft during a covert arms-buying mission'. According to his version, the CIA persuaded a Vienna-based arms dealer to add an extra thirty SA-7 anti-aircraft missiles, and ten launchers, to a larger Bulgarian contract destined for Libya. Carew's role was to act as loadmaster on the aircraft and supervise the cargo in Sofia. Once it was aboard, and over international airspace en route to Tripoli, he was to make the pilot divert to Frankfurt, and then land at Ramstein. The stated objective of Operation *Manta* was to acquire SAM missiles for the *Mujahideen*, but a more complicated and dangerous undertaking can hardly be imagined, especially when the desired commodity was relatively easily available on the international arms 'grey market' at minimal risk.

Carew's extraordinary story is interesting in a historical context because it shows British and American intelligence operations being conducted in Afghanistan several years earlier than has been disclosed previously, for he claims to be the first Western agent to operate inside Afghanistan, and the first to link up with the *Mujahideen*. In addition, he was engaged in firefights with Soviet *Spetsnaz* troops, and as such is probably the only British soldier ever to have done so. With such a remarkable tale, can he be believed?

It is certainly true that British personnel were 'de-badged' for deployment in Afghanistan, the proof being the embarrassing announcement in Kabul on 5 October 1983 that five Britons had been apprehended, and one, carrying documents identifying him as Stuart Bodman, had been killed. The others were identified as Roderick Macginnis, Stephen Elwick, 'Tim, Chris and Phil', and according to newspaper reports in England, had been on a weapon-collecting mission for the Americans, with SIS's support. However, does this incident amount to evidence that similar operations were being conducted three years earlier? Ken Connor, one of the longest-serving NCOs in the regiment, says that 'the SIS team began work in 1981, training the *Mujahideen* mainly in the use of communications equipment, in safe-houses in Pakistan' and that 'by 1982 the team was carrying out the training in-country', but the project inside Afghanistan was abandoned when the team was ambushed and lost some of their documents.[5] Thus the question arises, did Carew operate in Pakistan and Afghanistan much earlier than even Connor knew? It seems unlikely, as Connor was one of those who denounced Carew as a fraud.

In reality, Tom Carew's true name is Philip Sessarego, who served in the Royal Artillery, not the SAS, for which he applied, but was rejected, in 1973. According to BBC *Newsnight*'s investigation of him, based on a tip from Connor, he was also rejected for the reserve but allowed to stay on in the demonstration troop of non-members, also known as the 'goon troop', which sometimes played the role of the enemy in training. He was discharged in 1975.

Apparently Sessarego had not 'taken part in combat operations in Oman', nor ever visited the country, despite his claim to have 'spent enough time in Oman'; was not involved in establishing the SAS Northern Ireland cell, and did not re-join 22 SAS for a further eight-year period between 1983 and 1991, after working in Afghanistan. His true story, nonetheless, was quite remarkable, for his application to join the regiment occurred when his mother, who had moved to Hereford, had formed a relationship with one of the sergeants. This had helped him to remain in the demonstration troop in the hope of a further crack at selection, a privilege occasionally granted to candidates who, perhaps for medical reasons, had been unable to pass the very rigorous physical stages of the test. Sessarego had indeed been in the top group of candidates in selection, and had been expected to pass, but a knee problem had prevented him from completing it. Convinced that he would get through at another attempt, he had been assigned to the goon troop, but had never served in a sabre squadron, as he had claimed. However, he failed the second selection, and was RTU'd. A further application to join the regiment was turned down, apparently as a result of adverse comment made on his personal file, allegedly by an SAS sergeant whom Sessarego had surprised in a compromising situation, with a woman in a car on the firing range. Whatever the reason, Sessarego never got another chance to work with the SAS, and when he left the Army he worked for a freight handling company, run by an Icelandic-American, and was sent to Pakistan as ground crew. Later he was employed as a mercenary in the Maldives, and when his book was published he was living in Belgium, having changed his name by deed poll to Philip Anthony Stevenson.

Unlike many fantasists, Sessarego knew a great deal about 22 SAS and had spent a good deal of time around Stirling Lines, but it was almost inevitable, given that he had never served in a sabre squadron, that his embroidery would be discovered and exposed. One of those who worked on his book, not knowing his true name, was Adrian

Weale, an experienced Intelligence Corps reservist who challenged several of his claims, watered down some of the text but had been impressed when the manuscript, having been submitted for a clearance to the Ministry of Defence, was returned with a number of requests for deletions. Understandably, this response was interpreted, not just as a consent to publish, but as an endorsement of the book's authenticity. As it turned out, this was to be a spectacular miscalculation.

Chapter 10

Spooky 8: The Final Mission

Common to several of the books published by wannabe heroes is the central proposition that a government, or official agency, has deliberately abandoned or betrayed a team of patriots who have served their country faithfully, and deserved better treatment. Lawrence Gardella claims he was protected after his return from China in 1952 by the threat of his former comrades to disclose details of their secret mission. In *Spooky 8: The Final Mission*, published in New York in July 1999, Bob King makes a similar allegation, although his harrowing story is rather more contemporary, for the events he described occurred in 1992.

At the time King (although he acknowledges that this is not his real name) had been out of the U.S. Army for seventeen years, but during his service in Vietnam in 1973 he had participated in 'a couple of "untraceable" operations working for the CIA out of Thailand'.[1] According to his own account, he had joined the 82nd Airborne Division in 1971, apparently while still in high school.

Thereafter he had become the leader of a Special Projects team, designated W45B7S8, known as Spooky 8 'one of the few remaining TRTs (Tactical Reconnaissance Teams) made up of former military and ex-government employees'. According to King, these freelance units have been deployed in Central and South America to fight the drug war 'for several years on a clandestine operation known as Dark Eagle'.[2] As King explains, 'most of the time I was working for a suborganization of one of our many government's intelligence agencies' but he does not identify it directly.

King's story begins with his acceptance of a mission offered by a man named Bates, to gather together his team of volunteers and fly to Bogota for a straightforward assignment, to insert a pair of remote monitoring devices in the rainforest, close to an improvised airstrip being used by

145

suspected drug smugglers. The agency employing Bates is not identified, but it is explained that King's group had been selected for the task because 'many of the teams are scheduled to be debriefed and then reassigned. You are one of the few teams that have the experience we can count on.'[3]

They were to stay for a couple of days to ensure the hardware was working, and then be exfiltrated. Having arrived in Colombia as tourists, the group was met by Jack Springer who, with his Ray-Ban sunglasses and khaki photographer's vest 'had CIA written all over him' and flown in a private aircraft to an airfield, San Jose del Guaviare, where they were supplied by two other Americans, Baines and Valley, with communications equipment. Valley explained that the operation 'will benefit the DEA, but it will help other groups as well' while Springer revealed 'there might be a leak somewhere'.[4]

The following morning, they were flown in a helicopter to the target site, but after they had prepared the devices they were caught in an ambush, and three of their number were shot dead. Three others, including King, were wounded, and thirteen of their adversaries were killed, but King suspected they had been betrayed from the outset and deliberately led into a trap, with one of his own team being responsible for the death at very close range of his principal sniper. Anxious not to call up support, King independently arranged to be rescued by a friend who owed him a favour, and prepared to trek across the jungle to Sogamosa where, a couple of years earlier, he had established a safe-house. To mislead his unknown enemies, King burned the bodies of those who had been killed, having dressed them in their own clothes, thus giving the impression that his entire team had been wiped out.

However, three days later the survivors stumbled into a jungle clearing to find a helicopter, ostensibly on charter to a logging company. The Colombian pilots agreed to fly King and his men out, and soon afterwards they had landed at Tunja, where King promptly killed them with a single shot each to the head. They then acquired a car and drove the rest of the way to Sogamosa where they stayed in the safe-house and unearthed a cache of money and false American, British and Canadian passports. They then took a bus to Bucaramanga and then San Cristobal, and crossed the Venezuelan frontier to make their way to Caracas. There, with help from a friend who managed a hotel, King arranged for his team to fly back to the United States, and himself waited an extra day with his 'oldest and most trusted friend', known as 'Lucky' and 'fluent in several languages and a photography expert' whom he had met in the army in 1973, to take a flight via Jamaica.

King and Lucky landed in Montego Bay where King changed his

reservations and, instead of a twenty-minute wait, took a flight later the same evening for Miami. In the meantime, he strolled into Montego Bay where he was attacked by four men. He killed two with his bare hands, stabbed a third in the stomach with his assailant's own knife, and the fourth fled from the scene. Undeterred, King caught his flight to Miami and then made a connection to Colorado Springs where he made contact again with his team. He was now convinced that his group had been penetrated by a mole, and he decided that before he travelled to Washington DC to 'meet face-to-face with some people and get some answers', he would assemble what he termed his insurance. This material was a collection of highly compromising documents that had been gathered together by the members of Spooky 8, principally Mike, 'a civilian skydiving instructor with four thousand jumps' who looks 'around seventeen years old' but is 'a true assassin' and 'his baby face makes it easy for him to get real close to people, then kill them.' An orphan, Mike had been with King's group since 1978 and had 'worked behind the scenes to collect valuable government documents, memorandums and private notes implicating the higher-up officials who had the power to safeguard us'. Most importantly, Mike knew someone who was a maintenance supervisor responsible for repairing malfunctioning fax machines, copiers and shredders in 'top-secret government buildings', and for emptying the trash. 'Mike's prize document was a memo to then-President Reagan that I'm sure Congress and the press would have given anything for.' We also had things from the reign of Frank Carlucci, John McHanon, William Casey, George Bush, and our ace in the hole, Bill Colby, all while they worked with the CIA. Even William Crowell from the NSA wasn't immune to bits of information failing to reach the shredding machine.'

> We had copies of maps, directives to military leaders, shredded memos between CIA heads, code books, and tapes of radio intercepts.[5]

King called this material his 'collection of Cold War memorabilia' and included papers about 'black operations in Central and South America' and a list 'of drug lords and political puppets that had fallen from grace with the United States. I managed on a couple of occasions, to take pictures of good guys having meetings with bad guys. I even got a copy of a tape of a recorder that had been placed in a hotel room air vent and recorded one of the day's leading U.S. politicians having a little kinky sex with a Panamanian "professional". Possessing such documentation was incredibly dangerous.'

The members of Spook 8 gathered at Lucky's girlfriend's house in Manitou Springs and prepared for their survival by assembling the 'insurance' and making arrangements for it to be 'sent to the *Washington Post*, the *New York Times*, CNN and members of Congress'. King then placed a telephone call to the Central Intelligence Agency and asked to be put through to 'William Coltan', a man he knew to be a retiree. Surprisingly, the CIA telephone switchboard was able to divert the call straight to Coltan, who appeared well-informed about Spooky 8's recent experience, and invited King in to be debriefed.

Certainly King's supposed 'insurance' deserves some scrutiny, for this was the compromising material that he and his team were confident would give them a guarantee of protection. What was it, and where did it come from? King described it as information from six named individuals, three of whom had been Directors of Central Intelligence, one had been Director of the NSA, but Frank Carlucci and 'John McHanon' are harder to place. While John McMahon had been Deputy Director of Operations, there was no John McHanon in any senior position in the CIA. Similarly, Carlucci had been Reagan's National Security Adviser. Also, it is difficult to understand how William Colby, who had been DCI from 1973 to 1975, and who died in a boating accident in 1996, could have possessed information that would have been relevant to events in 1992.

Curiously, King only produces three letters in an appendix to *Spooky 8* to authenticate his tale. One, dated 17 August 1989, ostensibly from a 'Personnel Representative' of the CIA, is a redacted facsimile from an office in Dallas, Texas, and is entirely innocuous but contains a concealed message hidden in a single line on the bottom of the writing paper. The other two, from the U.S. Environmental Protection Agency's Office of Research and Development dated 6 April 1992, and the Department of Energy's Office of logistics, dated 12 February 1992, appear completely innocent, apart from some embarrassing errors that suggest they are rather poor forgeries. None seem to possess even the slightest potential for causing embarrassment to any American administration.

Chapter 11

The Patriot

There must be few more harrowing events that to have served one's country honourably, and then find oneself abandoned with no official acknowledgment nor even private recognition. Perhaps surprisingly, however, few people claim to have endured such an experience, although the exception is Oliver Upton, the author of *The Patriot*, 'based on a true story' which recounts 'a British agent's capture and his amazing escape from torture at the hands of the Russians'. In a preliminary Publisher's Statement, it is averred that 'the people who died in the operation have been given their real names, other names have been changed. Some place names have been changed, including that of the London office'.[1]

Upton's book, dedicated to the former Director-General of the Security Service MI5, was published in 1989 during the last days of the Cold War, and is founded on the author's own adventures, which date back to February 1971 when, at the age of twenty-five, he was working as a naval intelligence liaison officer at the Admiralty. Having served at sea and with the Special Boat Squadron of the Royal Marines, he was sent on a mission to East Germany to arrange the defection of a scientist who had developed a bullet that could penetrate Chobham armour. Upton, who wrote about himself as a character named 'Lieutenant Keith Finlay', was to meet the defector, a Professor Brennan, and collect a sample of the ingenious projectile in East Berlin, but instead of escorting him to the West he was to kill him. He was to travel under commercial cover, as an oil production engineer, equipped with a lethal pill concealed in a false tooth, and then fly home via Sweden, setting off from the U.S. Air Force base at RAF Greenham Common.

At a Berlin safe-house, Finlay teamed up with a friend with whom he previously had served in the Yemen, a British Army major who had spent five years in the SAS, and rather longer with the Defence

Intelligence Staff, but as their rental car had been destroyed by a bomb they travelled up to Denmark for a few days, assuming that their mission had been compromised. However, they soon returned to Berlin, entered the Soviet zone through the sewers, and made contact with Professor Brennan who drove them to a quiet stretch of the border. However, as they attempted to make the crossing through the wire, and Finlay tossed the Professor's bullet to some waiting patrol of British soldiers, the pair was ambushed. Finlay's companion, Patrick J. Canavan, shot dead two border guards, before being killed, and he himself received wounds in both legs.[2]

When Finlay regained consciousness he was in a KGB facility just outside Moscow, where he underwent a lengthy interrogation while being treated by two attractive nurses. He was also tortured with electric shocks and immersed in freezing cold water, but he refused to disclose the true nature of his mission. Finally, after three weeks, he was flown to a convalescent home at Muynak on the Aral Sea, where his nurse succumbed to his charms. Here he was spotted by a British agent, codenamed *Shoe*, who reported his survival to London, and a daring rescue was organised. During the exfiltration Finlay's nurse was shot dead, and he was disguised as a shepherd, but he was able to walk to Tashkent, and then reach Samarkand in a caravan of camels. Finally, after a spell in a U.S. Peace Corps hospital in Kabul, Finlay was flown to Karachi where he joined HMS *Aurora,* and the last leg of his journey home was on a Hercules to RAF Lyneham.[3]

Upton's remarkable adventure lasted nine months, but received no publicity, apart from a death notice inserted by his parents in the *Daily Telegraph* on 22 February 1971, and a report by the BBC of an exchange of gunfire between the Royal Green Jackets and an East German border patrol, the incident in which the SAS major was killed. Nevertheless, Upton insists that his tale is true, so who is he? Upton is sensitive about his true identity and insisted to his publisher that 'his anonymity shall be inviolate at all times'.[4] However, in Devon, where he ran the Shalden Shooting School near Bampton, until his death of lung cancer in February 2012, he called himself Rod Bremmer RN, but he has also been known as Keith Gray. He said of himself that he was born in 1941and attended the Royal Naval College Britannia in 1953. Thereafter he served on the motor torpedo boats *Dark Highwayman* and *Swordsman* before reading English Literature at the University of Bristol at Bath. He says his godfather was Earl Mountbatten of Burma, and that he was christened on Mountbatten's ship.

As for the rest of his naval career, Bremmer was somewhat vague. Saying only that he worked for a certain Admiral Inglis who operated from offices in London in Grosvenor Street and Admiralty Arch, and was trained at a shore establishment in Warwickshire in a group of a dozen to fourteen others. In 1972 he went onto the non-active list, but nevertheless participated thereafter in numerous clandestine operations, including one to Syria during the Six Day War; to Vietnam to work with the Australian SAS; to Beirut to watch American liaison with the Christian militias; to Finland to exfiltrate a Soviet, following the crash of the Comstock-13 satellite;[5] the murder of an Israeli woman in 1967; the identification of a South African BOSS agent in the Garden Room of 10 Downing Street; and kept Lord Kagan under surveillance.

While Bremmer asserts that all his contemporaries are dead, so it is hard to check some of his claims, there must be considerable doubt, for example, about his statement that Lionel 'Buster' Crabb was resettled in Canada following the incident in April 1956 in which he was presumed lost under a Soviet cruiser, the *Ordzhonikidze*, in Portsmouth Harbour. This particular tale is investigated in rather more depth in Chapter 5, but it is certainly possible to take a closer look at a couple of the author's assertions that can be checked. For example, he mentions having participated in an operation to identify a BOSS (South African Bureau for State Security) agent in Ten Downing Street, which must be a reference to Helen Keenan.

Although the publisher has stated that the names of those who died in Upton's adventure have not had their names changed, there is no record of an SAS major named Patrick J. Canavan being killed in February 1971, nor on any other date. That being said, there remain no other specifics in the book which can be verified easily. So is it likely that a lieutenant in the Royal Navy would be sent armed on a mission into East Germany to exfiltrate a scientist with a knowledge of a bullet capable of penetrating Chobham armour? This latter material is a part ceramic developed by British scientists at the Royal Ordnance plant at Chobham, Surrey, to give additional protection to the armour used to clad tanks and other armoured vehicles, and in 1971, it was considered a technological breakthrough that offered a substantial advantage until the introduction of anti-tank rounds tipped with depleted uranium.

Chapter 12

Sixteen Killers

The terrorist attack in America on 9 September 2001 served to swing the pendulum of public opinion back in favour of direct, extra-legal intervention by Special Forces to interdict suspected extremists before they can perpetrate an atrocity, and the ensuing debate about intelligence failures and the need for new homeland security measures prompted a former Royal Pioneer Corps soldier, John Urwin, to offer a new perspective on clandestine operations.

Unwin's contribution to the discussion about tackling terrorism was to reveal the existence, when he was doing his National Service in Cyprus in 1958, of a secret unit known as 'the sixteen', which became the title of his memoirs, with the subtitle *The Covert Assassination Squad that went Beyond the SAS*. 'The Sixteen' was not an official military designation, but apparently an informal name for a group of highly-trained soldiers who undertook deniable operations across the Middle East. As Urwin only served in the unit for a few months he learned little of its background, never discovered the true names of his fellow soldiers, saw no officers and evidently asked few questions.

Unusually, Urwin did not volunteer to join 'the Sixteen', but instead was selected after his arrival at a base in Cyprus, following the standard six weeks of squaddie training at Wrexham. A Geordie from Newcastle, with a debilitating stammer, Urwin had joined 524 Company, Royal Pioneer Corps soon after his eighteenth birthday in November 1957, and had been posted to a tented encampment outside Episkopi. While ostensibly serving as a waiter in the officers' mess he underwent a secret training course in unarmed combat and then participated in four operations. A fifth, intended to be the assassination of the Egyptian leader, Colonel Nasser, was cancelled at the last moment, but the others were spectacular, although Urwin was strangely uninquisitive about the precise identities of the men he says he killed.

Urwin's first operation was in Cyprus, a night-time mission in November 1958, to penetrate a cave in the Troodos mountains, four months after he had been recruited, where between ten and twelve terrorists of the EOKA, the Greek Cypriot nationalist guerrilla organisation, were hiding, and eliminate them. He killed one of three armed men with his bare hands while the other three members of his unit finished off the remaining pair. This was a 'totally clandestine, unofficial operation' and when it had been completed Urwin simply resumed his duties as a waiter until the next assignment.[1]

Urwin's second mission was to kill an unidentified man who was closely-guarded and worked in a government office in Beirut, and the method used to insert 'the Sixteen' into the Lebanon was oddly complicated. They were flown by a British Sycamore helicopter from Larnaca to a night rendezvous with a fishing boat stationed thirty miles off the Lebanese coast. Although Urwin had never been in a helicopter before he and his four companions successfully abseiled thirty feet down to the fishing boat, and later the same morning were landed on a beach some nine miles north of Beirut. Together they walked into the city, which Urwin recalls as 'a total shambles, like a shanty town' and made their way directly to the centre when their target was likely to be visiting a local café for lunch. As the victim approached the café, Urwin emerged from a rug shop carrying a carpet and stepped between him and his bodyguard. As the target attempted to fend off the carpet, Urwin deftly stabbed him in the chest with a long, sharp, needle-like weapon that had been fashioned the previous day especially for the task, and moments later the man collapsed and died. Satisfied that the target was dead, Urwin and his team then returned to the waiting fishing-boat and sailed back to Dhekelia in Cyprus, ready to re-join his unit at the end of the week, his absence having gone unnoticed.

Urwin's third mission, to murder Colonel Nasser, was called off at the last moment, but the plan was for his team to be dropped off from a specially modified Sycamore at a point fifteen to twenty miles north-north-west of Port Said and then, disguised as local workmen, make its way eighty miles to the centre of Cairo where Nasser was scheduled to visit a heavily protected headquarters building. Aided by aerial reconnaissance photographs of the area, Urwin prepared for the mission but, after the helicopter had arrived to fly them to Egypt, he was informed that Nasser had changed his schedule, and instead the target was to be a 'senior foreign military adviser'.[2]

Despite this last-moment change, the mission went ahead as planned, with the helicopter refuelling after a flight of 250 miles at a secret aviation fuel dump located near a beach in a remote area close to the

Israeli frontier, apparently one of several available. Although disturbed briefly by the unexpected appearance of an Israeli Meteor jet, the helicopter was quickly in the air again and ferried them to a marsh eighty-five miles from Cairo and, having dropped of Urwin and his team, flew off with a Mig-15 in pursuit. The five men then stole a boat, Urwin having broken the neck of the owner, his companions having knifed two others, and sailed upriver towards Cairo. Later, as they abandoned the boat, they killed three soldiers whom they encountered on the riverbank, and buried their bodies in shallow graves, having taken their blood-stained uniforms and their truck. They completed their journey to Cairo in the truck and made their way to the city centre where their target was scheduled to leave his office at ten in the evening. Although they had not been told the name of their target, he was, they guessed, 'a senior Soviet military adviser or an aide assisting the Egyptian government'.[3] They reached him in his office on the third floor of the office building, having reached the roof from a neighbouring derelict property using crossbows to secure a line high above the perimeter fence. Using ropes and pulleys, and distracting the guards by starting a fire in a storeroom on the other side of the compound, the four men crossed to the roof of the target building and then let themselves in through a skylight. Moments later they had found their surprised quarry by identifying him from a photograph, and then shot him in the head with a silenced gun, arranging the body and the room to make it look as though his death had been a suicide. The team then exited the building the way they had entered, and returned to their truck undetected to make their way back to rendezvous with the Sycamore. The helicopter pick-up was executed faultlessly and the team flew 140 miles east to refuel, and then crossed the Mediterranean towards Cyprus, and transferred to a small cabin cruiser boat waiting twenty miles off the coast which took them the rest of the way to Dhekelia. After an absence of just two days, Urwin re-joined his unit, nobody there realising that he had been on a secret mission to Cairo.

Urwin's fourth and final assignment, some months later, was a daring attack on a military conference held at Jaraba in Syria, and on this occasion the objective was to disrupt the meeting and prevent it from taking place. Once again, the team of four was flown by helicopter at night to a fishing boat waiting five miles south of Tyre, and then dropped on the beach where other members of the Sixteen were waiting. Having scrambled aboard a truck the group drove up into the mountains and then walked down into the Hileh basin to Jaraba where they kept a watch on a poorly-guarded military compound, the site of the meeting they planned to disrupt.

When all the participants had gathered in the compound, one of the Sixteen, a man named Rostin, slipped into the building and lobbed a grenade into the main room, killing all five people inside, Simultaneously Urwin and his companions opened up with automatic fire and grenades, destroying two trucks and finishing off all the guards. Having wreaked devastation, the men withdrew to the mountains but while they reassembled Urwin was taken by surprise by a Syrian Army truck. The two soldiers on board approached Urwin with knives, but he was able to kill one while his companions dealt with the other, silently, but received a stab wound to his leg. This prompted Urwin's evacuation by helicopter off the beach, and soon afterwards he was back with his unit in Cyprus, explaining that his wound had been caused by 'a broken bedspring'.[4]

Urwin's account of his adventures end on Christmas Eve, 1959, when he was shipped from Limassol on the SS *Devonshire* with his Royal Pioneer Corps company, having spent just eighteen months in Cyprus. The question that arises is what, if any, part of Urwin's story is true? The proposition that the British Army sanctioned an elite group of Special Forces to carry out a covert policy of murder across the Middle East in 1959 seems, on the face of it, entirely fanciful, yet it is true that on two occasions during the 1950s, the Prime Minister did request the assassination of two political figures, and both are well-documented. The first, of course, was Colonel Nasser in 1956, an event that so scandalised Sir Anthony Nutting that he resigned as Minister of State at the Foreign Office in November in protest of Anthony Eden's order, screamed hysterically down the telephone, not to 'neutralize' the Egyptian leader but to destroy him. Unwilling to undermine Eden's authority at a moment of national crisis, Nutting concealed the true reason for his departure from office and delayed it a week to combine it with an announcement of his resignation from the Commons, but the episode is now well-known. Nutting himself alluded to it obliquely twenty years later in an interview to the BBC, and referred to it again in his autobiography, *No End of a Lesson*, loyally omitting the details. Indeed, it was not until Peter Wright released *SpyCatcher* in 1987 that an insider revealed that SIS's plan to eliminate Nasser involved two plots. The first, to use nerve gas concealed in an air conditioning duct, was initially approved by Eden and then cancelled when the invasion took place. When the British and French troops were withdrawn, Eden renewed his interest and SIS came up with an alternative scheme, a bomb concealed behind a wall in a building he was scheduled to meet a group of senior army officers. Because SIS's local network had been rounded up by Nasser's highly efficient *Mukhabarat* it was forced to rely on a disaffected group within the Egyptian military, but their efforts apparently failed when their weapons proved defective. But if Eden's plans to assassinate Nasser had gone awry, had his successor at Number Ten, Harold Macmillan, tried to repeat the exercise three years later? There is no evidence to support such a proposition, and no reason to believe that Macmillan had any interest in assassinating anyone.

So could a group such as the 'Sixteen' really have existed? The fundamental contradiction in Urwin's version is that he insists he and his companions were entirely unofficial, yet he also says that their existence must have been approved at a high level, not least because they were using military facilities, including helicopters, trucks and boats, and were reliant on official intelligence, for example to find their target in Beirut, and locate the relevant headquarters building in Cairo. But if the group enjoyed this level of official support, why did they have to take measures to avoid encountering British troops on their operations? Why did their (unmarked) helicopter take evasive action to evade radar detection when leaving Cyprus?

Equally baffling is the suggestion that 'the Sixteen', or any other British clandestine force, had been deployed against EOKA terrorists, for this is the first time such a suggestion has been made. The EOKA campaign reached a peak in 1958 when an operation, codenamed *Sunshine*, had been initiated by MI5 to find and eliminate the organisation's leader, Colonel George Grivas. Included in the plan was a decorated SIS officer who was flown to the island to be the triggerman to deal with Grivas once he had been found. However, *Sunshine* was scrapped in February 1959, when a political settlement was reached after lengthy talks between the various warring Cypriot factions, so no further action was taken against Grivas who, overnight, was transformed from terrorist into a political leader. In other words, if 'the Sixteen' really existed and were available to be deployed against EOKA gunmen, why did SIS feel the need to import their own hitman?

Unfortunately, Urwin is frustratingly vague about the precise dates of each of the four operations he participated in, so it is impossible to pin down exactly when each is supposed to have taken place, but the impression is given that the Sixteen's mission to attack the EOKA cave happened at a time when British operations against the terrorists were winding down, not escalating. So was 'the Sixteen' simply a local, ad hoc expedient, or a more wide-ranging organisation? Urwin believes the latter explanation, and says that 'at that time British Intelligence, the government and the MOD had been deeply infiltrated by Soviet controlled and operated moles'.[5] Elaborating on this, the author asserts that 'following the discovery in 1951 of Burgess's and Maclean's defections to the Soviet Union, it was felt that no employee of either British Intelligence or government departments could be fully trusted … The Sixteen were there to carry out missions that no government could be seen to be endorsing'.[6] Thus 'the Sixteen' had been created to undertake deniable missions that could not be entrusted to the government's more conventional security and intelligence agencies.

Such an eventuality seems quite bizarre, and there is no other evidence to sustain the claim. On the contrary, there is plenty to suggest that both MI5 and SIS continued to undertake high-risk operations after the 1951 defections, and many of the most vulnerable, especially in the field of technical intelligence collection, proved worthwhile and were never compromised.

More generally, there are numerous other concerns about Urwin's claims which need to be addressed. How could a mess waiter with a speech impediment, just through his basic training, be a candidate to join an elite unit, especially when volunteers for the SAS are not eligible to apply for a transfer until they have served at least three years in their parent regiment? Why would his extra-curricular training in Cyprus not include working from helicopters when plenty were available, and why, given his complete lack of experience, was Urwin chosen to take part in the Beirut mission which required him not only to fly in a helicopter, but to abseil down from a Sycamore as it hovered over a fishing boat? It might also be asked why such a complicated route was taken to insert Urwin and his team into the Lebanon, when scheduled, commercial flights from Cyprus to Beirut, then the hub of Middle East Airlines, were available in 1958? In addition, Urwin's description of Beirut at that time as 'a shambles' is contradicted by the many British expatriates there who regarded it as 'the Switzerland of the Middle East' enjoying a long period of unprecedented peace and prosperity, following the arrival of the U.S. Marines in 1958 to support the pro-Western government. Urwin's recollection of the city, then a vibrant centre of international commerce, with famous seafront hotels such as the St George and the Phoenica serving a sophisticated cosmopolitan population, as a ruin patrolled by uniformed militias, certainly suggests his memory is at fault. The first signs of the civil war that was to wreck the Lebanon did not materialise until 1972, fourteen years later.

The problem of verifying Urwin's story are considerable, and not helped by the difficulty of identifying his victims. Whilst it is true that the British Army wished to locate and engage EOKA terrorists, is it likely that just four men (one being an untried novice) would be deployed against a force of 'ten or twelve' gunmen? Quite apart from military orthodoxy, common sense suggests that such an imbalance, even with the benefit of surprise, would invite disaster and certainly not guarantee success. But as EOKA was a prohibited organisation, what was the reason for mounting a deniable operation? As the gunmen were legitimate adversaries for the Army, why use 'the Sixteen', and not send a couple of platoons of infantry into the area? If specialist skills were required, in preference to the deployment of regular troops, the Army, after all, was not short of Special Forces, the Special Air Service regiment having been reformed in Penang, Malaya, in 1952 as the 22nd SAS. The regiment had been disbanded in October 1945, with a territorial unit, designated the 21st SAS, being formed in the north of England in 1947. The Malaya Emergency had prompted General Sir John Harding, Commander-in-Chief, Far East Land Forces, to authorise the creation by Colonel 'Mad Mike' Calvert of the Malayan Scouts which, in 1952, had changed its name to the 22nd SAS. By 1956 the original four squadrons, A, B, C, and D had been augmented by a Parachute Regiment Squadron, and all were operational in 1958, with the Rhodesian C Squadron having been replaced by New Zealand and Fijian soldiers. If battle-hardened Special Forces had been required in Cyprus, they were certainly available, which makes it puzzling that the Army might have considered using inexperienced squaddies of 'the Sixteen'.

What motive could anyone have had for murdering a senior Soviet military adviser in Cairo? The same query could be expressed about Urwin's anonymous target in Beirut, a city that in 1958 was a veritable centre of international espionage and, of course, then the home of Kim Philby and numerous other spies, among them a large SIS station headed by the legendary Frank Steele who had taken up his appointment in July 1958 from the New Zealander Donald Prater, later a distinguished biographer and historian. The proposition that a British-sponsored assassination could have taken place in the Lebanon without their knowledge is, to put it mildly, improbable. Equally unlikely is the assertion that half of 'the Sixteen' were engaged in collecting intelligence in Africa and the Middle East in support of operations undertaken by the other eight, and that this clandestine organisation had been in existence for 'several years' before Urwin joined it.

The hallmark of British covert operations has always been the degree of detailed planning that has gone into their preparation, allowing for only the very minimum margin of error. This orthodoxy stands in stark contrast to the way the Sixteen's Egyptian mission appears to have been handled, with nothing beyond improvisation to insert the team into Cairo, not to mention the very obvious trail of mayhem left in their wake. As for cover stories, it would be hard to explain the presence of a British helicopter, devoid of identification, manoeuvring in and out of Israeli and Egyptian airspace, and it would not have taken a very skilled interrogator to decide that Urwin, who had never previously travelled beyond his home city of Newcastle, was a British soldier, even if he was not dressed in any recognisable uniform.

Would it have been possible for one of the Sycamore HR.14s, then flown by the RAF's 284 Squadron and based at Lakatamia, Limassol and Akrotiri, and usually operating on search and rescue and internal security roles, to have performed as Urwin has described, flying the very long distance to Egypt?

Urwin says the Sycamore had been modified to allow an extended range, but could the aircraft have flown to Egypt from Cyprus, a distance of three hundred miles, with a pilot and four passengers when the Sycamore usually operated with a crew of two and a capacity of up to three passengers? His description of the flight, with the helicopter completing a take-off and landing in Cyprus prior to them climbing aboard, makes the story almost, but not quite, impracticable. If Urwin's version was true, and even allowing for the tanks to be topped up after the first landing (which is not mentioned by the author), and the helpful low ambient air temperature early in the morning, Egypt would have been well beyond the Sycamore's range, and it would have been a very foolhardy pilot who would have attempted a mission of this kind, with absolutely zero safety margin. Urwin's account omits any mention of what the pilot and helicopter did after it had dropped them off in Egypt, but if the plan called for a further flight back to Cyprus (and it is hard to imagine the aircraft loitering in the war zone for twenty-four hours) it also requires the solo pilot to refuel by himself on the return journey. Impossible? Not entirely, but certainly highly improbable.

The conclusion must be that Urwin, who now runs a survival course in the Orkneys, could not have taken part in the four operations he described in precisely the way he says they happened. Doubtless this is a consequence of the passage of time, and not a function of imagination, although his publishers, when asked to confirm that they accepted the veracity of their author's claims, declined to make any public statement whatever.

Chapter 13

Was The Prime Minister Really
A Spy?

Of all the most extravagant, extraordinary claims made by any writer
in the intelligence field, at any time, must be Anthony Grey's
exposé of Harold Holt, the former Prime Minister of Australia who
disappeared while swimming near his home in Portsea, Victoria, in
December 1967. The official police report into the incident concluded
the following year that, despite the absence of a body, he had most likely
died of drowning. This was the generally accepted verdict until 1983
when a respected Reuters journalist, Anthony Grey, published his
sensational book which claimed that Holt had been a lifelong spy,
working first for the Nationalist Chinese and then for the People's
Republic of China, who had been spirited away from his home by
submarine shortly before the Australian Security Intelligence
Organization (ASIO) closed in on him.

Under normal circumstances such a proposition would only be
expected to be given an airing in a supermarket tabloid, but Grey, the
author of four novels and the survivor of two years of solitary
confinement in his home in Beijing as a hostage during Mao's disastrous
Cultural Revolution, was an experienced foreign correspondent who
also presented a current affairs programme broadcast on the BBC World
Service. Grey did not identify the original source of his story but
described him as a retired Royal Australian Navy officer who, 'not
wishing to draw undue attention to himself, decided he would prefer to
remain anonymous'. With such a creditable author, *The Prime Minister
Was A Spy* was taken quite seriously by many commentators, and the
book appeared to be a very detailed dossier of a truly astonishing case
of top-level espionage.

According to Grey, Holt had been recruited in 1929 by Sung Fa-tsiang,
an official of the Chinese Consulate-General in Melbourne who had

bought a series of magazine articles from the young Queen's College law undergraduate. A year later, having signed receipts for several payments, Holt allegedly was asked by Sung's replacement, Li Hung, who was later to be China's vice-consul in Sydney, to act as a secret representative of the nationalist Kuomintang government, and thus began his clandestine relationship with the Chinese that was to last his lifetime. When, in August 1935 Holt had been elected to the House of Representatives for the right-wing United Australia Party, he was 'a fully-fledged spy' and had been given the nom-de-guerre 'H.K. Bors', which apparently the true name of a scrap iron exporter, by his new contact, Wang kung-fang, whom he met regularly in a park and instructed him on Parliamentary Questions he wished to be tabled. Later Wang was to insist that Holt airmail his information to an accommodation address in Gerrard Street, in London, and when he was appointed minister without portfolio in (Sir) Robert Menzies' government in 1939 'the quality of the material Holt was able to send to Gerrard Street improved dramatically'.[1] However, the following year, when Holt was dropped from the coalition government, he volunteered for the Australian Army, but was soon restored to ministerial office, in charge of Labour and National Service when, in August 1940, three ministers were killed in an aircraft accident in Canberra. He also acted as minister for Air and Civil Aviation when the minister was overseas, and this enabled him to get access to cabinet papers which he removed 'surreptitiously from the files whenever he could and forwarded them by airmail' to London.

Holt's ministerial career in the 1940s was to be short-lived as the AUP was to spend eight years in opposition, but during the period of the Labour administration he remained active and only became a 'sleeper' in December 1948, awaiting a call to resume espionage, which finally arrived in March 1952 from his controller, D.R. Wong. In the meantime, Holt developed a reputation as a fierce anti-Communist and did not realize that Wong had defected to the Communists. Far from helping the Kuomintang in Taiwan, as he believed, Holt, by then Minister of Immigration and Labour, was disclosing details of his discussions with the American ambassador about the possible use of an atomic bomb in Korea, to his contact. In the months that followed Holt kept in touch with the Chinese through a bogus newsletter which he circulated to a small group of friends, including Wong. Hidden in the text were replies to Wong's questionnaires, written in an elaborate colour code and concealed in ostensibly innocent references to Holt's visits to the theatre.

In 1954, after his appointment as a Privy Councillor, Holt was instructed by Wong to use a new system, involving newspaper

161

advertisements for second-hand cars, of arranging secret meetings in a local safe-house in Melbourne, and it was at one of these, still under the impression that he had been spying for Taiwan, that Holt announced that he was to suspend operations. He remained inactive until Wong visited him at his law offices in April 1957 and persuaded him to start spying again. Holt apparently agreed, imposing three conditions: that Chen Yi, the Communist Director of Intelligence, should be appointed Foreign Minister, that Mao should reject Soviet-style Communism, and that he make a public gesture confirming that he was not 'anti-intellectual'. With agreement to these terms, thrashed out over two and a half hours, Holt once again became a spy, this time working for Peking, while he was fulfilling his ministerial role as Federal Treasurer. Holt routinely removed classified documents and passed them to Wong, but in 1961, fearful of increased ASIO surveillance on suspected Communists, Holt became less productive, to the point that he 'did little spying of consequence between 1962 and 1964'. Wong, fearing that Holt was losing his nerve, arranged for a Whiskey-class diesel submarine to make a thirty-eight-day voyage to Australia and linger underwater off the coast at Port Stephens in case Holt needed to be exfiltrated. After waiting for eight days, the submarine made the return leg of the 5,500 mile round-trip, back to China, without its passenger.

When in August 1965 the Prime Minister, Sir Robert Menzies, announced to his ministers that Australian troops would fight in Vietnam, Holt was prompted to leave the Cabinet room and make a call from a pay-phone to alert Wong of the development. The news reached Peking before a press statement had been prepared in Canberra, and then was leaked to the media, prompting an ASIO enquiry into the breach of security. The investigation proved inconclusive, but Holt had been dismayed by the way the Chinese had handled his tip, and he held only one further secret rendezvous with Wong, on 16 December 1965, before Menzies unexpectedly resigned, and Holt was made his successor in January 1966.

Among Holt's first decisions as Prime Minister was to treble the number of Australian troops in Vietnam, and during a visit to the United States in June 1966, while supposedly taking time off to do some private sight-seeing while en route to Washington DC to meet President Johnson, he spent two days conferring with Liao Cheng-chih, one of his Chinese contacts whom he had previously met years earlier in Singapore, in San Francisco. However, in May 1967, Holt read an ASIO report referring to his own secret codename, 'H.K. Bors', and took fright, calling an emergency meeting with Wong, at which he asked to be rescued. Wong judged that Holt was close to a breakdown and plans

162

were made to exfiltrate the spy by submarine the following December from the beach off his holiday home.

According to Grey, Holt was seized by two Chinese frogmen as he snorkelled in shallow water, and conveyed aboard the escape hatch of a submarine lying submerged close by. The Prime Minister was then spirited to China where he was granted political asylum, and supposedly lived in quiet retirement for many years, advising Peking on international trade issues.

Taken as a whole, *The Prime Minister Was A Spy* is one of the most extraordinary stories ever to be published as non-fiction, but how did Anthony Grey come to write such an improbable tale? The answer lies with a mysterious Australian businessman, who Grey does not name in the book, who first approached him in May 1983, having undertaken much of the research while pretending to have been working on Holt's biography. The businessman was Donald Titcombe, a former Australian naval intelligence officer, who claimed that he had been tipped off in July 1973 by a Chinese official, and that after he had expressed interest in the story he had travelled to Hong Kong in 1975 to obtain semi-official confirmation. At a further meeting, organised in Macao in February 1983, Titcombe had sought further details, but although he had not received any conclusive proof he was able to persuade Grey that the central story had been corroborated and was supported by plenty circumstantial evidence.

While Grey apparently never questioned the credentials of his informant, it turned out that Lieutenant-Commander Titcombe had been accused in 1967 of sharing classified information with his mistress, and subsequently had been asked to resign his commission in the Royal Australian Navy. Since then Titcombe had pursued a controversial business career as an entrepreneur seeking to promote yachting marinas in such diverse locations as Grenada, Chichester and Conway, but none had proved viable. When the *Observer* and the *Sunday Telegraph* denounced the book as a hoax, Titcombe had sued for libel, and his litigation had been settled by the *Observer*, although in 1989 he abandoned the action against the *Sunday Telegraph*.

A careful analysis of the book itself shows that it is a little thin on specifics, and that much of the information, according to Grey, had come from 'detailed verbal information provided in Asia, Australia and Europe by different Chinese informants. These informants appear to have had access to intelligence files – of both Communist and Nationalist China – going back fifty years'.[2] In the book there are indeed references to these anonymous informants. One was 'a Chinese official who had apparently been given access' to 'a detailed intelligence dossier' whom Titcombe met in 'an Australian motel room in 1982'.[3] This was a 'file that had apparently been retained intact by Holt's Chinese controllers through fifty years of revolution and upheaval in China'. Details of Holt's recruitment had been provided by a 'Chinese informant who gave details of this period at meetings in South-East Asia in 1980' and had quoted 'from files of the period'.[4] This same informant claimed that in 1931 Chinese legations around the world had drawn up lists of suitable candidates for future recruitment, and the name of Kim Philby had appeared on one prepared at 'the universities of Oxford and Cambridge'.[5] Bearing in mind that Philby had not yet gone up to Cambridge in 1931, this seems a trifle prescient.

Grey revealed that when approached in late 1976 'a high-ranking Australian public official had expressed doubts about Holt's loyalty, and that at 'that time only the barest outline of the story had emerged from the Chinese informants'. The full story had emerged only after a series of meetings with various Chinese informants, but one 'admitted to being a high-ranking official in the Peking Ministry of Foreign Affairs'.[6] Altogether Grey quotes the mysterious Chinese informants no less 156 times in the text, noting only that Titcombe held an undisclosed number of meetings with them in Australia and South-East Asia between 1980 and February 1983, when he went to live in Europe.

Several of the items described by the author as having originated with the Chinese informants deserve scrutiny. One is the account given of Holt's first rendezvous with Wong in mid-March 1946 at the Prince of Wales Hotel in the St Kilda suburb of Melbourne, which originated with 'the file which the Chinese informant gleaned the detail of this meeting'. One of the pressing topics on that occasion had been the news that 'a Russian KGB agent, Igor Gouzenko, had defected to the West in 1945 bringing with him many documents which revealed the hitherto unknown scale of Soviet intelligence activities and subversion in capitalist countries'.[7] This version seemed flawed, for several reasons. Firstly, the KGB did not exist in 1945, and Gouzenko had been a GRU cipher clerk. Secondly, the documents purloined by Gouzenko only referred to GRU operations in Canada, and did not mention any other country. Finally, no public announcement had been made regarding Gouzenko's defection at the time of the meeting, so it seems unlikely that Holt would have been impressed by 'one of the most pressing topics of the day', as claimed.[8] Certainly Gouzenko's revelations were of considerable importance, and some say marked the opening of the Cold War, but in March 1946 this impact had not been appreciated.

This episode has the ring of material compiled years after the event, when the precise chronology has been blurred by the elapse of time, and this characteristic can be detected in other passages. For example, the author claimed that in 1948 the Chinese received a report concerning the interception of Soviet signals by the British at Darwin, and the news that 'MI5 had sent out a Chinese language specialist to help the Americans monitor' the diplomatic wireless traffic to and from Canberra. Once again, there is a strange aspect to this story, for MI5 did despatch Courtenay Young to Australia, but he was a Japanese expert, and not a Chinese linguist. Grey claimed that 'this information matched up with a report from Holt himself which showed the Soviet Union was clearly operating spy-rings in Australia – and that the authorities had discovered this through radio'.[9] Actually, this knowledge was not released in Australia until 1981, two years before Grey's book was published, and at the time the evidence (garnered from *Venona*) of Soviet espionage was never described as having emanated from signals intelligence. On the contrary, every effort had been made to conceal the true source, and nobody in Australia was indoctrinated into the secret. Even the most senior counter-intelligence personnel were deliberately given the strong impression that 'the source' was a well-placed spy in Moscow. Accordingly, the proposition that Holt, who was then an opposition back-bencher, might have learned about *Venona* seems improbable.

Holt's alleged method of communicating with his Chinese contacts also seems worth of scrutiny. Initially he had airmailed his reports to London, but later had concealed them in his seven newsletters, using an ingenious code 'based on colours and numbers where each colour and each number had its own meaning according to a prearranged "key"'. Six of the newsletters had been addressed to friends, while a seventh had gone to 'D.R. Wong', Holt's Chinese controller.[10] Holt and his wife were particularly fond of the theatre and never wasted an opportunity to see a show when they were travelling abroad. While on these trips Holt compiled detailed descriptions of his visits to musicals such as *South Pacific* and *Guys and Dolls*, and this struck Titcombe's researcher, who read the newsletters, as suspicious, although at the time she did not realize their significance.

> The colours and numbers that would convey the required answers were to be applied to the numbers of actors in a show, the colours of their costumes and the scenery back-drops.[11]

Later 'the codes had been extended to take in wine, food and clothes as well as theatre'. Naturally the obvious way to test this assertion is to submit the surviving copies of the newsletters to a detailed cryptographic examination to find evidence of the hidden text, as Grey acknowledged: 'Perhaps if a trained cryptographer were allowed access to them, some hint might be obtained of what coded information was locked up in those endless theatre commentaries; but, without the "key" invented by "Wong" and the knowledge of what questions the information was related to, it would be an extremely difficult task'. As this would represent the only direct, documentary proof of Holt's alleged espionage, it is surprising that no efforts were made to apply this test, even though the copies 'are still being stored in an accountant's office in the centre of Melbourne', the owner having insisted that 'as they were personal, no direct quotations should be made from them'.[12]

The volume of material supposedly supplied by Holt to his Chinese controllers naturally raises the issue of exactly what the politician was supposed to have produced. In 1980, Titcombe only saw four examples, typed in English on four faded, poor quality, sheets of paper:

> One referred to Holt's report about America's intention to bomb military bases in China in 1952 if the Korean armistice negotiations failed; another referred to the surprise Australian decision to commit more troops to Vietnam in support of the Americans in August 1965; a third concerned an assessment of Cambodia's future made in 1954; and the fourth contained an analysis of the strengths and weaknesses of two Pakistani politicians, the Governor-General Ghulam Muhammed and Foreign Minister Zafrullah Khan, whom Holt had met in 1952.[13]

The problem with these four items is that none of it amounts to evidence of espionage, and really falls more into the category of political controversy and personal opinion, but not secret intelligence. For example, General MacArthur's much-publicised wish to bomb the Chinese airbases in Manchuria, in direct contradiction of President Truman's declared policy, led to his very public dismissal, so there was no secrecy there. Similarly, the Australian commitment to deploy troops in Vietnam was announced openly and, although politically controversial, was not of any strategic significance as the numbers involved never exceeded more than 3,000. Since at the time the Chinese were hardly allies of the North Vietnamese, and certainly were not combatants, the news could not have had much impact in Peking although, according to Grey, the Chinese took the opportunity to indulge in a little mischief-making by leaking it to the media. Holt's August 1954 opinion of the future of Cambodia in an 'uncoded report' was apparently based on his personal observation, and did not contain any secret intelligence. Equally, his opinions of a pair of Pakistani politicians, who were probably much better known to the Chinese than to Holt, could not have carried much weight. Furthermore, Titcombe noticed that the wording of the report he had seen in 1980 was 'identical' to that contained in the newsletter he read two years later, and concluded 'it seemed to be an example of intelligence conveyed "in the clear"'. It might also be assumed that if this information was sent *en clair*, it probably was not secret.

So why, after thirty-eight years of top-level espionage, did the Chinese not produce anything rather more impressive by way of proof? Grey remarks that Titcombe's informants 'did not volunteer much information about the nature of the intelligence passed by Holt between 1957 and 1962' but he might just as well have made the same comment about the rest of his espionage. Writing articles for the Chinese as a student, and receiving remuneration for them, hardly amounts to evidence of espionage, and if it is indeed the case that Holt was paid up to $30,000 for his information, this may be more a matter for the income tax authorities than ASIO. Perhaps Holt used his political status as an agent of influence to given covert support to the Chinese, but again this sounds more like corruption and less like espionage. In short, *The Prime Minister Was a Spy* contains not a single example of actual espionage.

The truth is that Holt was a lacklustre politician in a country that has produced few politicians of international stature. He had no overseas experience until he travelled abroad, for the first time in October 1948 to attend a Commonwealth Parliamentary conference in London as a member of the Australian opposition. Thereafter Holt attended many of these international gatherings, organised by the Commonwealth Parliamentary Association but, whilst grand-sounding to the initiated, these annual meetings are usually of absolutely no significance, the delegates being minor-league players busy networking and freeloading. The proposition that Holt might have picked up secrets useful to the Chinese at these shindigs, appears unlikely, to put it mildly.

So what exactly is the evidence of Holt's association with the Chinese? He had been cultivated initially by the Chinese Consul General in Melbourne, Sung Ting-hua, who had paid for his articles, but when he had been withdrawn under a cloud 'early in 1931' his successor was the Vice Consul, Li Hung, who operated from Sydney. When he was sent home, the new Consul-General, Dr Chen Wei-ping, informed Holt that his new contact would be Wang Kung-fang who had 'an intense hatred of communism and all things Russian'.[14]

However, the decision was taken in Nanking, when he was elected to Parliament in 1935, that 'the handling of Harold Holt was now too important to be left solely in the hands of his controller Wang' and that a new contact, Hsu Mo, would be sent to Sydney as a diplomat, actually 'the Vice Minister, as head of the diplomatic mission' to assist in running the MP. Five weeks of intensive briefing took place at the Domain Street safe-house during June, July and August 1936 and the two Chinese ran Holt jointly until 1940 when it was decided that Wang had become 'more friendly' than was desirable with Holt, and he was withdrawn abruptly. Hsu Mo waited until October 1941 to meet Holt, and then did not see him again until a second series of meetings held over three days in February 1944. Soon afterwards Hsu Mo telephoned Holt to explain that he had been recalled urgently to Chungking, and it was a further two years before he was contacted again, in mid-March 1946 by a man who introduced himself as 'D.R. Wong', actually Y.M. Liu, an affable Chinese who had adopted the identity of a former graduate of Queen's College who would operate from 'a new Chinese Vice Consulate that had been opened in Swanston Street, Melbourne'.

There would be no further contact with the Chinese diplomatic mission in Canberra, where Hsu Mo had worked, and future communications would be through letters left under an azalea bush in Holt's garden. Holt was to cease using the mail-drop in Soho, London, which had been in use since 1938 but, despite this elaborate alternate arrangement, Wong did not contact him for a further two years, until December 1948. When he did so, it was to warn him that the turmoil in China made future contact unwise, thus turning Holt 'into a "sleeper" for the second time in ten years'.[15] Wong's next call was in March 1952, to arrange a meeting where Holt was informed, falsely, that Hsu Mo had been appointed Taiwan's Director of Intelligence. Bizarrely, he had by then defected to the Communists, and had been operating in Australia since 1949, not as a diplomat, but as an illegal. Apparently he had been given the task in August 1951 of reactivating Holt for the Communists, and had spent six months watching the minister to ensure he had not been in touch with Taiwan. Satisfied that Holt had been inactive, Wong then proceeded to run Holt under a 'false flag' for the next three years, until April 1957, when he finally explained that he was working for Mao, not Chiang Kai-shek. Surprisingly, Holt seemed to have been undismayed by the deception and readily agreed to serve Peking as faithfully as he had been working for Taiwan.

Whether this is even remotely credible must be left to the judgment of the reader, but there is a distinctly odd dimension to it and deserves further attention, especially as Titcombe said he discovered an old Ministry of Labour file bearing a request from Holt, dated February 1957, for information about a Chinese diplomat named D.R. Wong, and this represents 'the strongest single piece of Australian corroboration he had found of the story told to him by the different Chinese officials'.[16] The significance of the file was the denial from Holt's officials of any accredited diplomat named D.R. Wong, and the assertion that 'the only person showing any continuity of diplomatic accreditation since the early 1940s is a Y.M. Liu who was a vice Consul attached to the Chinese Consulate-General's office in Melbourne until 1949'.[17] In other words, Holt had expressed interest in a diplomat called Wong, and instead the ministry produced a reference to Liu, the man whom Holt had seen just twice in the 1940s, in March 1946 and December 1948. The advice that this individual had been 'the only person showing any continuity of diplomatic accreditation since the early 1940s' is bizarre when, quite obviously, Hsu Mo himself would have been a much better candidate, having arrived in Australia in 1940 and left in 1944, staying rather longer than Liu. Anthony Grey assumes that Holt would have immediately recognised the photograph of Liu as his contact Wong, but none of this amounts to anything approaching proof that Liu operated under the alias Wong, nor that Liu was ever in contact with Holt, or was even an intelligence officer and his handler. All it shows is that Titcombe says Holt called for a file on a Chinese diplomat and received Liu's.

There are several other contradictions in Grey's account regarding Holt's Chinese contacts, for although he says that Sung was withdrawn from Australia in early 1931, he is also mentioned as having attended 'further meetings in January 1932 … arranged with his colleague Sung Tang-hua, at a house in Domain Street, South Yarra'.[18] That Holt could have had so many dealings with Chinese intelligence personnel from both the Communist and Nationalist camps, that went completely unremarked at the time may not be strange, even if D.R. Wong was one of just seven recipients of his newsletter, but the proposition that the Prime Minister held five clandestine meetings with Wong between his appointment in January 1966 and his disappearance in December the following year, seems harder to swallow.

If, as Titcombe and Grey claim, Holt was a spy, what exactly had been his motivation? According to Grey, Holt believed he was helping the nationalists until 1957, and then enthusiastically worked for the Communists, undeterred by the false flag deception. But was he an idealist, or an opportunist driven by his secret income, estimated at about £30,000? With the best will in the world, none of it makes any sense at all.

After publication of *The Prime Minister Was A Spy* Grey continued his career in journalism and now lives in Norwich. In 2009, aged seventy-one, he released *The Hostage Handbook*.[19]

Chapter 14

Sins Of The Father

One of the more curious characteristics of the world of post-war clandestine intelligence operations is the resentment of some of the children of the practitioners. Often they grew up in a period of adolescent rebellion and resentment, and later in life, perhaps when they had learned the true profession of their parents, they underwent a cathartic experience by writing about how they perceived their life. Some of the children appear, from their own accounts, to have harboured massive irritation at learning, perhaps belatedly, that their father had been a senior CIA officer, or in the case of Corinne Souza, an SIS agent. Larry J. Kolb, for instance, wrote *Overworld: The Life and Times of a Reluctant Spy*, in which he revealed that his father had been 'a high-ranking American spymaster'.[1] Similarly, Harold Lloyd Goodall Jnr. wrote *A Need to Know*, alleging that his father had been a CIA veteran,[2] and in 2007 Lucinda Franks produced *My Father's Secret War*, yet, as we shall see, the evidence for any of these individuals having worked for a clandestine organization is rather slim.[3]

In his highly entertaining autobiography Larry Kolb describes his various occupations, as a sports agent and as Mohammad Ali's manager, and finally being married to Adnan Khashoggi's step-daughter, but it is in his role as a spy that he was to experience the most exciting of adventures, mentored by that legendary CIA officer, Miles Copeland. According to Kolb, espionage was in his blood, and he gives a detailed account of his father's career which began in the wartime Counter-Intelligence Corps and ended in the CIA. When Larry was born in 1953, he was teaching 'Sophisticated Assassination' at the War College in Washington DC, but his entry into the secret world had taken place during the war when he was at Fort Benning, Georgia. However, when Pearl Harbor was attacked, he had been transferred to Jacksonville as the CIC's Special Agent in Charge, and assigned the task of penetrating a local group of American Nazis. As he came from an authentic German-American background, Kolb was accepted by the group and was soon wearing a brownshirt uniform adorned with swastikas and attending meetings three or four times a week, He was promoted to second-in-command, but then was arrested by the FBI.

> We were supposed to go out to the beach and rendezvous with a German submarine, to meet some agents sent in from Germany. But instead one night the FBI swept in and rolled us all up.[4]

To preserve his cover, the FBI pretended that Kolb had been shot dead, in a fight right in front of the others, and this protected him from reprisals. As he explained to his son, 'some of them were executed. Some of them were sent to prison. But they all left friends and relatives back home in Jacksonville who knew me. And that I was killed that night. If one of them saw me alive, they'll know. They'd understand everything, That's why I never set foot in Jacksonville again.'[5]

This remarkable tale undoubtedly concerns Operation *Pastorius*, an attempt by the *Abwehr* to infiltrate eight saboteurs into the United States by submarine. The event took place on 18 June 1942, when the *U-584* dropped four saboteurs onto the beach at Ponte Vedra, twenty-five miles south of Jacksonville. Having buried some boxes of equipment and explosives in the sand-dunes they walked to a store on Highway 140 and then caught a bus to Jacksonville where Edward J. Kerling and Herman Neubauer checked into the Seminole Hotel. Their companions, Herbert Haupt and Werner Kiel, checked into another hotel and the following day the men caught two different trains to Cincinnati. All had been born in Germany, but had lived in the United States before the war, and they were led by Kerling, aged thirty-three, who had worked for four years in New York.

Haupt did not stay in Cincinnati, like the others, but instead travelled on to Chicago, where he had been brought up and trained as an apprentice optician, and he was followed there on 20 June by Neibauer, a former chef on the SS *Hamburg*. Meanwhile Kerling and Thiel went to New York, unaware that Georg Dasch, the thirty-nine-year-old head of operation *Pastorius*, who had landed on Long Island, New York, on 14 June from the same U-boat, had turned himself in to the FBI in Washington DC, revealing that his three companions were staying at the Governor Clinton Hotel in New York. They had been quickly arrested, and another suspect, Helmut Leiner, whose name had been found on a list of sixteen contacts supplied to Dasch, written in secret writing on a handkerchief, had been placed under surveillance. He was seen to meet Kerling, who was then followed to a rendezvous with Thiel. All three were detained and, on 27 June, Haupt was arrested in Chicago. Under interrogation he revealed that Neubauer was staying at a hotel in Chicago, and later the same evening he was arrested at the Sheridan Plaza. All eight men were then reunited in Washington D.C. where they were placed on trial and convicted of espionage.

The problem with Kolb's version of events is that the group of four saboteurs who landed in Florida were not met by any local Nazis, and none of the sixteen contacts given by the *Abwehr* to Dasch and Kerling even lived in Florida. Nor was there a fight on the beach, and the only deaths occurred after the Nazi spies had been convicted in Washington D.C. In other words, Kolb's tale was sheer fiction.

This episode was an important milestone in Kolb's life, for he was personally selected and thanked by J. Edgar Hoover for his participation in the coup, and was thereafter quickly promoted, receiving a commission and a transfer to Atlanta with his friend, the Coca-Cola heir, Asa Candler. A year later he was serving in Washington, and then was given an undercover assignment at MacDill Field in Tampa. The investigation centred on the mysteriously high losses of B-26 bombers on training flights. Thirty crashed in the last few months of 1942, and another sixty in 1943, until the culprit was detected. 'It was sabotage. A German-American maintenance crew chief was bringing down those planes. We arrested him right there in the hangar. Asa came down from Atlanta and we took him down together. However, the incident was covered up, and the crashes were attributed to design flaws and poor training procedures.'[6]

Kolb arrived in Paris in 1944 with the rank of lieutenant-colonel, where he encountered Miles Copeland. the son of an Alabama physician who, in February 1942 had joined the CIC before transferring in London to the Office of Strategic Services. When OSS was wound up in October 1945 Copeland worked for the Central Intelligence Group (which became the CIA in 1947) operating in Damascus and across the Middle East. A colourful character, he would become an independent businessman and later write a series of semi-autobiographical accounts of the intelligence business, *The Game of Nations: The Amorality of Power Politics* in 1969;[7] *The Game Player: Confessions of The CIA's Original Political Operative* in 1989;[8] and *The Real Spy World* in 1974.[9] Always mischievous, Copeland maintained contact with the CIA for the remainder of his life, but his direct employment ended in 1953 while he was in Egypt. The fact that he knew Larry Kolb and his father did not make either a spy, and certainly the embellished version of PASTORIUS, which is among the best documented cases of espionage in American history, does not prove anything beyond possession of a vivid imagination.

Kolb evidently believed, with only the flimsiest of evidence, that both he and his father had been employed by the CIA, and it turns out that this is not such an unusual phenomenon. Another example is Roland W. Haas, the author of *Enter the Past Tense: My Secret Life as a CIA Assassin*.[10] According to Haas, who came from a German immigrant family and was born in Buffalo, New York, in August 1952, he had been approached to work for the CIA in March 1971 while he was attending Purdue University in Indiana on a scholarship as a Naval Reserve Naval Officer Training Candidate. Fluent in German and Russian because of his family background, he was told by a mysterious civilian he would be known only as 'Phil' that, as part of his cover, he would be expelled from his college and then work as an assassin, murdering victims to order. Apparently amenable to this proposal, Haas was arrested in March 1972 and convicted of breaking into the Reserve Officers' Training Corps armoury and starting a fire.

In October 1972 Haas enrolled at the Ludwig Maximillians University in Munich but not long after his arrival he was contacted by Phil who instructed him to travel to Turkey, Iran, Afghanistan and Pakistan and, posing as a well-funded buyer, was to kill the head of a major heroin smuggling ring in Kabul. Adopting the role of a student on the hippie trail to spiritual enlightenment to Katmandu in the Himalayas, he caught the Orient Express to Turkey. During a week in Istanbul he made contact with a Akhun Berka al Zarqa, a known drug dealer and, having announced his intention to make a significant investment, hitched a ride on a French Volkswagon van from Ankara to Tabriz and then Tehran. After a few days of sight-seeing in Iran he continued his journey to Kabul where checked in at the Hotel Najib and, a few days later, arranged to meet his target, a Tajik named Abdunabi. At their second meeting, where a drug deal was to be negotiated, Haas broke Abdunabi's neck and then cut the throat of his brother who was there to protect him. He also knifed a second brother, and then caught a bus over the Khyber Pass to Pakistan. After a stay in Lahore, Haas moved on to Delhi, eventually returning to Istanbul on the much the same route, taking in Kabul and then Tehran where he spent a week in prison on unknown charges, being released on 3 April. Having checked into the Taksim Hilton, Haas broke into al Zarqa's empty home and awaited his return the same evening. As Zarqa entered his house, accompanied by three men, Haas shot all four of them with a silenced pistol and then drove to the Sirkeci railway station to catch a train for Vienna. His mission had lasted five months, and had been financed by occasional deliveries of cash to various American Express offices during the journey.

Once back in Munich Maas received another visit from Phil who instructed him to parachute into East Germany and meet 'Klaus' in an Erfurt church, and then drive with him in his car across the border into Czechoslovakia and then enter the Federal Republic.

Haas's new assignment began on 1 June when he was flown from an air base at Wiesbaden along the frontier and dropped into East Germany carrying false papers identifying him as a student at Leipzig University. Having made contact with Klaus, and driven to within a few miles of the Czech frontier near Zwota, he then abandoned the car and climbed through the border fence into Czechoslovakia at a predetermined spot where the wire had been cut. Then, once in Czechoslovakia, Haas and his companion hot-wired an unlocked Skoda and drove to Cheb where they hid the car in a wood and walked to the final fence, emerging in West Germany near Schirnding. The entire exfiltration had taken less than twenty-eight hours.

In July 1973 Haas returned home to Lakewood, Ohio, to complete his studies at Purdue, and graduated in May 1974. He then took a master's degree in German and Russian and, having graduated in May 1976, moved to California to do a PhD at Berkeley. While a student Haas worked first as a bouncer at a bar, and then in Oakland as a carpet salesman, but in 1981 opened a gym which proved to be a very successful business. However, the gym became a haunt for a Hell's Angels motorcycle gang and, having fallen out with his partner, he moved to Würzburg, Germany, in 1982. There, once again, he was contacted by Phil who suggested a teaching job on an American base, the Downs barracks, at Meiningen, a convenient cover for a mission into East Germany to murder three women, all suspected Red Army Faction terrorists living in Suhl. Haas crossed the border through a tunnel near Ostheim and killed the trio after having forced their Trabant off the road near Dietzhausen.

In July 1982 Haas received instructions to cross the border again and make contact with a Soviet *Spetsnaz* officer who would pass him 'highly classified military documents.'[11] On his third mission as a courier Haas learned from the officer that he wanted to defect, and was told to exfiltrate him in September, but while driving the hooded officer towards the tunnel they were stopped by an East German policeman, whom he promptly shot dead. The rest of the mission was uneventful, and upon his return to West Germany Haas found a job as a civilian on the U.S. Army's training area at Wildflecken. Then, in January 1987, he was temporarily appointed the base's Security, Plans and Operations

Officer, a post in which he was responsible for drawing up and maintaining contingency war mobilization plans. During this period Haas continued to live in Meinigen and in 1988 also investigated a local bar owner suspected of being an East German spy. Haas followed him, watched while he passed an envelope to his contact, and after he submitted a report the suspect was arrested and charged, but later amnestied. Haas would later say that from 1987 he had been 'drinking every day – usually to the point of total intoxication'.[12]

In November 1990, coinciding with the birth of his second son, Haas was diagnosed as a diabetic but nevertheless he continued his clandestine work for the CIA while being hired from August 1991 as a U.S. Army weapons inspector under the Conventional Armed Forces in Europe agreement. He also arranged for the desertion of three Soviet soldiers, all 'Spetsnaz field grade officers' accompanied by a wife and her child. Two of the men turned out to be a 'Spetsnaz battalion commander and his executive officer', but his episode had not been authorized by the CIA. Consequently, Haas was the subject of an investigation 'which lasted a few months', but evidently he was cleared of any misconduct.[13]

When the Meinigen base was scheduled for closure in 1992 Haas applied for a transfer to an intelligence job at Fort Bragg, North Carolina, but through Phil's intervention acquired a post in Atlanta as a U.S. Army Reserve's Command Information officer, and five months later was promoted chief of the Security Division before being appointed assistant deputy chief of staff for intelligence.

During two years in Atlanta Haas says he conducted four further clandestine missions for the CIA, and 'each of them involved a permanent removal of a very real threat to U.S. national security' although he would not go into detail.[14] Despite being 'a chronic alcoholic' Haas remained in the U.S. Army Reserve intelligence command until December 2002 when he was sent on an assignment to Camp X-Ray at Guantanamo Bay. Haas's visit to Guantanamo Bay included the opportunity to sit in on the interrogation of an Al Qaida terrorist, Mohammed Al Qahtani, who had been subjected to sixteen enhanced interrogation techniques approved by Defense Secretary Donald Rumsfeld on 2 December. Haas then returned to Fort McPherson in Atlanta, but in February 2004 was hospitalised for detoxification, counselling and psychiatric evaluation. At the time of writing his book, in 2007, he had retained his job as the assistant deputy chief of staff at the U.S. Army Reserve Command, and was living in Peachtree, Georgia.

In conclusion, Haas claims to have killed eighteen people and insists that 'the only one person who knew'[15] of his covert CIA career, which had lasted thirty years, was 'Phil' who kept his identity secret. 'Nobody else connected my name with any operation' he says, but could any of this really be true? The answer is certainly not, but Haas's motives will never be known because, according to the Coweta, Georgia, sheriff's department, he was found dead in August 2010, having bled to death in his car from a self-inflicted gunshot wound in his thigh.

A more recent contribution to this genre is *My Father's Secret War*, written in 2007 by a Pulitzer Prize-winning journalist, Lucinda Franks, the wife of the then New York district attorney, Robert Morgenthau. As her elderly father, a veteran of the U.S. Navy and the war in the Pacific, lapsed into dementia she became increasingly intrigued by her discovery of an SS officer's cap among his stored possessions. Under any circumstances such an item would provoke understandable curiosity, but in a Jewish family an explanation was required, and Cindy Franks began to research such information as she could extract from her ailing father.

According to his official service records, Tom Franks had enlisted at the end of 1942, aged nearly thirty, and served as a junior officer in a radar unit that had island-hopped across the Pacific towards Okinawa, but in 1944 much of the Advanced Reconnaissance Group (U.S.) was disbanded and ostensibly he had been transferred to the Navy Yard at Washington DC in December 1944. However, according to his version, part of which was videotaped for a holocaust museum in New York, he had been based in England in early 1945, had undertaken two secret missions to Sweden, had worn a Nazi uniform (from which he had retained the cap as a souvenir) and had killed a suspected double agent and a German sergeant in a Gestapo office somewhere in Nazi-occupied Europe.

Apart from Tom Franks' personnel file, his daughter had a collection of his letters to his mother which provided an indication of his whereabouts as he was posted from Port Hueneme, California, to await embarkation for the Pacific. Over the following year Franks would serve with his unit in Guadalcanal, Emirau and Ulithi Atoll, but by January 1945 he was back in Washington. So when had he operated as an assassin in Europe? Franks recalled that 'I was sent on a couple of European missions before I went to the Pacific' and went on to describe two missions to Sweden, saying 'a time or two I was in Sweden,' adding that 'it must have been spring of '43.' He had 'checked in with some British intelligence chaps,' noting that 'I had a lot of specialized training in England' and 'sometimes I'd get no more than a few hours' notice' of his mission. On one of these assignments 'they sent me over from England to Stockholm and I stayed there for a few days.' His objective, apparently, was to visit a storehouse to 'inspect a shipment of roller bearings'. He had been accompanied on one mission to Stockholm by a friend, 'we both made deliveries there at one time or another, and I honestly never was sure which intelligence agency was sending me on my errand.' On a second mission, completed alone, he 'was disguised as a fisherman and a dockworker' and was instructed to photograph 'certain people under suspicion and the exact geography of certain fjords'. For this he was equipped with a Minox camera, 'a gadget classified for wartime use' and had been 'deposited in Lysekil', a town chosen 'for its quiet discretion and lack of spies.'[16]

Thus, according to Tom Franks, in the spring of 1943 he had been based in England, liaising with some unknown British intelligence agency that his daughter would speculate was most likely Special Operations Executive, and had undertaken at least two missions, one to Stockholm and the other to Lysekil. However, according to his 'abbreviated military file' that Cindy recovered, her father had spent January 1943 at a navy induction centre in the Bronx, and then at the Ordnance School at the Navy yard before being posted to Norfolk, Virginia. On 23 February he received orders to inspect naval ordnance in Norfolk and Charleston, and on 20 May he went on an inspection tour to Pontiac, Michigan, and then attended an anti-aircraft artillery course for eight weeks before reporting to Port Hueneme in July. Missing from the file was any deployment to Europe, but Cindy's explanation for the omission is simply that the details had been deliberately excised to preserve secrecy.

Cindy would claim that her father's second period as a secret agent in Europe took place after his return to the United States from the Pacific, when he was a member of a 'special operations group in the Bureaux of Ordnance.'[17] He said 'I was based in England for a while. Then I'd go in and out of Axis territory. Quickly.' Later he would recall 'I usually spent only a short time in occupied Europe, the rest of the time I would spend in London.' On the question of his role, he was emphatic. 'I was an assassin,' mentioning that he had been 'dressed as one of the Waffen SS.' He had 'gone in by parachute before but later on I went in on a small plane, a bomber'.[18]

Thus, during his second period in the European theatre, Franks had infiltrated enemy-occupied territory and had killed two people. One had been a German sergeant who had disturbed him while he had broken into the Gestapo's headquarters. 'I was there to pick locks' he asserted, 'I shot him and took my satchel'. When asked why he had been selected for the mission he had replied, 'I guess they liked the way I used a small camera'.[19]

The other person Franks killed was a man he described as a friend and a double agent. 'He was a good man. A first-rate operative.' Later he would recall that 'I knew his wife and two children. I had been to his home', but nevertheless he had 'recommended that he be eliminated' and 'I shot him with a Colt .45 fitted with a silencer'. As for timing, Franks said 'I was attached to the Army, officially as an ordnance officer in Alsace. We may have already crossed the Rhine. It was toward the end of the war'. Apparently the unnamed double agent 'this defector' had switched sides and was working for 'the Russians, the damn Communists. He was a traitor. He was going to let the Russians know where a store of German materiel, unassembled parts, blueprints, could be found.'[20]

Although Franks had recommended his friend's death, he insisted that 'my superiors had planned it.' Exactly who these superiors were, Franks did not recall, but he did say that 'my superior was an army intelligence man.'[21]

In April 1945 Franks visited a German concentration camp at Ohrdruf, and afterwards his principal role seems to have been to question some of the minor rocket scientists. He was qualified to do so because he had 'spent a year in Germany before the war studying chemistry' and therefore he had 'helped interpret statements taken from German prisoners of war incarcerated in German camps'. After he had 'studied the V-1, the V-2, and other much smaller rockets' his task had been to collect intelligence on 'chemical and bacterial weapons', and on one occasion he had 'busted right into Nazi headquarters … we photographed blueprints and plans'. In addition, according to Cindy, he had also found time to participate in the delivery of weapons, '.38 calibre Enfields,' to the Danish resistance.[22]

Whilst it might not be improbable that someone with Franks' technical qualifications and experience might have been transferred from the Pacific to Europe at the end of 1944, the deployment trend was rather more in the opposite direction but, setting that small doubt aside, it seems reasonable that he might have been tasked to analyse the interrogation transcripts of German prisoners to glean nuggets of scientific intelligence. However, the suggestion that as an expert on clandestine photography, lock-picking and radar, he had by then parachuted into France to assist the resistance, had masqueraded as a Waffen-SS officer to penetrate a Gestapo office, had delivered weapons to Denmark and been employed as an assassin beggars belief. Making the tale harder to swallow is his daughter's willingness to overlook the obvious contradictions in her father's official file which shows his presence in Washington on 2 January 1945, when he was granted four weeks of leave, and his orders dated 20 April 1945 to inspect ordnance in Charleston, North Carolina.

The question arises of how a professional journalist could reconcile the official record and claim 'it all fits'. One clue may lie in her apparent predisposition to believe that intelligence agencies routinely indulged in murder, claiming that 'the OSS and CIA had long ago admitted to terminating those who knew too much'.[23] For a well-informed contributor to the *New York Times* to make such an observation is indeed remarkable, for this is in fact the precise opposite of the evidence submitted, and accepted by the Pike and Church Committee congressional investigations conducted in 1975. Her attitude to the FBI and the CIA is illustrated by her assertion that she had 'learned from my research that the FBI and CIA tapped the phones of many intelligence agents after the war', the implication being that the FBI and CIA had spied on American retirees. She made no effort to substantiate such a sweeping allegation, and it is, of course, impossible to support.

So much of what her father had told Cindy was so patently improbable, such as his claim to have undergone 'Chinese water torture' to prepare himself for his clandestine role, that she managed to lose all objectivity in assessing his reliability.

Self-delusion might appear to be a common denominator in the cases of Roland Haas and Tom Franks, but what does the same apply to 'David Anderson', the author of *NOC: Non-official Cover. British Secret Operations*?

Within the international secret intelligence community the most vulnerable officers are undoubtedly the personnel known by the Russians as illegals, and by others as agents operating under 'non-official cover', often referred to by the acronym NOC. Within the CIA these individuals, who work outside the protection of the Vienna Convention which offers immunity to accredited diplomatic and consular staff, are managed by the Directorate of Operations' super-secret and innocuously-titled Office of External Development. During the Soviet era illegals were operated by the elite Directorate S of the KGB's First Chief Directorate and enjoyed a reputation that dated back to the era of 'the great illegals' before the Second World War when Arnold Deutsch, Theodore Maly and Richard Sorge were running networks across Europe and recruiting some of Moscow's most famous spies, among them the notorious Cambridge Five.

Within the CIA, NOC's also have a special status, and legal protection under the Intelligence Identities Protection Act, a statute passed in 1986 following the damaging disclosures made by the renegade Philip Agee.

Within the organization, one NOC, Paul Redmond, is revered. Having been arrested in Shanghai in 1951, he died in prison nineteen years later, still refusing to admit being a CIA officer. The only book to have been written by a former NOC, Valerie Plame, caused controversy in 2007 when she gave an account in *Fair Game*[24] of her role after she had ostensibly dropped out of the CIA after serving one tour in Athens under diplomatic cover. One other CIA officer, David Doyle, also served a period of his career as a NOC under journalistic cover in the Far East, but omitted all reference to his experiences in his 2000 autobiography, *Inside Espionage*.[25]

Another tale, released by James Waste in 2010, purports to be his recollections as a NOC, whereas in fact he was simply a 'directed traveller,' one of hundreds of legitimate businessman recruited during the Cold War as an agent to undertake tasks for the CIA, rather than as a NOC.[26]

It is into this relative vacuum that an author using the pen-name Nicholas Anderson has released *NOC. Non-Official Cover: British Secret Operations*, in which he describes in what he terms 'informed fiction' his activities working undercover for the Secret Intelligence Service between 1973, when he was a helicopter pilot with the rank of 'flight lieutenant', one that is limited to the RAF and unknown in the Royal Navy, qualified marksman, and champion swimmer fluent in Chinese and Russian, seconded from the Royal Navy after just two years of service, having graduated from the Royal Naval College at Dartmouth, until early 1983, when he resigned and emigrated to the United States. In his short career he 'visited well over 50 foreign nations in 10 years' and was considered 'an expert on Chinese, Russian and Arabic affairs specializing in new technology mainly relating to defence programmes'.[27] Although Anderson does not seem to be aware of Plame's memoir, for he claims to be the very first NOC in either the US or the UK to have written on the topic, it seems that he wrote his manuscript in 1989, and then faced a decade of unreported legal obstacles before publication or a drastically reduced version.

The text contains some clues to Anderson's background, for he says he was born in Bombay, his parents having met in Aden, and was educated at a boarding school in Hurworth, County Durham, before joining the 'British Schools swimming team' at the age of fifteen and then being selected at eighteen for Newcastle United as a reserve player for two seasons. His father had been posted to Singapore, and had worked at Little Sai Wan, the GCHQ analytical facility in Hong Kong, and is described as having been 'MI6's Foreign Office liaison with the French government' when Yuri Krotkov defected in London in

September 1963. His uncle Len, his father's elder brother, had been a Trotskyite union organizer in Yorkshire. According to Anderson's publisher, who offers a slightly different version, Anderson joined SIS in 1971 and is a '19-year covert action veteran', working until 2008 when he was granted political asylum in France.[28]

Anderson says he studied at Patrice Lumumba University in Moscow in 1970, aged eighteen, where one of his contemporaries had been Carlos the Jackal and, after having been interviewed by the FCO's Coordinating Staff at Queen Anne's Gate, and surviving 'a lie-detector test on a monthly basis', underwent training at Fort Monckton and Bletchley Park, with nine months in the 'analytical directorate' before being posted by SIS, first for two years to Copenhagen, where he also found the time to study for a PhD in social anthropology, and then to Berne. The author insists that he was one of only a dozen SIS NOCs, and was handled by a senior officer named only as 'Martin Mackenzie' which he says 'is a take on his real name. Insiders can figure it out and know that I know.' Indeed, Anderson boldly says 'I do invite investigative journalists to closely follow my story: They will see truth emerge and that my "imagined characters" do exist in real life.' Indeed, he repeats, 'my narrative … is accurate to the spirit and the letter of what transpired.' The book, he insists 'is a documentary novel.'[29]

The author says that after leaving SIS in 1983, he returned to the organization for twenty months between 1992 and 1993, despite having been 'officially disgraced' and served with a Public Interest Immunity Certificate, which he describes as 'a UK legal mechanism exclusively signed by the Foreign Secretary' to block the release of details of his 'entire career at SIS and Royal Navy Fleet Air Arm.' He also received a 'six-figure gratuity in one payment in cash' and the offer of a decoration in the form of a CMG.[30]

Anderson describes a series of secret missions, including one in which he was parachuted into Kazakhstan in December 1977, carrying papers identifying him as a Red Air Force officer, to find undeclared SS-18 missiles near Semipalatinsk, before traveling by train to Vladivostok and joining a freighter bound for Japan. In another assignment completed 'in the mid-seventies' he crossed the Tunisian border, equipped with a miniature camera and a suicide pill, dressed in Arab garb, to examine a Libyan facility at Tiji suspected of developing chemical weapons. The compound, which he succeeded in penetrating, covered six square miles and although officially described as a 'water irrigation storage system' was of interest to analysts who had reported that 'biological manufactured weapons can produce tons of poison gas per day.' Having taken photographs of his objective Anderson headed back to Tunisia on a stolen bicycle, pausing only to snatch a picture of a Provisional IRA leader, Patrick O'Neill, inside a military training camp.[31]

Some years later, while on holiday in Cyprus in 1976, Anderson spotted the same Provisional IRA leader watching a British military base accompanied by a Libyan, and on the spur of the moment he followed the Irishman to Rome and then acquired a new alias and travel papers to pursue him to Sofia. Anderson's decision to pursue Paddy O'Neill (not his real name, although he is described as having been Sinn Fein's director of publicity) had been conveyed to London by a Cypriot immigration officer whom he had approached shortly before embarking on his unscheduled flight:

> This is an official request from the UK's Secret Intelligence Service. On Her Majesty's duty I command you to inform the British consulate here in Cyprus of my imminent unexpected departure to Rome. Please make a note of my name and provide those details to them immediately.[32]

However, when he checked in at the Hotel Vitosha he was drugged, abducted and questioned for eleven weeks before being released at the Turkish frontier into the custody of a Mossad officer. Having acknowledged his true identity, Anderson was flown from Edirne on a private aircraft to the Tel Nof airbase where he was questioned by an Israeli security officer about his knowledge of Abu Nidal, before continuing his journey on the same Lockheed Jetstar to Bournemouth airport. Finally, Anderson was delivered to a house in Hampshire where he underwent five days of debriefing at the hands of an MI-19 veteran, described as 'the German Department – that oversaw the return of prisoners of war into normal life.'[33]

According to Anderson, his movements while in Bulgarian captivity had been monitored by a GPS satellite which had picked up signals transmitted from a device implanted in one of his teeth. Although there had been some delay caused by a bureaucratic problem with the Pentagon that controlled the GPS system, GCHQ at Cheltenham had located him via the KH-9 HEXAGON Crystals satellite array which had defeated Bulgarian attempts to jam his signals. In this way SIS had traced him to a facility just south of the industrial city of Plovdiv. He had contemplated suicide, a capsule of poison having been concealed in another of his teeth, but had resisted the temptation, confident that he would be found and freed. The involvement of the Israelis had been an act of gratitude for a tip to the identity of a Palestinian terrorist who had been responsible for the murder of an Aman intelligence officer. This information had been left on a slip of paper in the rental car he had abandoned at Larnaca airport.

Anderson offers no indication of precisely when he endured his months of imprisonment in Bulgaria during 1976, but mentions that his Israeli friends had been preoccupied at the time by the hijacking of a Lufthansa Boeing airliner by four Palestinians, one of whom was a woman, who had taken the plane to Rome and Larnaca.

Another of Anderson's missions was the exfiltration from Poland in 1976 of a GRU officer, Mayor Irena Puchovskaya, who had been cultivated by the *Bundesnachrichtendienst* for three years. Although ostensibly GRU, she was 'a head assistant to the chief of staff of the KGB's First Chief Directorate' who had been assigned to the Soviet embassy in Warsaw for the past month. 'In her official capacity as GRU liaison at the KGB's First Chief Directorate foreign intelligence headquarters at Yasenevo, she had access to all of its active measures files at Department A'. Helpfully, Anderson explains that 'the "A" in Department A stood for America.' He also described her as 'a high-class whore' who had been engaged seven times in seven years, and among her lovers had been 'the current bosses of Gosatomnadzor, Minatom, and the Kurchatov Institute.'[34]

SIS's team of three, headed by a former British Army paratroop captain, Ian McIntyre, included David Brennan, another former Fleet Air Arm helicopter pilot. In 1988 Brennan, a Roman Catholic originally from Glenoe in Northern Ireland, and the nephew of the leader of the Provisional IRA, had been posted to Belize 'in the newly formed Counter Narcotics Section in the makeshift British Consulate' where the British High Commissioner never knew he existed. His alleged task was 'to regularly check up on the several violent peasant uprising in Central America' and had lost the use of his legs after being captured and tortured by a drug gang in Nicaragua. Wheelchair-bound, he would later gas himself, having suffered from depression for years.[35]

In preparation for their mission, Anderson, McIntyre and Brennan had undergone a 'minimal warfare crash course training' which 'included skiing and climbing' at Arisaig House near Lochailort and then received their final instructions at 'the SIS' farm manor in Godmanchester'. They had then flown to Krakow as 'summer holidaymakers' for a week's package stay with the Orbis official travel organization, working 'under the auspices of NATO' because the company 'only brought Britons to Poland.' Accordingly, the trio slipped away from the rest of their group at the ski resort of Zakopane and held a rendezvous twenty miles away on the edge of the Morskie Oko lake with a BND officer, Dr Ralf Marczewski, based in Warsaw under cultural attaché cover, who supplied them with three automatic weapons, a quantity of plastic explosive grenades and a 'specially camouflaged liferaft'.[36] All radar-reflecting metal had been stripped from the craft, later described as 'a rigid inflatable boat' and the men were required to remove their GPS teeth:

> SIS men on deep cover foreign duty had built-in radio signals continuously emitting to within 300 yards of the exact position, monitored by 24 satellites equally divided among six orbits, 11,000 miles out in space, courtesy of the United States Air Force's Global Positioning System.[37]

In elaborating further, Anderson confirmed that his left molar 'was fitted with either a tiny recording transmitter or a cyanide capsule', while the right 'had a satellite finding device'.[38]

The plan was to row the Soviet defector 325 miles to the German town of Hof, carrying the boat around un-navigable obstacles, a journey that was estimated to take 'four or five days' but when she turned up she was followed by a track-suited Soviet intelligence officer. Brennan felled him with a single blow to the head but then the unconscious man was shot dead by Puchovskaya using a silenced pistol.

The remainder of the mission was uneventful and, with the help of 'a specially-made non-ferrous miniature compass' and a map tattooed temporarily on McIntyre's wrist, the four crossed Czechoslovakia undetected and reached West Germany, where a helicopter met them. Having 'climbed up the winch ladder' the party was flown to safety, the raft destroyed by gunfire, and back in London Anderson 'filed an after action review CX on my findings from her. Those two initials, which stand for Cummings Exclusive (after the first ever SIS chief, Mansfield Cummings), have always been an SIS acronym for classified top secret reports on agents. Hers was my first. (Up to then I had only filed YZ reports, which were marked under sensitive.)'[39]

In January 1978 'Flight Lieutenant Anderson' underwent training at the Royal Marines 'Special Boat Service' headquarters in Poole in preparation for Operation *Seed*, a clandestine infiltration by air from Turkey and then sea into the Crimea to reconnoitre 'a secret nuclear facility' near Feodosiya, and then be established as a NOC in Moscow. His journey took him by an RAF C-130 Hercules via Malta to Rhodes where he transferred to a twin-engine Yak transport flown by Turkish aircrew for the final leg to Gölcük. Finally, he was dropped into the Black Sea to swim, with the aid of a silently-propelled underwater diver vehicle, to the coast where, upon landing, he encountered a local peasant who died as he raised his handgun to hit him. He then stayed the night in a cheap hostel in Yalta and the following day held a rendezvous outside a military museum with a Jew codenamed Hilazon, who supplied him with identification papers and drove him to Sevastopol where they caught a series of trains to Vol'sk, the closed city in which his contact worked as an entomologist and headed a facility researching 'in alphabetical order chemical, bacteriological, biological, entomological, nuclear, organic, radiological' weapons.[40] Then, while acting as Hilazon's assistant while his regular assistant was on a three-week visit to East Germany, Anderson collected information about the site and the personnel working there, photographed documents, and attended a concert in Vol'sk with Zhenya, a beautiful twenty-two-year-old blonde KGB officer who played the cello. He also took a soil sample which, when analysed later in England, revealed 'the exact power of an atomic test that had occurred in the region five months earlier.'[41]

Having completed his task in Vol'sk, Anderson resumed his journey to Moscow by train, carrying photographs Hilazon had taken previously of a secret military installation at Cape Onuk in the eastern Crimea. Once in Moscow, enjoying the spring weather, he stayed with a Jewish family briefly before taking the metro to receive, during the rush-hour, a package containing money, a new identity and coded instructions.

Five months later, and 'less than a year' after his release from Bulgaria, Anderson participated in Operation *Kantele*, the exfiltration of a medical researcher, Dr Michal Molody, and his wife Caterina, across the Finnish frontier. He had known Molody since his student period in Moscow in 1970 and now the physician wanted to defect with a mass of accumulated scientific knowledge.

According to Anderson, although he had known Molody in 1970, he had met him again in a Moscow bar nine years later when he had adopted the identity of a Russian from Rostov-on-Don. Evidently the doctor had not given much thought to the transformation from the English undergraduate into a Russian businessman importing musical instruments, traveling on a 'perfectly legal red passport belonging to the Soviet Union' but also using 'a dozen illegal exit-entry routes in Poland, Czechoslovakia and Hungary that were carefully arranged by expert MI6 operatives'.[42] At that time his greatest coup had been the purchase 'from a retired training professor at Voroshilov Naval Academy in Leningrad' of details of the Northern and Pacific Fleets' submarine bases. He also identified the plants manufacturing ICBMs in the southern Ukraine, found the hamlet of Malakhovka where only

English was spoken, and discovered a facility producing hundreds of tons of anthrax at Pokrov.

Molody's value was his cures for Parkinson's disease, Down's Syndrome and diabetes, not to mention effective treatments for AIDS and malaria, based on a potent mix of human foetal tissue and the brain of the African fruit fly. On 6 December the trio, led by a Finnish guide, strolled across the border at dawn near Virojoki and caught a local bus to Helsinki where the Russians were issued with false British passports and flown by Swissair to Lugano to undergo a lengthy debriefing. Once in Switzerland Molody began to make some startling disclosures, including three closed cities, Oblensk, Arzamas-16, and Krasnoyarsk-26, 'each previously unknown' that 'produced nuclear warheads'.

> He told us of the existence of a space launch pad it turned out neither London nor I had ever heard of, at Pleseck in the Archangel region, 400 miles north of Moscow.[43]

Anderson bid Molody farewell at the Royal Navy's helicopter training station at Portland in 1979, when the scientist and his wife were flown to Fort Monckton to attend 'induction courses' before being resettled by the CIA in the United States.

These five missions into the Soviet Bloc are the core of Anderson's book, although he covers plenty of other ground, and makes some surprising assertions. For example, when 'in between jobs' he says 'highly observant MI6 international men like me were assigned a week or two in Northern Ireland' to give 'a personal overview on each of Northern Ireland's political parties', mentioning Sinn Fein as 'legally being the IRA's official political wing.'[44] This is a very strange assertion as Sinn Fein was the legal overt political wing of the Provisional IRA, and emphatically not anything to do with the official IRA.

While none of Anderson's missions seem to stand up to any scrutiny, his involvement in the exfiltration of the GRU major from Poland in 1976 is perhaps the oddest. Despite weeks of preparation and training, which supposedly included skiing in Scotland during the summer, Anderson accompanied two other SIS officers to Zakopane in a legitimate tour group of twenty other British tourists. Their task, which apparently they were unaware of at the time of their departure, was to escort a GRU officer, who was a BND asset, to West Germany. Naturally, one might wonder why SIS was ever involved in such an undertaking, nor why any sensible planner had selected a route that required not just one, but four international frontiers to be negotiated.

Aside from these concerns, there is the curious problem of how to explain the disappearance of three British adults from their tourist group. Surely one of the other tourists would have raised the alarm when the trio vanished? They were clients of the Polish state-owned tour agency that itself could be expected to take an interest in the men, and doubtless the media, in search of a human interest story, would ferret to find distraught relatives in England, anxious for news of their loved ones. Unless SIS had taken some quite extraordinarily elaborate precautions, the authorities, and indeed everyone else, would soon discover that the three were no ordinary travellers, but were equipped with alias documentation 'provided by G/REP, SIS forgery department'.[45] The SIS trio apparently shared a chalet with an entirely innocent married couple who had not been indoctrinated into the operation, so could have been expected to raise the alarm. Even if they did not, the SIS men slipped away from their group 'two days from the end of the holiday' so the news of their disappearance would have reached Britain from the other fifteen holidaymakers within forty-eight hours, while the team were still at large, guiding their rigid inflatable across Czechoslovakia and East Germany.

Any competent search by the authorities for the missing men would have revealed that they had been taken 'by an old Polish Fiat driven by an elderly but clearly sharp local' who had shaken their hands before delivering them to a lake twenty miles away. Was he an SIS agent too, or simply a hapless dupe who would have cooperated with the authorities? If he was involved, then he had been put at considerable risk. If not, he would have been able to lead investigators to the lake where no doubt forensic evidence existed of weapons, a boat, a shooting and perhaps a murder.

Setting aside the fate of the elderly sharp local with his Fiat, there is the question of why the SIS men were given 'three fully-loaded automatic weapons', instructed to carry them with the safety switch off, 'ready for action', and issued with twenty-five grenades. For reasons unclear, the grenades contained Semtex, and detonators that would trigger an explosion four seconds after being exposed to air. Also unexplained were their rules of engagement, or what the team was supposed to do with their weapons, apart from trying to avoid an accident with the grenades. One might also wonder why the BND had taken the trouble to employ a craft that 'has had all objects with any amount of metal removed from it' in an attempt to defeat radar, and demand that the men discard their watches, belts and rings, and yet carry three Heckler & Koch MP5SDs, made of metal, and loaded with metal ammunition.

Dr Marczewski, the BND officer briefing the team for their four-day voyage with the woman described variously as a 'Russian senior secretary' and 'an administrative worker', revealed much of his own background, his name, his occupation as an anthropologist, his cover role as the cultural attaché at the embassy in Warsaw, his recruitment of the GRU woman and even his access to KH-9 imagery of the intended route to West Germany.

The man killed by the GRU major was, so the BND officer claimed, a member of the Soviet *rezidentura* in Warsaw, and 'her forced lover'. However, Anderson later learns that the relationships were altogether more complicated. In fact, the dead man was not a Soviet, nor the Warsaw *rezident*, but an Iranian to whom Dr Marczewski had sold the blueprints of a Chinese-designed nuclear weapon. Apparently Marczewski had employed Major Puchovskaya 'to lure him into the Polish countryside, have sex, then drug him, whereupon she could repossess the blueprint's capsule for Dr Ralf. In return for succeeding he rewarded her with defection to the West.'[46]

Evidently Puchovskaya had failed in her simple task of recovering the capsule from the Iranian's rectum, thus preventing Marczewski from selling the blueprint to the Pakistanis, and so had shot the man. Nevertheless, we are told Marczewski did later succeed in passing the blueprint to Farooq Ahmed, a Pakistani and close associate of A.Q. Khan. When Ahmed was arrested in West Germany he denounced Dr Marczewski, who had by then abandoned the BND.

This labyrinthine tale deserves some scrutiny because it involves some familiar names, such as A.Q. Khan. The first question that arises is why Iran would have wanted a nuclear weapon design in 1976 when the Shah's entirely legitimate and internationally-supervised civil atomic programme had foresworn a military capability? Secondly, in 1976 Pakistan had not even contemplated the development of an atomic weapon, and would not accumulate sufficient fissionable material for a test for a further twenty-two years. Thirdly, it is inherently improbable that A.Q. khan would have been interested in buying a Chinese blueprint for 'millions' from Marczewski when the Chinese would give him the design for free. Far from being in the market to buy blueprints, Khan was in the business of *selling* them. Like so much else in Anderson's account, it only makes sense when viewed as rather poorly-crafter fiction without even a scintilla of verisimilitude.

By writing his story Anderson says he has broken the Official Secrets Act, but a question arises about the proportion of the book which might be considered breaches of the law because virtually every detail that might be verified turns out to be untrue, and the legion of internal inconsistencies suggest the entire tale is a rather poor fabrication. For instance, any layman with a knowledge of GPS systems knows they are passive receivers of satellite signals, not active transmitters, so the proposition that such devices are routinely concealed in the teeth of SIS officers is bizarre. Similarly, if Anderson was recruited as an illegal, why was he posted to British diplomatic missions in Copenhagen and Berne? And why, if he was known to the Soviet authorities as a British student in Moscow in 1970, could he so easily switch identities and live in the Soviet Union and Eastern Bloc for months at a time? And if it was so easy for him to enter and leave the country, why the need to be infiltrated by sea and by parachute?

In the chronology of the experiences Anderson describes, there are some definite time markers, but they tend to undermine his version. For example, he states that the KH-9 HEXAGON' satellite system was employed to locate him during his captivity in Bulgaria, which allegedly took place in 1976, yet the first KH-9 HEXAGON satellite was not launched into orbit until June 1984. This is a strange error for an expert in new military technology to make, not unlike his stated belief that the ECHELON discrimination software program is actually 'a global satellite communications spy cosmos', but he seems to betray a curious ignorance about SIS which never had an office in 'the London Borough of SW7', does not refer to itself as 'the 'Foreign Service' and does not use the definite article, as in 'the SIS'.

Anderson's purported SIS career, which included a posting 'in my first year – 1974' to Copenhagen where he handled Oleg Gordievsky, does not ring true either. He says he played badminton with Gordievsky on three occasions and received Kodak film canisters from him which he handed to his 'SIS number two (COP/1) right after the matches were over'. Several problems arise from this claim, as Anderson was not the SIS station commander in Copenhagen in 1974, a role fulfilled by Robert Browning, later succeeded by John Davies. Anderson was never the SIS head of station in Denmark, and the station consisted of a single officer and a secretary. Perhaps significantly, no SIS officer served in Copenhagen and then followed Anderson' claimed career pattern to Berne. Furthermore, only Browning ever played badminton with Gordievsky, who never held the rank of colonel, and no film canisters were ever passed in the way the author describes. In other words, the entire episode is fiction, and of course the very notion that a newly-recruited SIS officer would be posted to a European capital as station commander is strange.

Anderson's claim that Ellen Blyton was 'the personal assistant for nearly two decades to three "C"s, the male heads of SIS who never used their real names' is also odd as the author's purported service with SIS covered the period from 1973, when John Rennie was Chief, to 1993 when Colin McColl held the post, during a period when there were six different Chiefs.

The information Anderson says he collected in Russia, about Red Banner Fleet submarine bases, was well-known to Western intelligence analysts while he was still at school with, for instance, Plesetsk having been photographed regularly since it was first overflown by the Discoverer -29 satellite in August 1961. Furthermore, the details that one would expect an SIS officer to know, such as the correct name of the organisation's first chief, Mansfield Cumming, have escaped Anderson who even misnamed the SBS a year after it had changed its name from the Special Boat Section to the Special Boat Squadron. It was *never* the Special Boat Service. Similarly, there is no 'Forensic Explosives Laboratory unit in Sevenoaks, Kent' but there is a Home Office Forensic Science Service, and a separate Royal Armaments Research and Development Agency at Fort Halstead near Sevenoaks in Kent. Nor is there a 'Federal Drug Administration (FDA)' although there is a Food and Drug Administration which has the acronym FDA. The British armed forces do not have a 'Special Investigations Branch'; FBI personnel are not 'called agents' but Special Agents. As North Sea gas is not toxic like old town gas, it is simply not possible for David Brennan to have committed suicide in the way described, having gassed himself in his own oven.

Anderson's supposed knowledge of Moscow is demonstrably flawed, there never having been an 'old KGB library' open to the public, and the proposition that the Hotel Mezhdunarodnaya possessed 'a cheap suite' is incredible as the Hammer centre, as it was better known, was probably Moscow's most modern and expensive Western hostelry at the time the author described.

In dealing with the KGB, Anderson says Irena Puchovskaya was a GRU officer, and was 'a head assistant to the chief of staff of the KGB's First Chief Directorate'.[47] However, there was no such post, and no GRU officer could anyway have ever held such an appointment. The KGB did not move out of the Lubyanka in 'around 1976' and his claim the 'SVR and the SVRR had been the KGB's successors' is incorrect. So too is his belief that the KGB structure included a 'Department A'. Indeed, his grasp of British Intelligence organizations is not much better, for MI-19 was the War Office designation of the Combined Services Detailed Interrogation Centre, and not an organization dedicated to the rehabilitation of released prisoners of war.

There was no SIS station in Belize in 1988, and Anderson seems confused between a high commission, an embassy and a consulate. The wartime SIS facilities in Godmanchester and Bletchley Park closed down in 1945; Arisaig House in Inverness-shire is a hotel; and a Public Interest Immunity Certificate is not 'a gagging order' but an application, signed by any minister, to the High Court judge seeking an order, usually to protect the identity of a witness in a criminal trial, but also to protect national security. While Anderson claims that the certificate itself has the impact of a non-appealable order, it is actually a request that, like any other application, can be argued at a hearing, opposed and appealed. Nor was the Foreign Office's Coordinating Staff ever located in Queen Anne's Gate.

Anderson says on 12 September 1993, he murdered a pair of ex-French Foreign Legionnaires in Cabinda, Angola, because they had been responsible for the bomb that had killed the British ambassador to Dublin, Christopher Ewart-Biggs, in July 1976, an assassination that he had witnessed, and had compromised his colleague David Brennan. It is alleged that Ewart-Biggs had served as a Jedburgh during the Second World War in Team *Hubert*, and then had pursued a diplomatic career, although his radical views had singled him out for assassination. In reality, of course, Ewart-Biggs was never a Jedburgh, and he was indeed murdered by Irish republicans.

Anderson's behaviour, confiding in several people of his SIS work; of working under diplomatic cover; of identifying himself as an SIS officer to Cypriot immigration; of demanding a tour from British Army personnel in Larnaca; of dictating secret messages over an open telephone line in Moscow to the British embassy; of reading classified documents while on regular flight; and receiving secrets in an envelope marked 'British embassy' at his hotel in Moscow suggest that the author did not know much about operating clandestinely. His account also includes eating a boiled baby in China, and being detained in Miami when returning from the Caribbean in January 1994, leaving the reader bemused by Anderson's tale. Did he ever have anything to do with SIS? It would seem that apart from having read a couple of books on intelligence operations, and having studied Richard Tomlinson's *The Big Breach*, Anderson simply relied on his own imagination. The book is littered with evidence to show he has never even met an intelligence professional, and particularly telling is his recollection of what he calls 'an intelligence training directive' that instructed officers 'under no circumstances negotiate with terrorists, to talk to them is to surrender to them'. So how does this square with SIS's key role during the conflict in Ulster when for years SIS maintained a back-channel to the PIRA leadership for the precise purpose of conducting negotiations?

Anderson's central plot concerns his relationship with the genius Dr Molody, but it is unclear why SIS should have responded to his request, apparently made to the British ambassador in Moscow in January 1992, for Anderson to be flown to see him. The urgency required an MI5 officer to be flown from Washington, DC to Los Angeles, to escort Anderson back to London, and then be flown on to Moscow, all first class and at HMG's expense. Perhaps equally bizarrely, the Russians seem to have been uncharacteristically unconcerned about the fact that Molody had been exfiltrated to Britain in 1978, and then moved to the United States under CIA sponsorship the following year.

Equally puzzling is why, after Anderson had spent eleven weeks under interrogation in a Bulgarian gaol in 1976, he would ever have been placed at risk again by being employed 'black', that is to say under alias in a hostile environment. Having been involved in the murder in Poland of Irena Puchovskaya's companion, and his true identity known to the BND officer who had planned her exfiltration to Germany, who later turned out have been spying for the Chinese, Anderson's clandestine career, such as it was, should have been terminated, but instead he was entrusted with yet more high-risk missions with no discernible value.

Whilst it is true that SIS has always managed a few officers working under non-official cover, usually in commercial enterprises, the investment is a heavy one and they are not placed in unnecessary jeopardy by being sent to SIS stations in Europe where they will probably be spotted and may even come under hostile surveillance, and definitely not employed to handle serving KGB officers such as Oleg Gordievsky. Accordingly, Anderson's tale cannot be regarded as anything other than sheer invention, built on a very poor foundation by someone who cannot distinguish between an expatriate and an ex-patriot.

Chapter 15

Gestapo Müller

One of the more notorious figures of the Second World War was undoubtedly Heinrich Müller, the head of the most notorious secret police apparatus which exacted almost total control over Nazi Germany and the occupied countries. A former First World War pilot, and later a senior police officer in Munich, where he had cracked down on the Nazis as a subversive movement, 'Gestapo' Müller proved himself to be a faithful, if undiscriminating, servant of the state who was transferred to the *Sicherheitsdienst* in 1936, and in November 1940 he was promoted *SS-Gruppenführer* and the Reich's most senior police official. In that capacity he had tracked down enemy spies, dealt ruthlessly with subversives and after the attempt to assassinate Hitler in July 1944, had investigated the plotters and delivered those who had not committed suicide to the People's Court that had sentenced them all to various forms of execution.

Müller, accordingly, acquired a reputation that made him even more feared than most in a regime built on fear, torture and inhumanity, but in April 1945 he simply disappeared. Although he was always high on the list of wanted Nazi war criminals, Müller vanished without trace, and unlike Dr Josef Mengele and Adolf Eichmann, he left absolutely no trace. His remaining family, being his wife, son and handicapped daughter, continued to live in Munich, but of Müller himself there was no clue to indicate that he had escaped from the Führer's bunker in Berlin in last days of the war. Rumours later circulated that Müller had been a lifelong Communist, and had taken refuge in the Soviet Union where he had been given a new identity, but there was never any evidence to suggest that he had not perished in the ruins of Berlin, where there was a grave with his headstone.

That remained the position until 1973 when the Federal German Republic issued a warrant for Müller's arrest as a precaution in case he really was still alive, and nothing more was heard of him until 1995 when an American author made an astonishing disclosure. He claimed that a collector of historic wartime documents had recently purchased a collection of papers that included material that had belonged to Müller, including an 800-page transcript of an interrogation conducted by a CIA officer in Switzerland over two months in the late summer and autumn of 1948. According to Gregory Douglas, who claimed to have examined Müller's archive, the Nazi had flown out of Berlin in a light aircraft, just as the Soviets were closing in on the *Führerbunker*, and had adopted a new identity in Switzerland. There he had remained until September 1948 when his former Gestapo deputy, Willi Krichbaum, had contacted him and acted as an intermediary for the newly created CIA. Thereafter the CIA had recruited him and brought him to the United States where he had provided invaluable information about his contacts in eastern Europe. This covert role apparently had continued into the 1960s.

At the time of Douglas's revelation, it was common knowledge that several former Nazis had developed relationships of various kinds with a variety of American intelligence agencies in Europe immediately after the war. More than a few had found employment in the *Bundesnachrichtendienst*, the Federal Republic's foreign intelligence service, headed by General Reinhard Gehlen, and only recently Klaus Barbie, the notorious 'Butcher of Lyons' had been found to have helped the U.S. Counter-Intelligence Corps while a fugitive. In such an environment, therefore, it did not seem so unlikely that Müller might have evaded capture and been perceived as a potentially attractive source of information by an agency concentrating, not on ex-Nazis, but the new Soviet threat.

According to Douglas, who released *Gestapo Müller* in 1995, the Nazi had been persuaded to join the CIA in 1948, and had been supplied with a copy of the transcripts of his interviews, which he had annotated and placed in his personal archive. Thus the original Müller documents, purchased in Switzerland by the unnamed collector, consisted of the interrogation transcripts and another, equally astonishing item, the transcripts of conversations held between President Franklin D. Roosevelt and Winston Churchill over the scrambled transatlantic radio-telephone channel between the White House and the Cabinet War Room in Whitehall.[1]

This latter material had never been disclosed previously, and according to Douglas, the channel had been compromised by the *Reichpost*'s radio intercept service from 7 September 1941, and had produced between thirty and sixty transcripts a day. Although the source had been considered top secret, some of the English transcripts had been distributed to Müller who had retained some of the more interesting ones, even if they were slightly fragmented. Two had been selected by Douglas for reproduction in their entirety, and their content was indeed explosive. The first, dated 26 November 1941, was an exchange in which Churchill warned that a Japanese battle group of six aircraft carriers and two battleships, accompanied by numerous other ships, had put to sea the previous day and was headed for Pearl Harbor. Thus, a clear twelve days before the Japanese raid on Hawaii, Roosevelt had been given the most detailed advance notice of Tokyo's intention to carry out a surprise attack on the United States. Indeed, without being asked for the source of his news, the Prime Minister volunteered that his information had come 'from our agents in Japan as well as the most specific intelligence in the form of the highest level Japanese naval coded messages'.[2] As if to emphasize the reliability of the reports, Churchill explained that 'one of the sources is the individual who supplied us the material on the diplomatic codes that [conversation broken] and a naval offices [sic] whom our service has compromised'.[3]

The second transcript chosen by Douglas for inclusion does not have quite the same implications for history, but apparently recorded on Monday, 19 July 1943, in which the two statesmen had discussed the recent air accident in which the Polish leader, General Wladisalw Sikorski, had been killed when his Liberator bomber had attempted to take-off from Gibraltar. Ostensibly the purpose of the discussion had been the Allies' plans for Benito Mussolini who had just been placed under arrest by the new Italian government, but Roosevelt had taken the opportunity to upbraid Churchill for the recent death of Admiral Darlan, asserting that 'It's well known to my intelligence circles and elsewhere that you had the man murdered'. He then complained that Sikorski had died while 'under your protection and control' and that 'too many people who disagree with you seem to have fatal aircraft accidents'.[4] Even more remarkably, the President had pleaded 'Surely the pattern could be varied. Ships do sink after all. I do remember the Lusitania.'[5]

Far from denying these extraordinary charges, Churchill seems to have acknowledged the truth of them by saying 'we shoot spies here' and then equating the former U.S. ambassador in London, Joseph Kennedy, to a traitor. Roosevelt then responded by saying 'you have your Dukes of Windsor and Kent and I have Joe Kennedy.'[6]

Of the transcripts cited by Douglas, clearly the transatlantic conversations are the most significant, for their import is obvious. In the first, Churchill had provided the most detailed warning of the imminent Japanese attack, yet Roosevelt had not acted upon it. By any standards, this was an important contribution to the long-standing controversy over whether the White House had deliberately suppressed advance knowledge of the Japanese raid in an effort to end America's neutrality. Ever since the admission that some Japanese naval and diplomatic ciphers had been read by the U.S. Navy's cryptographers, a debate had raged about the extent, if any, that Roosevelt had foreknowledge of Japanese intentions, but until the publication of the Müller intercepts there had never been any reliable evidence to suggest that the President had engaged in a conspiracy, much less plotted with Churchill who, supposedly, had enjoyed access to secret Japanese communications.

Despite the absence of any independent confirmation of the authenticity of the transcripts, or forensic analysis of the actual documents, there is some reason to question whether the conversations, as described, could ever have taken place. In regard to the Pearl Harbor transcript, it does seem extraordinary that Churchill might have referred to the two sources he said he was reliant upon, being individual agents (in the plural) and the signals intelligence. Coincidentally, there was apparently a link between the two, for one of the agents had been the very same man who had compromised the 'diplomatic codes'. Thus, according to Churchill, Britain possessed more than one agent in Japan in September 1941, was in contact with them, and could receive information from them about events within a few hours of them occurring. Churchill's conversation with Roosevelt supposedly had taken place at 13.15 hours on Wednesday, 26 November 1941, describing the departure of the Japanese battle group 'yesterday from a secret base in the northern Japanese islands'.[7] However, according to the official histories of British wartime cryptography, the codebreakers at Bletchley Park did not succeed in reading any of the Japanese diplomatic machine-generated cipher traffic before until after the attack, even though the Americans had donated a replica of the PURPLE machine to the British in January 1941. Previously, the breaks into the Japanese naval communications had been achieved manually, and without the assistance of anyone in Japan. Although by September 1941 Britain was not yet at war with Japan, the Secret Intelligence Service representative in Tokyo had no agents on the loose in Japan with the means of communicating almost instantly to the British. Thus, apart from the intrinsic unlikelihood of the Prime Minister claiming that a particular naval officer had been coerced into providing his country's cipher secrets, there is the absolute impossibility that SIS had any agents in Japan, and certainly none with access to the Japanese navy's future plans.

That the transatlantic conversations between Downing Street and the White House were being monitored by the enemy was known, according to Ruth Ive (nee Magnus), the telephone operator who supervised the calls, listened in to prevent any breaches of security, and issued a stern reminder before each conversation. In her recollection, retained in a manuscript held by the Churchill Archive in Cambridge, she insists that the stilted dialogue was choreographed by references to telegrams exchanged earlier in the day between the two men, so they only referred to numbered paragraphs and not specific topics. In other words, the transcript described by Douglas could not be authentic.

On the basis that the transcript is a rather improbable fabrication, there is further internal evidence to suggest that it had been created rather more recently than 1941, and the passing reference to Vice President Harry Hopkins as a Soviet sympathiser is quite significant. According to the transcript, Churchill had said 'we cannot compromise our codebreaking' and then had insisted than 'not even Hopkins' should be told about the decryption. 'It will go straight to Moscow' he supposedly said, yet Roosevelt made absolutely no response, the implication being that the President was either already aware, or content, for his Vice President to be in constant direct contact with the Soviets.[8] Actually, the assertion that Hopkins had been a source for the Kremlin had been mooted first by Christopher Andrew in *Inside the KGB* in 1989, and the claim had sparked a major controversy among historians. Later the Cambridge historian would modify his claim by suggesting that Hopkins had been an unconscious source for the Russians, but if the transcript were genuine, it would imply that Roosevelt and Churchill knew of Hopkins' unreliability in at least September 1941, if not earlier, although there is absolutely no other evidence to substantiate the allegation.

If this first transcript is deeply suspect, what about the second? Is it likely that Roosevelt would have accused Churchill of murdering Admiral Darlan and the Duke of Kent, or of having engineered the loss of the *Lusitania* in 1916? Actually, Admiral Darlan had been shot dead by a French assassin who had been undergone training in a camp in Algiers run by the American Office of Strategic Services, and the Duke of Kent had perished in an air disaster when his plane had flown into a mountainside in Scotland. Only in the 1980s had a conspiracy theory emerged that the crash in which the homosexual Kent had died might not have been an accident. Similarly, there had been speculation in the 1980s about the sinking of the *Lusitania* because the disaster had so jeopardised the Kaiser's relationship with the United States. However, the proposition that Churchill might have played any sinister role in

197

the maritime catastrophe was emphatically a very modern phenomenon. And yet, here was the assertion, made directly to Churchill in 1943, and allowed to go uncontested. Thus, on the face of the 1943 transcript, the prime minister was effectively admitting to a whole series of crimes he would not be accused of in his lifetime. As if that were not improbable enough, there is the very curious comment, attributed to Churchill that 'we shoot spies here'.[9] In fact, the British only executed a single spy during the entire war by firing-squad. As Churchill knew only too well, enemy spies caught in Britain were hanged, not shot. A small error, perhaps, but not one that Churchill would ever have made as he is recorder as having taken a particular interest in the fate of Nazi agents convicted of espionage in England.

Having looked at the two radio-telephone transcripts, and concluded that they are of doubtful authenticity, one can wonder why Müller might have retained them, for he did not speak English. But putting this detail aside, what of the interrogation transcripts? Do they hold up to scrutiny? The author supplies few details about the three American intelligence officers who supervised the interviews, but the unnamed main interrogator seems extraordinarily ignorant of wartime Soviet intelligence operations, considering that he had been selected to question Müller, an undoubted expert in the field. Oddly, the interrogator knew nothing about Henri Robertson, one of the most important Soviet espionage cases of the entire war, even if Müller mistakenly refers to him as a saboteur, saying 'sabotage was his speciality'. Actually, Robinson was never a saboteur, but the controller of a very large Soviet GRU intelligence network based in Western Europe but centred in Paris, where he had been arrested in December 1942. The extent to which Robinson, who died in German hands, collaborated with his captors is unknown, although Müller claims to have 'turned him around rather quickly' and to have faked his execution.[10]

In addition to this relatively small item, there are three other references in the interview transcripts which jar. Of course, supposedly Müller is only reflecting his own opinions, and talking of what he claims are his own experiences, but placed in the context of 1948 they are decidedly strange. Take, for example, Muller's account of the execution of the British traitor, Sir Roger Casement in August 1916. Casement had been convicted of attempting to lead a rebellion in Ireland after he had returned to that country, in the middle of the war, from Germany on a U-boat. His plea for clemency, in view of his past service to the Crown in the consular service, had dissolved after a document circulated which showed Casement to have been a predatory homosexual paedophile who had recorded his experiences in graphic detail. But was the document, later known as 'the Black Diary', genuine, or a forgery concocted by nefarious British intelligence officers determined to silence the protests about Casement's imminent execution? The issue became a cause celebre, especially in Ireland during the 1980s, but forensic examination of the diaries undertaken in Dublin in recent years have proved them to be authentic. However, when Müller supposedly raised the issue in 1948, he claimed that the diaries had been forged by an unidentified 'Swiss expert' employed under instructions from Captain Reginald Hall, then the British Admiralty's Director of Naval Intelligence. On this allegation, at least Müller was dead wrong, but what of his other assertions? One was the curious claim that two notorious war criminals, Odilo Globocnik and Christian Wirth, had been transferred from British to American custody in return for a collection of incriminating letters written before the war by the Duke of Windsor to Adolf Hitler. This, of course, is a familiar theme, with the former King guilty of treacherously attempting to betray his country to the Nazis, and Müller claimed to have kept copies of the correspondence. Could this really be true? Since Müller's documents have never been examined independently, it is impossible to say, but it is curious that an issue raised in the 1980s is claimed to have been mentioned in 1948. Similarly, Müller is reported as having stated that a British propaganda radio, transmitting from England during the war, had assisted the Gestapo investigation into the 20 July plot by broadcasting the names of those involved. Could this really have been true? Even Müller himself was unable to explain the motives of those supposedly involved in such an act, but the allegation raises the question about quite how the British could ever have known who had participated?

The publication of *Gestapo Chief* in 1995 was greeted initially with some scepticism, although it was obvious that the author had undertaken some considerable research, but he was unwilling to allow any independent scrutiny of his archive, and claimed not to know the identity of Müller's supposed CIA interrogators. One biographer, Gitta Sereny, who spent some considerable time checking on a couple of the documents relating to Odilo Globocnik, concluded that the material she had seen had been skilful forgeries, and other historians expressed dismay at Müller's claims about the numbers who had perished in the holocaust, and his belief that Hitler had escaped from Berlin to live in Spain. There was also some controversy concerning Gregory Douglas himself, for he was also said to have used the names Peter Stahl and Walter Storch, although when traced to his home in Detroit the author denied it.

The debate about *Getsapo Chief* would be revived with a second volume in 1997 which, although devoid of the reproduction of the numerous facsimile documents in the first volume, contained more extracts from the Müller interrogation transcripts, and an interesting disclosure concerning the identity of the CIA interrogator. The author revealed that hitherto he had only known the officer by the codename *Welborn-II*, and had discerned from remarks in the transcripts that he had been a wartime OSS officer who had been operational in northern Italy, and had been acquainted with Allen Dulles. However, in February 1996 he had been contacted by William Corson, an author who had written on intelligence and espionage topics, who had claimed to have recognised *Welborn-II* as James Kronthal, a CIA officer who had committed suicide at his home in Washington DC in April 1953. According to Corson and his co-author Bill Crowley, with whom he had collaborated to write *Widows* in 1989, Kronthal had been a Soviet mole, perhaps having been compromised by the KGB because of his homosexualty. Corson's theory was slightly undermined by his inaccurate description of Kronthal as having been the CIA's station chief in Berne from April 1947 (a post he never held), but the identification of one of the CIA interrogators, and the apparent endorsement of Bill Corson reopened interest in Douglas's revelations.

In this second volume Müller is reported to have made more disclosures of a historical significance, among them his belief that the *Hindenburg* disaster of 1937 had been sabotage and not, as previously believed, a tragic accident. Müller apparently supervised a secret investigation into the loss of the airship and concluded that a bomb attached to a clockwork timer had been responsible for the fire which had so quickly consumed the aircraft as it had come in to dock in New Jersey, and the perpetrator had been motivated by personal gain, and not politics. Although the Gestapo was never known to have conducted such an investigation, there is no reason to suppose that this account is flawed, but some of the other assertions attributed to Müller seem worthy of greater examination. One concerns the Duke of Windsor, and the allegation that he had acted as a Nazi spy when he had been attached to the British Expeditionary Force in France in 1940. Müller insisted that 'he supplied very important information about troop positions and joint British-French military plans' and conveyed it through Charles Bedaux when 'he went on leave to Paris.'[11] Bedaux apparently had then carried the information to the German embassy in Holland. But could this really be true? Müller would not appear to be the most reliable of sources on the Duke, for he went on to say that 'the British government warned him discreetly that if he didn't go to the

Bahamas as Governor, they would kill his wife, so he went.'[12] Actually, there is no evidence whatever to support this novel proposition.

Although the basis of the CIA's alleged interest in Müller in 1948 had been his expertise in pre-war and wartime Soviet espionage, very little of the first volume of *Gestapo Chief* had been devoted to that topic, whereas the second compensated for the earlier omission by giving him an opportunity to show his value. For example, when his interrogator raised the topic of a Nazi atomic weapons research program, Müller claimed that the SS had established its own scheme, independent of the Army, in 1943, and that although he was unaware of what progress had been achieved, he knew that it had been assisted by information gleaned from wireless messages sent by Soviet agents inside the Manhattan Project. Müller described 'the interception and decryption of radio messages sent by Soviet spies in your country to Moscow concerning this business'.

> If you know where to look and what to look for, radio messages can be intercepted. Reading them is quite another matter. There were a number of levels of codes. Some we had broken and others were a one-time type of encoding that was extremely difficult to break. A spy ring operating out of Ottawa in Canada also sent messages to Moscow and many of these we could read. These fools often sent identical messages so that by tracking backwards, we could discover what was in the more complex codes. We didn't get everything, but certainly enough to keep my office informed as to your progress on the bomb.[13]

The fact that the Soviets had taken a close interest in the Anglo-American atomic bomb project had been public knowledge, of course, since the conviction in 1946 of the Soviet spy, Dr Alan Nunn May, and by 1948 much of the testimony of the GRU defector Igor Gouzenko had received huge publicity, but in this short passage, Müller made three astonishing claims which deserve close analysis because they certainly had not been given wide circulation. Firstly, the assertion that Soviet spies in the United States and Canada during the Second World War had relied upon wireless signals to communicate with Moscow; secondly, that some of these messages had been intercepted and read, and thirdly that the even more surprising claim that these messages had given the Nazis an accurate picture of the progress achieved by scientists developing an atomic bomb.

The first major problem with this scenario is the fact that the Soviet espionage networks in Canada and the United States relied upon commercial telegraph lines to transmit their messages to and from Moscow, so wireless interception was a physical impossibility. The German radio interception service had been adept at monitoring Soviet traffic in the Balkans, but was never able to study the north American messages because they had been sent on secure landlines.

When this particular transcript had been published by Gregory, in 1997, several thousand Soviet telegrams, known collectively as *Venona*, had been declassified by the U.S. National Security Agency, and had attracted considerable attention, but since their release in July 1995, there had been widespread misunderstanding about exactly how the material had been gathered. In fact, the Soviets had sent their enciphered messages, twice a day, from regular Western Union offices in Washington D.C., New York and San Francisco, and copies of all their traffic had been retained by the cable company and subsequently turned over to the American authorities. Müller's version of events, in respect of how the Soviets had communicated with Moscow, was entirely mistaken, and undermines the rest of his claims concerning the significance of the traffic. His description of the Soviets having replicated important messages on low-level and high-grade ciphers was an interesting misrepresentation of what had actually been achieved by the codebreakers who had worked on the Soviet traffic and had discovered that some messages, containing rather dull trade data, had been encrypted on one-time pads which had been compromised by the duplication of some one-time pad pages which, under normal circumstances, should have been unique. Where there was this duplication, with some of the same pages used for trade traffic (consisting often of cargo manifests which were known in plain-text to the cryptanalysts) it had been possible to read fragments of the rather more interesting GRU and NKVD telegrams which contained information about the spy-rings. Of this material a proportion concerned atomic espionage, but none of this related to Soviet networks in Canada, and the texts concerning the Manhattan Project were so sparse that they certainly could not have allowed an outsider to assess the progress achieved by the physicists at Los Alamos. Most of the messages had been confined to administrative arrangements for the handling of agents who had penetrated the Berkeley Radiation Laboratory, Oak Ridge and Los Alamos, but by no stretch of the imagination did this material give any indication on what the project had accomplished. Indeed, the Allies learned from the group of leading German scientists incarcerated at Farm Hall, Cambridgeshire, when the atom bombs were dropped on Hiroshima and Nagasaki, that none of the physicists led by Werner Heisenberg had ever contemplated that the Americans or British had perfected fission or a chain-reaction in the form of a weapon. The surprise expressed by the prisoners had been entirely genuine, and their reaction and subsequent private discussions had been recorded by hidden microphones, yet according to Müller's account they should have been fully aware of what had been achieved at Los Alamos. How was it possible that Müller could have known what the Reich's leading scientists did not?

The existence of a major Soviet spy-ring in wartime Canada had become known to the British, Canadian and American authorities in September 1945 with the defection of a cipher clerk, Igor Gouzenko, who revealed the GRU's interest in physicists such as Nunn May and others who had been working on the Manhattan Project at the Chalk River site. However, none of the embassy's communications had been intercepted by the Americans, or the Canadians, and it would have been impossible for the Nazis to have done so because of the Soviet reliance on commercial landlines. So where does that leave Müller's recollection that the Gestapo had been reading the Soviet traffic? He was surely mistaken, but then so was Frank Wisner, the CIA officer identified by Douglas Gregory as Müller's second interrogator, designated 'Q-2'.

Wisner had been a wartime OSS officer who would direct the Office of Policy Coordination, the CIA's original clandestine service, and according to Douglas Gregory, in the autumn of 1948 had interrogated Müller, and the transcripts had caught this strange assertion:

> We discovered that any attempt to expose or punish Soviet spies would be grounds for immediate dismissal from the service. When we found their spies operating inside the atomic bomb project, we were told that Roosevelt personally forbade us to touch any of these people. We were also strictly forbidden to listen in on their radio contact with Moscow, but of course we paid no attention to the President, because that was an area he had no control over.[14]

Thus Frank Wisner is confirming in 1948 that during the war OSS, or maybe the American authorities, had monitored a spy-ring's 'radio contact with Moscow', in spite of the fact that no such wireless link ever existed. Indeed, the CIA was not even indoctrinated into the *Venona* programme until 1952, which leaves one wondering how Wisner could have been in a position to discuss it so freely with a Nazi war criminal *five years* before he had been informed of it. The transcript also states that Wisner and his OSS colleagues had known of spies inside the Manhattan Project before the death of President Roosevelt, whereas no OSS personnel had ever been indoctrinated into the project, at any time.

Curiously, the transcripts reveal that both Müller and Wisner had made the same mistake about the origins of the *Venona* material. One possible explanation is that the transcripts were faked by someone who had not understood the precise nature of *Venona*. In any event, both Müller and Wisner were completely wrong in their understanding of this valuable source, and the error is a significant one for the Gestapo chief's value to the CIA was supposedly his knowledge of Soviet espionage, and this, he had explained, had been gleaned from intercepts of this identical traffic. Another odd aspect of Wisner's remarks is his insistence that President Roosevelt had placed a ban on the investigation of Soviet espionage, and that anyone caught in pursuit of Soviet spies would suffer 'immediate dismissal from the service'.[15] This is a strange observation because, of course, OSS was not engaged in any Soviet counter-espionage operations, and was unaware of the Manhattan project, whereas the FBI was fully committed to such investigations and had accumulated enough information to force the expulsion in 1944 of the NKVD *resident* in Washington D.C., Vasili Zarubin. The FBI ran numerous Soviet counter-espionage operations, kept dozens of suspects under surveillance, and played a vital role in the investigation of leaks from inside the Manhattan project, so Wisner's claim makes no sense.

When invited to compile a list of Soviet agents active in the United States, Müller had produced forty-three names, including those of Alger Hiss, Samuel Dickstein, Harry Dexter White and Robert Oppenheimer. Furthermore, Müller had declared that 'all of these sources have been identified by their names in various communications with Moscow. We were intercepting radio traffic, both from the United States and Canada, and their names are a compilation of both sources, plus information gained from my own interrogations.'[16] Thus Müller had claimed that the names of Hiss, Dickstein, White and Oppenheimer had been compromised in the Soviet radio traffic, whereas actually they could not have been. In the NKVD's telegrams the identities of most spies were concealed by codenames, and this was particularly true of Alger Hiss and Harry Dexter White. The codenames of both men appear in the *Venona* traffic, and the contexts suggest they had acted as spies, but the reference to Oppenheimer had not been incriminating, and Dickstein's name appeared in none of the Soviet traffic. In fact, his role as an NKVD mole had been revealed by Oleg Gordievsky in his book *Inside the KGB*. What makes this all so peculiar is Gregory's eccentric (and wholly bogus) assertion that 'it was later discovered by U.S. intelligence that Gordievsky was a double agent'.

Even if there might have been some confusion about precisely where Müller had acquired his information, his evidence concerning Hiss and White would have been considered very important in 1948 when both men were active espionage suspects. Hiss would eventually be convicted of perjury, whereas the former Assistant Secretary of the Treasury would die of a heart attack a week after testifying before Congress. If either Kronthal or Wisner had any knowledge of Soviet counter-espionage investigations conducted in the United States, they would have known that Müller's evidence concerning these notorious traitors would have been seized upon as potentially vital corroboration. As for a Presidential ban on any Soviet espionage investigations, or on the interception of Soviet communications, Wisner must have been very mistaken. There was never any such prohibition, and the cryptanalytic programme conducted by the Army Signal Security Service began in 1943 at Arlington Hall and continued under the auspices of its successor organisations, including the National Security Agency, until it was concluded in 1979.

Müller's list of forty-three spies, described as 'very important sources for the Soviets' of whom some he knew were 'paid agents of Moscow' seems inconclusive, for the context of the relevant transcript suggests a distinction between the two categories which he said he would clarify 'in the event our negotiations are successful'.[17] Müller appeared to be on rather stronger ground in discussing British traitors, and asked his interrogator 'do you have a list of the British you want to check on?' suggesting that 'I can give you one very good name for your people: Victor Rothschild'.[18]

This offer, apparently made in 1948, rings hollow, for at the time Lord Rothschild had no intelligence role, and was following an independent career as a biochemist. Between 1940 and 1945 he had served in MI5 as a scientific adviser and counter-sabotage expert, but he was never an influential nor senior figure in the British security apparatus. His access to classified information was more than four years out of date, and he seems a curious name for Müller to have mentioned as important in 1948. Perhaps significantly, Rothschild had become highly controversial shortly before the publication of Gregory's second volume, partly because of lingering doubts in some quarters about his loyalty, based on his old friendships with the notorious moles Guy Burgess, Kim Philby and Anthony Blunt. Also Cambridge-educated and a suspected former member of the CPGB, Rothschild had been headline news before his death in 1990, although he had been virtually unknown in 1948 when Müller apparently selected him, over all others, as a significant revelation.

The natural inclination is to suspect that the relevant transcript, in which Lord Rothschild's name was mentioned, did not originate in 1948, but was of rather more recent manufacture. Its impact in 1948 would have been minimal, whereas if Müller really had a knowledge of Soviet penetration of the Manhattan Project there are other names that would have been served his purpose rather more efficiently, if he was intending to offer the CIA a glimpse of the authenticity and value of his material. For instance, in 1948 the FBI was still preoccupied with the mole-hunt to identify a key spy in Los Alamos whose codenames in the Soviet traffic had been *Rest* and *Charles*. The net was closing in on a couple of candidates in 1948, both of whom remained at work in the atomic field in England, perhaps still engaged in espionage, so the investigation, which was by then three years old, was a major priority. A year later, of course, the culprit would be identified as the physicist Klaus Fuchs, and he had been responsible for some of the information contained in the intercepted *Venona* texts which had proved so valuable to the Soviets. Indeed, of all the *Venona* material, it was the messages from Fuchs which appeared to provide the most important data about the Manhattan project, and if this was the same as that available to Müller, why had he not disclosed Fuchs's name? His choice of Rothschild, in preference to any other name, seems very peculiar.

Thus, when analysing Douglas Gregory's second volume, there appears to be a problem running through much of it concerning Müller's reliability. Although neither of his interrogators appears to have pressed him on the point, his claim to have received wireless intercepts which compromised Soviet spies in the United States was a practical impossibility. That neither Kronthal nor Wisner realised this, and seemed to be under the same misapprehension, suggests a single hand might have been behind the fabrication of the transcripts.

As for the third volume of *Gestapo Chief*, released in 1997, there were fewer sensational revelations, and the author returned to Müller's earlier remarks about Victor Rothschild, revealing that he had been a member of the Soviet spy-ring headed by Henri Robinson, and his name had been included in the papers seized from his Paris apartment in 1943, along some forty others, among them such improbable Soviet agents as Ernest Bevin, Sir Charles Hambro and Sir Maurice Hankey.

Chapter 16

Brigadier Alexander Wilson

'Writers of thrillers tend to gravitate to the secret
service as surely as the mentally unstable become
psychiatrists, or the impotent pornographers.'
Malcolm Muggeridge

On 4 April 1963 an elderly man dropped dead from a heart attack in
the kitchen of his home at 13 Lancaster Gardens, Ealing, in west
London; a few days later he was buried in a family plot beside his
mother in the cemetery at Miton in Portsmouth. According to his death
certificate, Alexander Joseph Wilson was a retired brigadier in the
Indian Army aged sixty-eight, and during his lifetime he had claimed
to have spent much of his career in the British Secret Intelligence
Service. He was also the prolific author of some twenty-one spy books
and detective mysteries published in London between 1928 and 1940.
Among his characters were the spymaster Sir Leonard Wallace, who
sported a wooden arm, and his monocle-wearing subordinate Captain
Hugh Shannon. The books included *The Mystery of Tunnel 51*, *The Devil's
Cocktail* and the aptly-titled *Confessions of a Scoundrel* and *The Sentimental
Crook*.

Although none of his books would be released after the war, Wilson
continued to write, completing further manuscripts, and told his wife
that he was engaged on clandestine work for a department of the
Foreign Office. However, almost nothing about Alexander Wilson was
quite what it seemed. Indeed, at the time of his death he was married
to no less than four wives simultaneously. All bore his children and
lived in different parts of the county, but were unaware of each other's
existence. His seven children, which included a City businessman, an
Army officer and a captain in the Royal Navy, did not learn about each

other until years after his death. Furthermore, apart from thirteen months of service as a subaltern in the Army Service Corps during the First World War, there was no record of his ever having served in the Indian Army or of having achieved a higher rank.

Even Wilson's exact age, real name, true parentage and educational background seemed uncertain, for he had offered conflicting evidence at various times to identify himself as Lieutenant Colonel Alexander Chesney Wilson DSO, DFC, born in Grosvenor Square in November 1894, formerly of the Middlesex Regiment and the Royal Flying Corps, educated at Repton and Cambridge, and the son of Colonel Gordon Wilson who had married the Duke of Marlborough's daughter, Lady Mary. This version was contradicted by a birth certificate from Dover dated October 1993, criminal records showing he had three convictions – two for theft and one for wearing a uniform and medals to which he was not entitled – and a chancery order for bankruptcy.

After his death, Wilson's widow, Alison, the mother of two of his sons Gordon and Nigel, discovered papers that showed her husband had been married previously to a woman in Southampton named Gladys. Later it would emerge that he had also been married to Dorothy, a woman living in Maida Vale who had borne him a son, Michael, an actor with the adopted stage name Mike Shannon. According to Michael, his father had been reported killed at El Alamein in 1941, but the reality was that Wilson had faked his death to marry Alison McKelvie who was by then pregnant with their first son, Gordon.

In reality, Wilson had been working as a Special Constable in Hammersmith between September 1939 and March 1940, and had been convicted in October 1944, the year of Nigel's birth, on a charge of wearing a colonel's uniform and medals to which he was not entitled. In January 1944 he had been bankrupted after he failed to repay a loan. Four years later, in August 1948, he was sentenced to three years' imprisonment for embezzling £148 from the Hampstead cinema he was managing, and, after his release, he had found a job in a Sanderson wallpaper factory in Pinner, and then as a porter at the West Middlesex Hospital's casualty department in Isleworth. In January 1955 he met and married a twenty-six year-old nurse, Elizabeth Hill, and they had another child, Douglas, but she quickly moved to Scotland.

Wilson's real background was rather different to the claimed SIS career he used to dupe his various wives. He was actually the son of an Army Hospital Corps sergeant who served in the Boer War, was posted to Mauritius, Hong Kong, Singapore and Ceylon, and rose through the ranks to be a colonel, and died in 1919. His son was educated at St Joseph's College in Hong Kong and St Boniface's College in Plymouth, joined the Royal Navy as a cadet, was trained by the Royal Naval Air Service as a pilot, but was injured in a plane crash.

In 1915 he was commissioned into the Royal Army Service Corps but was badly wounded by shrapnel. In 1916 he married Gladys, and their son Adrian was born the following year. After the war he joined the Merchant Navy, working on the liner SS *Prinzessin* as a purser on a voyage to Vancouver via Cape Town. In September 1919 he was convicted of stealing £151, serving six months' hard labour Oakalla Prison Farm in British Columbia, Canada.

After his release Wilson and his wife managed a repertory theatre company and she bore him two more children, Dennis and Daphne. It was at this point that he began writing, and in 1925 he abandoned his family in England and was appointed professor of English literature at Islamia College, part of the University of Punjab in Lahore, where he started to produce espionage fiction. In 1928 he published *The Mystery of Tunnel 51*, which was followed by *The Devil's Cocktail* and *Wallace of the Secret Service*. The plot of the first centred on a murder in Simla of a military intelligence officer, investigated by Sir Leonard Wallace. In the second, Wallace intervenes in Lahore after his agent, sent on a mission from London to investigate local unrest, uncovers a Soviet plot masterminded by Nikolai Bukharin. The third, *Wallace of the Secret Service*, is prefaced by a contribution from an unnamed former Home Secretary, who signs himself 'C', in which he claims the credit for having spotted the talents of the young Major Wallace, described as 'Chief of the Intelligence Corps', when he uncovered a German U-boat base in Dorset.[1]

During the years that followed Wilson travelled across the region learning several languages, and as commander of the university's training corps he acquired an honorary rank in the Indian Army Reserve. This he resigned in 1931 to take up a post editing a local daily newspaper.

In 1933 Wilson married the actress Dorothy Wick, who was touring with the Grand Guignol theatre company, and their son Michael was born later the same year. Meanwhile, Wilson had adopted the spy genre, producing *The Factory Mystery* and *The Boxing Mystery* as Gregory Wilson. He also published three thrillers, *Callaghan of Intelligence*, *"Steel" Callaghan*, and *Callaghan Meets His Fate* as Michael Chesney but featuring Colonel Geoffrey Callaghan, described as the Chief of Military Intelligence.[2] In 1935 the family returned to the UK and settled in London, but Wilson returned to Gladys in Southampton and joined SIS in October 1940 while Dorothy and her son moved to Yorkshire.

During 1939 Wilson had made numerous applications to the War Office to be re-employed as a reservist, but in none of the forms he completed did he refer to any previous intelligence experience. His subsequent position in SIS, as one of a team of linguists monitoring the foreign language telephone calls made to and from neutral diplomatic missions in London, and circulated in Whitehall as 'Special Material', coincided in 1940 with the release of his last novel, *Chronicles of the Secret Service*. It was the tenth publication to star Sir Leonard Wallace, a book that boasted 'Major Alexander Wilson probably knows as much about the Secret Service as any living novelist'.[3]

However, Wilson was sacked by SIS in October 1942 for submitting embellished reports of his eavesdropping on the Turkish embassy's telephone conversations. Wilson spoke fluent Hindi, Persian and Arabic, but his behaviour was that of a fabricator, producing information that was contradicted by an investigation conducted by an MI5 officer, Alex Kellar, who concluded that Wilson's imagination had led to a massive misdirection of MI5's scarce counter-espionage resources. Unaware of what was happening, the distinguished Turkish ambassador, Rauf Orbey, a former naval officer and prime minister, had been the subject of a thorough investigation, which had exonerated him and cast doubt on Wilson's transcripts. In anticipation of a major row, and a formal complaint from MI5's Director-General, David Petrie, the SIS Chief, Stewart Menzies, explained the incident to Peter Loxley at the Foreign Office in June 1943:

> You will shortly be receiving from Petrie a further report prepared by Kellar on his investigation into the alleged intelligence activities of the Egyptian ambassador.
>
> The conclusion of this report is that the intelligence activities attributed to the Egyptian ambassador and his agents in Special Material have in fact been pure fiction.
>
> I have studied the report carefully, and I feel bound to accept the conclusions. This is of course a very serious matter, and I can only express my regret for all the unnecessary work and trouble which has been caused to all concerned. You will doubtless wish to have the following information about the case. All the conversations which purported to show the Egyptian Ambassador and his circle engaging in intelligence activities were recorded and translated by one member of my Section concerned … This officer joined my organisation in October 1939. He was of course vetted in the usual way. He was taken on as an interpreter in Hindustani, Persian and Arabic and he passed the usual tests. Another officer of the Section concerned, who was an examiner in Hindustani, Persian und Arabic, and who sat next to him for some time, said that Wilson was the finest natural interpreter he

had met. In these circumstances it is not surprising that it was a long time before his translations of conversations were called in question.

Wilson was eventually dismissed in October 1942 for reasons entirely unconnected with his work in this office. He was found to have staged a fake burglary in his flat. He has subsequently been in further serious trouble with the police.

Wilson previously had been a professional writer of fiction. When some of his reports were questioned towards the end of his service here, the possibility that he was embroidering on what he heard was taken into account and he was given a very serious warning that he was not to report what he thought was meant in the Egyptian conversations but to keep to the literal translation or the words used. From this time all his reports were carefully scrutinised, and he was questioned constantly to ascertain if he was sure his interpretation was accurate. On no occasion would he admit any doubt. Another officer who sat next to him listened in to the Egyptian conversations on several occasions, but heard nothing that was not reported substantially correctly. While therefore we must now admit that a great deal of what Wilson recorded was pure invention (though I think it probable that in many cases he did no more than embroider on what he actually heard), I do not think that we can hold ourselves greatly to blame for not having discovered earlier what was happening.

There are only two ways of making absolutely sure that this sort of thing cannot occur:

(1) to have two men constantly listening together on a particular line;

(2) to have every call recorded and read by two different men.

In practice it is quite impossible to adopt either of these methods. We have 230 separate lines on the boards. Three-quarters of the calls are purely social ones or calls between servants, which are of no interest to anyone. We could not possibly provide a separate recording machine for every line, and we must therefore rely on the staff to judge, as a conversation proceeds, whether a verbatim report is necessary.

Nor of course, could we spare the manpower required to have two men listening in on every line. In any case such a practice would lead to bad feeling among the staff, whose nerves are naturally strained by the very nature of their work.

I think that the only possible course is to continue as at present, picking our men carefully and trusting them to do the best they can. If any reports are called in question by the Foreign Office or anyone else, then immediate steps can be taken to check any further conversations in the same series. I do not think it at all likely that we shall again have the bad luck to strike a man who combines a blameless record, first rate linguistic abilities, remarkable gifts as a writer of fiction, and no sense of responsibility in using them. As far as I know, there has never been the slightest suspicion against any other of the staff of having faked or written up reports. In general I think we can claim that on extremely difficult and trying job has been consistently carried out with meticulous attention to the accuracy of the report.[4]

That unhappy episode ended Wilson's brief intelligence career, and it was not until an enterprising journalist, Tim Crook, was persuaded by a friend, the actor Michael Shannon, to research his father's background and write *The Secret Lives of a Secret Agent: the Mysterious Life and Times of Alexander Wilson*, which was published in 2010.[5] Crook was able to trace the rest of Wilson's descendents, and introduced all his grandchildren, among them the actress Ruth Wilson, who is Nigel's daughter, and her brother Sam, a BBC journalist, to each other for the first time, Dorothy's son Adrian having died in 1998.

Naturally the family wanted to believe that Wilson's philandering and financial misconduct was all part of an elaborate cover-story created by SIS to insert him into various environments, such as prison, where he could collect information for the authorities. Crook encouraged this view, suggesting that numerous official documents had been doctored or fabricated to cover up Wilson's real missions.

The truth, alas, is rather more banal. Wilson was a serial bigamist and a thief, attributes that tarnished his unquestioned talents as a linguist and novelist. Nor, contrary to Crook's view, do any of his books reveal any inside knowledge of SIS, or even the British Intelligence organisation in India where, according to his biographer, he must have been engaged in espionage. For instance, his first espionage novel, published in 1928, is supposedly filled with inside information that, according to Crook, proves that Wilson not only knew SIS's first Chief, Sir Mansfield Smith-Cumming, but had actually worked for him.

Firstly, it is suggested that Wilson's hero, Sir Leonard Wallace, was a character based on Mansfield Smith-Cumming, mainly because both men were amputees. Wallace sported a wooden arm, having been wounded by a German spy, whereas Smith-Cumming had a prosthetic foot following a road accident. There the similarities ended, for Smith-Cumming had died in June 1923, at the age of sixty-four, whereas Wallace was described as being aged thirty-two. Captain Smith-

Cumming was a naval officer answerable to the Foreign Office, while Wallace had been an infantry officer working under the auspices of the Home Office.

The Mystery of Tunnel 51 has nothing in the plot to suggest the author has anything but the shallowest knowledge of British Intelligence, either in London or in Delhi. Indeed, the story concerns the theft of a vital military document by Soviet agents, a crime requiring an investigation conducted by Wallace, Chief of the Secret Service. Although the Indian Police Special Branch is mentioned once, in passing, there is no reference to the Delhi Intelligence Bureau, the large, highly efficient regional intelligence agency which had prime responsibility for counter-espionage and counter-subversion. Contrary to the view expressed by his biographer, there is not a hint in the novel of any inside knowledge manifested by Wallace. Rather, Wilson's style is more Buchanesque, with traces of Bulldog Drummond and a serious dose of anti-Semitism, the principal villain being a dastardly Russian spy named Levinsky.

In his second novel in the Wallace of the Secret Service series, *The Devil's Cocktail*, which centres on a British officer being sent on a mission to Lahore under the academic cover of a university professor teaching English literature, the author says explicitly that 'India possesses a very fine police service, but there is no Intelligence Department worth the name'.

For all its flavour of *Greenmantle*, it is nonetheless significant that someone was writing in the Bond vein as early as 1928, when Fleming himself was then aged nineteen and would not introduce 007 for a further quarter century. It is equally remarkable that Wilson joined SIS, which is more than can be said of Fleming, whose wartime role was restricted to the Naval Intelligence Division. However, while it definitely can be said of the creator of James Bond that he based many of his plots and characters on real life, this is demonstrably untrue of Alexander Wilson.

Chapter 17

Operation Vengeance

Of the many tragic atrocities to have been committed in the cause of the Palestinians, the attack on the Israeli team at the Munich Olympics in September 1972 was one of the most horrific, because the appalling events, which led to the deaths of eleven athletes, were broadcast around the globe by television cameras which covered the hostage-taking at the Games themselves, and then the firefight which followed at Fürstenfeldbruck airbase, fifteen miles west of Munich Airport, as the eight Black September terrorists, two of whom had been employed as builders at the stadium, clambered out of two helicopters to make what they had been told would be their getaway flight to Libya in a Lufthansa 727. The German police had only managed to deploy five snipers, armed with bolt-action rifles without telescopic scopes, and they were heavily outgunned by the terrorists equipped with AK-47s and grenades. Finally, after an hour and a quarter of shooting, five of the gunmen lay dead, two were wounded and one was arrested while pretending to have been hit. However, there was also further carnage, with five bodies in the burnt-out wreck of one of the Bell Hueys, and four more dead hostages in the other.

The disaster had been the culmination of a series of blunders committed by the Munich police which underestimated the number of terrorists, initially counting only five, possessed no specialist counter-terrorist unit, and had failed to clear the area of spectators and news cameramen, thus allowing the gunmen to monitor the police counter-measures on television. Realising the Palestinians had anticipated a police raid, having watched the preparations on the news broadcasts, it was called off. With no trained snipers, and dependent on ordinary street cops, the police had planned to ambush the terrorists when they arrived with their nine hostages at Fürstenfeldbruck, but then failed to pass on the news to the airfield that there were actually eight terrorists, and not five. Then the two helicopters landed at an angle that made clear shots impossible, and a plan to seize the terrorist leader and his deputy as they inspected the Boeing 727 was abandoned at the last moment when the designated police officers spotted the gunmen carrying grenades.

When the first sniper eventually received orders to open fire, he missed the leader, and only wounded his deputy in the thigh. The unequal gun-battle that followed was essentially between two police riflemen and eight terrorists, with the three other snipers exposed and pinned down on the control tower, until army armoured cars belatedly intervened, prompting the gunmen to kill all their hostages.

Unknown to the rest of the public, while the country went into mourning and the remainder of the Israeli Olympiads withdrew from the games and flew home, Prime Minister Golda Meir had ordered Mossad to track down all those involved in the planning of the attack, and over the months that followed eight members of the Black September leadership died. In the middle of the following month Wael Zwaiter was hit by twelve bullets fired at close range in the entrance hall of his apartment block in Rome. In December the PLO representative Mahmoud Hamshari was killed in Paris by an ingenious bomb that detonated inside his telephone. In January 1973, *al-Fatah*'s Abad al-Chir died in an explosion under his bed in his room at the Olympic Hotel in Nicosia. In April Basil al-Kubaisi was shot in a Paris street. Three days later Kamal Nasser, Mahmoud Yussuf Najjer and Kemal Adwan were assassinated separately in their three Beirut apartments by thirty commandos that had slipped ashore from six darkened Zodiac inflatables.

Three days after that raid Zaid Muchassi was killed by a bomb in his Athens hotel room. Finally, in July 1974, a Mossad team was arrested in Norway after a Moroccan waiter had been shot dead in Lillehammer in front of his pregnant wife. Until this last, disastrous shooting, when an entirely innocent Arab, Ahmed Bouchiki, had been gunned down in a quiet residential street in the off-season ski resort, nobody publicly had linked the killings, but the .22 Beretta used to kill with Bouchiki fourteen bullets was linked by ballistics to the bullets that had killed Zwaiter in Paris and al-Kubaissi in Rome. Although the Norwegian *Overaaksingstejeste* estimated that at least eleven Israeli agents had participated in the surveillance on Bouchiki, which had incorrectly identified him as Ali Hassan Salameh, only seven were arrested. One, Yigal Eyal, listed at the embassy as a security guard, claimed diplomatic immunity and was expelled, Michael Dorf, the comms expert, was acquitted and the other five (Zwi Steinberg, Marianne Gladnikoff,

Sylvia Rafael, Dan Aerbel and Abraham Geimer) were convicted of murder and imprisoned.

The last chapter in this extraordinary chronology was the death in a massive car bomb in Beirut of Ali Hassan Salameh in January 1979. Sometimes known as 'the Red Prince', Salameh had been Black September's chief planner, and he was thought to have masterminded the Munich attack.[1]

The first, necessarily incomplete account of these extraordinary events, was provided by two *Time* journalists in 1976, with the publication of *Hit Team* which revealed that a Mossad officer named 'Mike' had led the team of fifteen covert surveillance, logistics, support and communications specialists who had acted on the authority of Golda Meir. They also benefited from the Norwegian police report which included details of eight Mossad safe-houses in Paris, compromised in documents recovered from the flat in Oslo where some of the Lillehammer team had been based at the time of their arrest. Later, similar accounts were to be given by Richard Deacon in 1977 in *The Israeli Secret Service*,[2] by Elaine Davenport, Paul Eddy and Peter Gillman in *The Plumbat Affair* in 1979,[3] by Edgar O'Ballance in *The Language of Violence* in 1979, by Stewart Steven in *The Spymasters of Israel* in 1980[4] and Michael Bar-Zohar and Eitan Haber *in The Quest for the Red Prince* in 1983.[5] To a greater or lesser extent, all the authors were dependent on *Hit Team*, but collectively they provided a mass of detail concerning Mossad's spree of revenge killings. In particular, the two well-connected Israeli journalists had established that three of the Lillehammer squad, travelling under the aliases Jonathan Ingleby, Rolf Baehr and Gerhard Emile Lafond, had left Norway, and revealed that *memuneh*, General Zvi Zamir, himself had been in Oslo during the operation, carrying an Israeli passport in the name of Tal Sarig, and had visited an advance command post at a motel forty miles south of Lillehammer.

Then, in 1984, a Canadian journalist, George Jonas, revealed in *Vengeance* that he had been approached by a former Mossad hitman named 'Avner' who claimed to have been one of the gunmen who had shot Zwaiter in Rome.[6] The other he identified as 'Robert' a member of an English family that had manufactured toys. He also gave a detailed description of how he had been parked in a van outside Dr Hamshari's second floor apartment in the Rue d'Alesia when Robert had activated the remote device which had detonated the plastic explosive concealed inside his telephone handset; and had accompanied Robert to Nicosia to place a pressure bomb under al-Chir's hotel bed. With a German-born Israeli named Hans, Avner had followed al-Kubaisi from his hotel in the Rue de l'Arcade, and then shot him dead as he crossed the Rue

Chauveau-Lagarde, near the Place de la Madeleine. It had been Avner who had been in lobby of the Hotel Aristides when Hans and Robert had blown up a suitcase-bomb placed in Muchassi's ninth floor room, and then had shot dead a KGB officer sitting in a car outside whom they suspected had spotted them. He had also maintained a watch on Boudia's Renault parked in the Rue des Fossés in Paris as Robert had placed a bomb under the driver's seat, and had watched it detonate as Boudia attempted to drive away. Finally, Avner claimed to have been given a tip that Ali Hassan Salameh and another Palestinian terrorist, Abu Daoud, were due to meet in a church in the Swiss town of Glarus in January 1974. Avner and two of his team, 'Steve' and Robert visited the church, but instead of finding their targets, the two Black September leaders, they instead walked in on three armed bodyguards, so they shot all three dead with their Berettas and fled to Zurich, unchallenged.

Altogether Avner claimed to have killed ten Arabs, the KGB *rezident* in Athens, plus a woman at her houseboat in Hoorn, on the Dutch coast in August 1974, who had shot his friend Carl in his room in the Europe Hotel in London three months earlier.[7] This particular murder apparently had not been sanctioned by Mossad, but had been an act of loyalty by Avner determined to take revenge for the death of his friend at the hands of a professional, allegedly contracted to kill him by the PLO. Three weeks later, Robert blew himself up in a field near the Belgian town of Battice while preparing another bomb, and in January 1975 Hans had been found dead, seated on a park bench near his home in Frankfurt's Ostpark. This further setback had served to persuade Avner to retire, and he had abandoned Mossad and emigrated with his wife and child to the United States where he had worked illegally as a taxi driver until he had made contact with *Vengeance*'s author, the Hungarian-born George Jonas, in Toronto with an offer to collaborate on a book which was to net $500,000 in foreign rights and $126,000 from Simon & Schuster in New York.

According to George Jonas, Avner had been born in Israel in 1947 but at the age of twelve, in 1959, he and his younger brother Ber had spent a year with his paternal grandfather in Frankfurt, where he had learned German. Later, his father had divorced his mother and had gone on a mission overseas for Mossad. By the time he had returned to settle in Rehovot in Isreal, with his new wife Wilma, Avner had spent three years on a kibbutz and completed his military service, which had included an attachment lasting four years to an elite commando unit that had seen combat in the 1967 Six Day War. Leaving the army with the rank of captain, Avner had been recruited by Mossad and had worked as an El Al spy marshal and courier before being invited by Mossad's General

Zamir, in September 1972, to meet Golda Meir at her apartment in Jerusalem and be invited to lead the team that would track down and kill the Black September terrorists responsible for the massacre at Munich. Having accepted the mission, Avner was order to resign from Mossad, and to report to his newly-appointed case officer, 'Ephraim' who introduced him to the other members of his team, and gave him a list of eleven targets. Curiously, they made no special arrangements for contacting each other regularly, with Ephraim remarking that he would follow Avner's progress through newspaper reports. This comment would later become significant.

According to Avner, the additional information he acquired about his targets came not from Ephraim, but from a former French wartime *resistant* who ran a freelance organization known as 'Le Group'. This impressive collection of mercenaries, all surveillance experts, drivers, locksmiths and other skilled craftsmen, routinely disposed of dead bodies across Europe, monitored the movements of terrorists and supplied accurate intelligence to the highest bidder.

Jonas did not identify Le Group's leader, but he did leave sufficient clues in the text for 'Ephraim' to be named as Mike Harari, a legendary former member of the Haganah and Mossad's director of operations who had made a timely exit from Oslo the day after his team shot Abdel Bouchiki. Reportedly Ephraim had made an unsuccessful attempt to lure Avner back to Mossad after he had emigrated to the United States. Even easier to give a real name to was Avner's father, the Mossad spy who supposedly had been imprisoned while on a mission abroad and, upon his release in 1967, had written a book and achieved the fame gained by Eli Cohen. The only person fitting this description was Wolfgang Lotz, the Mossad agent who had been arrested in Cairo in 1965, sentenced to life imprisonment for espionage and then released with his wife Waltraud in an exchange of prisoners in 1968. Originally from Mannheim, Lotz's mother had been Jewish and he had served as an officer in the Jewish Brigade of the British Army, and simultaneously had joined the Haganah. Undoubtedly Avner's description of his father fitted only Lotz, but the problem was that he had not been married before he had wed Waltraud in 1961, and they had not had any children. Furthermore, by 1984 when *Vengeance* was published, Lotz had moved back to Germany, and from his home in Munich he issued an emphatic denial that 'Avner' was his son. Jonas responded with the assertion that the character described as Avner's father had in fact been a composite of five different people. This admission suddenly cast doubt over the authenticity of the rest of the book, although Avner himself continued to refuse to reveal his true name. Why would Mossad have chosen an

El Al sky marshal as the leader of a murder squad going after the most ruthless terrorists in the world? Did it seem likely that so many of the deaths described by Avner had been unreported at the time they supposedly occurred? Were there any details of the well-documented assassinations that only the killer could have provided? Who would have wanted to cover-up the death of a Soviet diplomat in Athens in April 1973? In short, was there any evidence at all to support Avner's claims?

One important aspect to the assassinations which apparently was unknown to Avner, who failed to mention it, was the elaborate arrangements made to obtain a political sanction for each individual operation. When an approved target had been identified Mossad initiated a method of obtaining approval from a Cabinet committee, known as Committee-X, which gave its consent for each hit once a positive identification had been made. Obviously with matters of such political sensitivity, high-risk operations are usually conducted with an element of deniability to insulate a country's government from embarrassment, so the existence of Committee-X was not revealed until *Ha'aretz* broke the story in June 1986, naming General Moshe Dayan as having been a member. Having gained confirmation that Committee-X had given the final go-ahead on each individual hit, it is hard to reconcile this with Avner's version where he was not in direct communication even with 'Ephraim', and decided on each hit himself. The options are that either Avner had deliberately concealed Committee-X's existence, or that he had fabricated his entire story. Considering that he had anyway implicated Golda Meir by giving a detailed account of how she personally had invited him to take the assignment, it is hard to know why he would have omitted such an important detail, and one that gave his activities a moral, if not entirely legal, justification.

Another curiosity in Avner's account was his failure to mention the presence of Zvi Zamir in a parked car, watching the operation as Zwaiter had been shot in the entrance lobby of his apartment block in Rome. David Tinnin had mentioned this detail in *Hit Team*, but George Jonas has made a point of addressing this issue, and had observed that his sources had ridiculed 'the idea that the head of Mossad would expose himself in such a fashion' and further, had dismissed Zamir's alleged presence in Norway during the Lillehammer fiasco as 'a fairy tale'. However, Zamir's presence in Norway that weekend is well documented, and was perhaps not entirely surprising. As soon as the first hostages had been taken in the Olympic village, back in September 1972, Zamir had flown straight to Germany to be on the scene, and he had been an eye-witness to the tragedy. He had also personally supervised Golda Meir's security arrangements in January 1973 when she had flown to the Vatican to have a historic, private audience with Pope Paul VI and, according to *Hit Team*, had also been watching with Mike Harari when Mohammed Boudia had been blown up in his car. If he had been in Norway in July 1974, why not Rome in October 1972, or Paris in June 1973? Strangely, Jonas had not mentioned the suggestion that Zamir and 'Ephraim' had been present during Boudia's assassination.

The Lillehammer episode proved to be a major catastrophe for Mossad, arguably the greatest in the organization's history, yet Avner's stated reaction to it, as described by George Jonas, is distinctly odd. Under such circumstances the first concern for any clandestine agent would be the integrity of his own cover, and that of his network. News quickly spread that although most of those arrested had been entirely professional, sticking to their cover stories and giving away as little as possible, Marianne Gladnikoff, a twenty-five-year-old Swedish trainee, had fallen apart under interrogation and had made highly incriminating statements, while Dan Aerbel, a lifelong claustrophobic, had signed a long confession to avoid being returned to his cell. Indeed, Aerbel had not only volunteered a detailed account of the Lillehammer operation, and explained how surveillance on a Black September suspect, an Algerian named Kemal Benamane, had led his watchers from Geneva to Lillehammer, but had also revealed his participation in another highly secret Mossad operation conducted in 1968. Aerbel admitted that he had worked for Mossad since 1963, and had once owned a cargo ship, the *Scheersberg A*, which had later disappeared. In fact, as he revealed, the freighter had been used to transport a cargo of uranium yellowcake to Israel for refinement as fuel for the Dimona nuclear plant in the Negev desert. The consignment had been bought in Antwerp, supposedly for delivery to Naples, but mid-voyage in the Mediterranean the ship had changed its course for Israel and delivered 560 barrels of the precious ore. With Aerbel haemorrhaging secrets of this magnitude, Avner might have been forgiven for wondering if his own activities had been compromised, especially as the murder weapon used in Lillehammer had been traced to the two earlier hits in which he himself had played a role. Strangely, according to Jonas's version, these thoughts never occurred to Avner.

In summary, Avner admits to having participated in a dozen murders, and been a witness to another in London. His three fellow assassins were themselves shot dead, leaving few apparently in a position to corroborate his tale. Many of his other assertions, such as his claim to have spent two nights in a Paris safe-house with the notorious terrorist Carlos the Jackal, posing as a member of the Baader-Meinhof gang 'in the spring of 1973', are equally hard to verify. Nevertheless, despite the many gaps in his tale, it became the basis of *Munich*, a big-budget movie made by Stephen Spielberg in 2005 which purported to document Avner's role as a Mossad assassin, collaborating with a mysterious French-run organization that had the ability to locate Black September terrorists across the world. Evidently entranced by Avner's story, Spielberg stuck closely to his version of events, right down to the murders in Holland, London and Athens that have proved so hard to authenticate, resulting in a splendid example of art mimicking art.

The theme of vengeance taken in the post-war era against surviving Nazis and their adherents is a popular one, and has attracted some unusual authors, some of whom claim to have participated in the murder of individuals alleged to have been involved in wartime atrocities.

In one example of retribution meted out by a victim of the Nazis, Grace Stoddard, describes in *No Cloak, No Dagger*, the experienced of a man she refers to as Keith Armstrong, although she acknowledges that this is not his true name.[8] According to her account, he was born in 1924 and after having been educated at a grammar school, a preparatory school in Sussex and Ambleton, a public school in Yorkshire, enlisted in the Royal Army Service Corps at the age of seventeen, joined Special Operations Executive and was posted to N Section for operations in Holland while also working for 'Section Z' of MI6. He also met and married a beautiful Belgian Arlette de Roche, a telephonist 'at SOE headquarters in Dorset Square', who would bear him a son, Stephen before she was sent on a mission by F Section to France.

Armstrong's initial training took place at 'Camp X' in Canada, having been flown across the Atlantic in an aircraft flown by an Air Training Auxiliary woman pilot. Later he would attend courses at RAF Ringway in Manchester, at Beaulieu in the New Forest, and at Wanborough Manor in Surrey where he was order to kill a man, a prisoner from Dartmoor, by knifing him during a night exercise.

His mission, given to him personally by Winston Churchill, was 'of the utmost importance and the utmost secrecy' and started either at 'a secret airfield in Sussex' or, a page later, at 'a secret airfield in Bedfordshire'.[9] Equipped with a false tooth containing cyanide, Armstrong was parachuted into the Netherlands near Arnhem to deliver a message from Churchill to the *Ordedienst* resistance movement. Unable to return to England by air or by boat as planned, Armstrong remained in Holland and participated in two sabotage operations. One destroyed a train carrying Jews to concentration camps, and the other was an attack on a power plant, guarded by 'Volkstrum' during which Armstrong killed a German sentry.

Soon after the destruction of the power station Armstrong was arrested for breaking the curfew and was imprisoned briefly at Scheveningen before being rescued as he was being transferred to another prison. He then was put in touch with the Comet Line and was passed down the underground railroad to Bordeaux and then across the Pyrenees to Spain where he was detained at the Miranda del Ebro internment camp. Finally, 'after some weeks', Armstrong was released and travelled to Lisbon for a flight to London where he was debriefed at 'the Royal Patriotic School, Wandsworth'.[10]

Upon his return to London, Armstrong had been reunited with his wife, Arlette, who worked as a telephonist at 'SOE headquarters in Dorset Square' where, even though she was Belgian, she was assigned to 'F Section.' Armstrong underwent further training, this time 'with the airborne troops at Thame Park, near Oxford' and meanwhile Arlette was sent on a mission to Nazi-occupied France.[11] In September 1944 Armstrong was landed by glider near Oostereck as part of Operation *Market Garden* and in heavy street-fighting seized a Bren gun and shot dead Major-General Kassin, 'the field commander of Arnhem'. Badly wounded, Armstrong was treated in hospital where he was arrested by the Gestapo and tortured by 'Oberstleutnant Joseph Schreider. He was then sentenced to death 'by Heinrich Himmler and Heinrich Mueller' and put on a train for Buchenwald where he arrived in 'late October of 1944'.[12]

Armstrong survived a harrowing captivity at Buchenwald to be freed in April 1945 by American forces and then escorted back to England by a member of the 'VAD (Voluntary Air Detachment)' to be welcomed home by Claude Dansey, Colin Gubbins and even Winston Churchill who entertained him to tea at Downing Street. Apparently Churchill explained that Armstrong had been 'singled out with certain others in a plan to deceive German intelligence' by disclosing to the enemy deliberately fabricated information while under interrogation. Nevertheless, Armstrong remained on good terms with Churchill, was invited to Chequers 'a few times' and became friends with Randolph Churchill's wife, June.

When he had recovered from his ordeal Armstrong was given an office 'in the basement of Northumberland House' and his 'birth certificate was changed to make' him older. Soon afterwards, Armstrong discovered a photograph of his wife Arlette at Ravensbruck concentration camp and set out to discover her fate, hitching a ride with Squadron Leader Giles on a flight to Paris from RAF Wittering.

After a short search he discovers a Dutch woman who was a witness to her execution and, determined to revenge her death, traces her killer to Lüchow, a village near Celle and Hanover, where he finds his quarry, an SS soldier, and shoots both him and his wife.

Upon his return to London Armstrong is assigned as an interrogator to the London Cage in Kensington Palace Gardens where he worked under Colonel A.P. Scotland and served on a court-martial, sitting as a major, which tries eight German soldiers who had murdered a sergeant-major in a prison camp. According to the author, five of the defendants were hanged at Pentonville prison. Armstrong also assisted Oreste Pinto and travelled to Holland with him to investigate the activities of Christian Lindemanns, 'a known double agent' and his death. Among his other duties was to work with the Palestine Police but after showing 'signs of stress' he was posted to Malta to recover.[13]

On 28 January 1947 Armstrong went to Buckingham Palace to receive a Military Cross from King George VI, and there he met Field Marshal Lord Wavell. This medal he added to his 'Croix de Guerre, three from Belgium and the two from France'[14] and his conversation with the King would lead him to be invited to join the royal family for tea at Windsor Castle in 1947. In the meantime, Armstrong worked 'as a dishwaster and cleaner at the Lyons Corner House' although he was actually working for 'MI6, a department of the Foreign Office.' He underwent further training and then participated in a mission to Groningen with four others to take delivery of a pair of dangerous Nazis in the Baltic off the Polish city of Utska. However, on the return journey they were ambushed and one of his companions was shot dead.

In the spring of 1949 Armstrong was ostensibly working as a photographer in a holiday camp but, while living in Eastbourne with his new wife, Audrey, was really was under secret instruction to 'keep an eye on shipping and report conversations I heard which might have some bearing on the activities of a foreign power.' In September 1956 Armstrong says he was arrested by the police on a charge of theft of sixpence having 'come from a store with marked coins in my pocket,' but this was really cover for another clandestine mission, this time to Budapest where, equipped with a false passport, he made contact with his Hungarian contact to receive 'a precious microfilm' but was obliged to shoot a pair of Soviet soldiers on the landing outside his apartment. To hide the two bodies, he simply stuffed them into a large chest inside his apartment.[15]

Upon his return to England, via Prestwick and Manchester, Armstrong completed his sentence at an open prison but was sent to Dublin with a bodyguard to lie low. Having checked in at the Shelbourne Hotel he was attacked by a mid-European hitman who was shot dead by his Scottish minder. Later they were ambushed in their car and, having split up, Armstrong was able to kill one of them, breaking his neck.

Having recovered from this adventure with a week in hospital Armstrong was promptly sent to Dresden posing as an electrical engineer, but was caught by the Stasi on his first day in East Germany. Nevertheless, he managed to escape to the West, but the following spring he was sent back, this time as a New Zealander, Neil MacDonald Smith. On this occasion he was soon arrested outside his hotel while taking a morning stroll after breakfast. He was sentenced to ten years' imprisonment and transferred to Moscow where he was incarcerated at the Lubyanka. However, 'eleven months, two weeks and four days later' he was exchanged at the Berlin Wall for a Soviet spy, and greeted by his MI6 colleague Maurice Oldfield.

Suspecting he had been betrayed by a mole inside MI6, Armstrong learned that the traitor had been found, and was being confined in a Ministry of Defence compound in Dorset, prior to being released to Moscow. Infuriated, Armstrong climbed over the fence with the aid of a folding ladder he hid in the trunk of his car and killed the man instantly with a karate chop to the neck. When challenged about the murder, Armstrong denied his involvement and continued to be employed 'in London and acting as a courier abroad.' His role was 'listening for moles and subversives at various levels of society in London' but in 1960 he was also living with his wife Audrey and their son in Devon where he spotted two suspicious men following him. When one evening the men fired into his house, killing 'Pip' Hargreaves a local fisherman, Armstrong responded by shooting one man dead, one with a bullet through the brain, and leaving two others, both Hungarians, to be detained by the police.

In 1961 Armstrong was granted a 'grace and favour' apartment at Windsor Castle, but later in the year he was informed that his son Stephen, his child by Arlette, had been knocked down by a car in a road accident outside the Gare Central in Brussels. He recovered but, two years later, after he had started an engineering course at Heidelberg university, he succumbed to complications in June 1963 and, 'just twenty years old' he was 'stricken with a complication' and died.[16]

Despite this tragedy Armstrong continued to work for MI6 and went on missions to South Africa, where he refused to work with the Bureau of State Security, to the former Belgian Congo, to Algeria and to Uganda where he met 'the infamous Idi Amin.' In one final attempt to assassinate him at his home on Dorset's border with Hampshire, Armstrong shot two potential assassins dead in his garden, leaving his son Nigel traumatised by the experience. He then moved to a flat in London where one of his 'main assignments was to look for subversives' but he also served in the British Army of the Rhine and was in uniform in Northern Ireland when another officer standing beside him was shot by a sniper. He also briefed Prime Minister Edward Heath and completed missions in Rome, France and Corfu. Finally, he was summoned to London to face charges, at a trial held before a judge sitting 'in camera', concerning his 'efforts to have the Official Secrets Act amended or repealed.' Having been found guilty, Armstrong was told he was 'no longer a member of Military Intelligence' and was ordered to live abroad without a pension.

Grace Stoddard assures her readers that 'the story is true' but it seems incredible that Armstrong could have killed at least nineteen people with all his activities concealed by a D-Notice. Furthermore, anyone attempting to research Armstrong's background, or even that of his first wife Arlette, would have been stymied by a very determined effort to 'blot out all traces' of his 'recent past, marriage, military record, everything, so that if a hostile power ever attempted to check up on me they would run up against a stone wall.' His birth certificate at Somerset House had been altered, as had his marriage records and Stephen's surname on his birth certificate.[17]

So could any of this be true? An analysis of Armstrong's activities makes it all hard to believe. He was 'told to find a civilian job' in 1947 and found work as 'a roving photographer', but mentions going to the Gehlen organisation in Pullach in 1948 on some unexplained visit. Bizarrely, Armstrong 'posed as a Canadian doctor in one of the remote villages of the Midlands,' although there is no explanation about his purpose.

By 1949 he was working at 'a holiday camp that needed a seasonal photographer' while living in Eastbourne and keeping 'an eye on shipping'. It was not until September 1956 that Armstrong was given a mission, while ostensibly serving a prison sentence for theft, to go to Budapest to collect a valuable microfilm. Under business cover and an alias he was also to learn all he could and 'receive intelligence from our embassy and get it back to London' which seems very odd. Why employ an extremely vulnerable agent to collect the microfilm, rather than an officer with diplomatic protection from the local SIS station? Why entrust material from the embassy to someone using a false passport when a fully protected diplomatic channel of communication was also available? As for his return journey, Armstrong allegedly was driven by the British Minister [sic] out of Budapest, and then made the rest of the journey to Austria on foot. Once in Vienna, he refused to hand over the microfilm to 'our people' but stayed in the city a day to rest before flying to Scotland and then Manchester. If the 'precious microfilm' really was 'very valuable' and contained information of the 'utmost importance,' why did Armstrong delay and not give it to the MI6 station in Vienna?[18]

Nothing about Armstrong's mission really makes sense but it is the key to subsequent events for, according to him, he became a marked man when the Soviets learned details of his successful mission from a mole and was forced to drop out of sight. Armstrong felt that he had been betrayed by a senior officer and 'that person had to be on a very high rung of the ladder because my mission was a very closely guarded secret.' Of course, one is bound to wonder just how secret his mission could have been if he had been given instructions 'by London to contact the British Consul, Joan Fish, if I found myself in trouble', which implies that a consular official had been indoctrinated as well as the British minister, Leslie Fry, who made contact with Armstrong by shouting from the street up at the window of his apartment 'I'm the British Minister here, and I've had word to look after you.'

On the basis of his prowess as an agent, and having thus attracted the attention of the Soviets who 'don't like it when agents operate successfully against them' Armstrong was sent to Dublin where he was nearly the victim of an assassination and that episode cost three lives, including two gunmen, both 'skilled professionals' and a Glasgow police sergeant. As for Armstrong, his injuries required him to be treated for a week in Belfast's Royal Victoria Hospital.

Curiously, MI6's reaction to these dramatic events was to despatch Armstrong on a mission to East Germany 'the last place they will be looking for you, right under their noses,' and here one should pause to consider precisely what has occurred.[19] Armstrong has received a criminal conviction under his own true identity and been sent to prison in England as cover for a mission conducted under alias to Budapest. Apparently angered by the success of his mission, the Soviets had responded by sending a team of killers to Ireland. When the gunmen failed, MI6 decided to send Armstrong 'only days' later' and a companion, a former 'member of SAS (Special Air Services) [sic]' to Eindhoven posing as members of 'a company of electrical engineers'. Their mission, expected to last just 'a day or two', was to travel to Dresden equipped with explosive briefcases containing a concealed compartment in which to carry microfilms. He was to deliver the briefcase but upon their arrival they had been arrested by the Stasi but having been badly injured by the exploding briefcase, they had been treated in a hospital from which they were able to escape. According to Armstring, both men were driven, in separate cars, to safety in West Germany and flown home to undergo a debriefing. They 'followed a route that was then a closely guarded secret and probably for many years to come' but since there were a limited number of official crossing-points between the zones of occupation the ease with which the pair was exfiltrated is remarkable.

Stoddard's explanation for the Stasi's uncharacteristic incompetence is interesting: 'The Stasi were trying to identify us and were having difficulty because of the various diversions that had been set up over time. As I was to find out, the Soviets knew very well who I was, but the information had not been shared with the East Germans.'[20]

Thus, according to Stoddard, the East Germans seized the two British agents without realising who they were, although the Soviets knew perfectly well, but had not shared the information. Equally improbable is the release of both prisoners from Stasi custody and their subsequent exfitration. Such an event would be the stuff of espionage folklore, but seems to have gone unremarked and unrecorded elsewhere.

If this seems improbable, so does the decision made by Armstrong's superiors in the spring, to send him back to Dresden. As he rightly observed, 'returning so soon to Dresden seemed suicidal' but nevertheless he went, this time carrying a New Zealand passport, to deliver a microfilm. When undergoing a brutal interrogation, he 'was astounded by the information they had about me. There was no doubt whatever that I had been betrayed by someone within the system who had access to my confidential files.' At his subsequent trial 'the most unexpected evidence came from a shopkeeper that I had known, this supposedly ordinary tradesman was anything but what he had appeared, he did not know everything, but enough to enable him to tell about me being in contact with certain people in the area.' Exactly what this incriminating testimony amounted to is unclear, but the implication is that Armstrong had been watched, perhaps at home in Devon, where he had met intelligence personnel who had inadvertently compromised him. Quite why this evidence was required, considering that Armstrong was in East Germany with false documentation and was engaged in espionage, is not clear. As his chief interrogator reportedly observed, 'a wonderful cover, but you did not have us fooled for long.'[21]

Sentenced to ten years' imprisonment, Armstrong was transferred to Moscow for further interrogation, torture, the administration of pentothal and 'physical abuse' but, after just over eleven months, he was exchanged in Berlin, although there is no mention of the individual or others for whom he was released. Once back in London, Armstrong revealed that inadvertently his interrogators had 'let slip the name of a friend in the department who they said was working for them'. Although not directly identified by Armstrong, he says 'that respected and successful man was knighted, pensioned and eventually raised to the peerage'.[22]

This is indeed a remarkable, indeed incredible, allegation, Firstly, it seems astonishing that the Soviets would have blundered by telling Armstrong the name of their mole inside MI6. Secondly, no SIS officer in the history of the organisation matches the description of an officer who received a knighthood, retired, and then sent to the House of Lords. In fact, since 1945 only two retired SIS officers have received life peerages, and both were women (Meta Ramsay and Daphne Park).

The first clue to Armstrong's identity can be found in the extraordinary similarity between his career and that claimed by a fraudster, John Cottell, who claimed an OBE, MVO and MC, and attempted in 1990 to have his entirely bogus memoirs published as *Codename Badger*.[23] The project, headed by the Savannah author and *Reader's Digest* writer Arthur Gordon, who died in 2002, was abandoned when Cottell was revealed to be convicted conman. He too claimed to have been born in 1924, to have joined SOE's Dutch Section, to have been recruited also by Colonel Claude Dansey's 'Z Section' as a teenager, to have married a beautiful Belgian, Marianne de Roubaix, who had worked as a telephonist in the Belgian embassy in London before she joined SOE. Cottell had been trained at Wanborough Manor, had knifed a prison convict at Beaulieu, completed a course at Camp X in Canada and had been dropped into Holland. His experience was so similar to Armstrong that his recollection of his inability to return to London is worth recounting. He said it,

> was going to be difficult if not impossible for me to get back to England. Nazi patrol boats had closed the Channel ports. Escape by Lysander was too risky. German intelligence seemed to know the plans of SOE in advance. Drops of arms and ammunition constantly fell into Nazi hands. Many agents were being picked up and made to transmit radio messages back to Britain at gunpoint. Even when they included prearranged distress signals to indicate that the message was being sent under duress, the signals were ignored, or perhaps suppressed by some traitor within SOE itself.[24]

This passage is curiously reminiscent of Grace Stoddard's treatment of Armstrong's experience. In her version she said that it, would be difficult, no impossible, for me to get back to England. Nazi patrol boats had closed the ports and it was too risky for a Lysander to taxi in. He told me that German intelligence seemed to know of SOE plans in advance. Drops of ammunition constantly fell into Nazi hands and so many agents were picked up and, at gun point, made to transmit radio messages back to England. Even when the messages included pre-arranged warning signals they were ignored, or perhaps suppressed by someone in SOE.[25]

Just like Armstrong, Cottell escaped to Spain by the Comet Line, was detained at the Miranda del Ebro prison, was debriefed at the RVPS in London by Colin Gubbins, and then underwent training to participate in the airborne attack on Arnhem where he killed General Kassin. When Cottell first made this claim, military historians pointed out that the death of Major-General Friedrich Kassin on the evening of 17 September, as his staff car approached a roadblock manned by Lieutenant James Cleminson's 5 Platoon, B Company, of the 3rd Parachute Battalion, is exceptionally well-documented, and no account refers to Cottell's alleged contribution. As for his award of the Military Cross for this engagement, the proposition is quite absurd. The MC is a decoration for gallantry, but no British troops were under fire when General Kassin's staff car accidentally blundered into the path of the paratroopers who opened fire, not with a Bren gun, but with rifles and Sten sub-machineguns. Since the four Germans fired not a shot there was no act of courage to be rewarded or recognised.

Cottell says he was captured at Arnhem and then forced to endure Buchenwald until his liberation in April 1945. After the war he hitched a ride with Squadron Leader Giles from RAF Wittering to Paris and having traced the SS corporal who had killed Marianne, shot him dead at his home near Lüchow, together with his wife.

The rest of Cottell's post-war career exactly mirrors Armstrong's, although his investiture at Buckingham Palace took place a week earlier, on 20 January 1947, but it was also attended by Field Marshal Lord Wavell. Cottell collected two Nazi prisoners in a boat off Ustka, worked as a dishwasher in a Lyons Corner House and undertook secret missions for MI6, including an assignment in Budapest and one to Dresden using the alias Neil McDonald Smith which resulted in his capture. After eleven months in prison he was exchanged in Berlin where he was welcomed by Maurice Oldfield. Cottell also escaped an assassination attempt in his hotel in Dublin, murdered an MI6 traitor after he had climbed into a Ministry of Defence establishment in Dorset, and had killed a gunman who had tried to break into his house, the two other culprits, both Hungarians, being arrested by the police. Cottell also claimed to have served in the British Army in Northern Ireland and to have briefed Edward Heath. His son Peter is also described as having been an engineering student at Heidelberg and to have died at the age of twenty, but of leukaemia.

A comparison between Armstrong's story and that of Cottell's past tale reveals a few differences, apart from Armstrong's assertion that his SOE codename was *Vapor*. Cottell said he was educated at Stamford in Leicestershire. Armstrong supposedly attended 'the local grammar school' before going to 'a good public school in Yorkshire, Ambleton', at the age of ten. The problem with the latter version, apart from the fact that there is no school in Yorkshire or anywhere else called Ambleton, is that pupils did not go to a grammar school until they are eleven years or older. Cottell was married 'in the church of St Paul's before an elderly priest with no witnesses except my best man and Marianne's parents.' Armstrong was 'married in Saint Paul's Church with her parents and my best man as the only attendees.' In almost every other respect the sequence of events described in both books is identical, with both men experiencing incarceration for 'eleven months, two weeks and four days'.

The similarities are so great between *No Cloak No Dagger* and John Cottell's discredited *Codename Badger* that it is hard to resist the conclusion that Grace Stoddard must have a strong connection with the first book, and this turns out to be the case. Actually, 'Grace Stoddard' is Mrs Candace Cottell, and when contacted at their home in St Croix Street, Eugene, Oregon, where her husband still claims a military rank and medals to which he is not entitled, she acknowledged that she was indeed Grace Stoddard, but declined to explain the similarity between the two books apparently written nineteen years apart. Even her husband's admonition that 'in Britain to claim a high decoration that in fact has not been awarded is the worst kind of deception and dishonour imaginable' is mirrored in *No Cloak No Dagger* where Armstrong observes that 'to claim a high decoration that has not been awarded would be the worst kind of deception and dishonour imaginable'.

Postscript

The extent to which authors have invented pasts for themselves, or have imagined their participation in clandestine operations, or simply have reported the fabricated exploits of others, is quite remarkable, especially when so many examples are concentrated together, and although the analysis of these books has an entertainment value, there is another, more sinister aspect to them, which has only become apparent in recent times.

Whereas few of the suspect tales investigated here are backed by any documentation, there has been a tendency for revisionists to interpret some post-war events based upon newly discovered documents, often of a wartime vintage, but only recently declassified. Of course, such research is not only relevant but extremely important and the release of secret files, in College Park, Kew and Moscow, has shed new light on many secret operations and political judgments and enabled the public to gain a better understanding of how the war had been fought and victory achieved. New areas of study, including the previously taboo subjects of codebreaking, double agents, strategic deception and interrogation techniques, enthralled historians and their readers who previously had been reliant on a rather thin diet of memoirs and sanitised official histories. The opening of the archives offered tremendous opportunities to researchers, and the reading rooms were quickly filled with veterans seeking further details of operations in which they had participated, journalists in search of a scoop, and other researchers eager to learn more from official papers that in some cases were intended to remain closed for scores more years.

Among the more assiduous of those toiling in London's Public Record Office (PRO) was Martin Allen, the Welsh-educated son of Professor Peter Allen of the University of Toronto, the author in 1978 of *The Cambridge Apostles: The Early Years*, and in 1983 *The Crown and the*

Swastika, in which he revealed a Nazi scheme in which the Deputy Führer, Rudolf Hess, made contact with the Duke of Windsor in Portugal in 1940. In May 2005 Martin Allen published *Himmler's Secret War* in which he revealed the fruit of his searches in the PRO, an assassination plot approved at the highest levels of the British government which had arranged for the murder of *SS-Reichfuhrer* Heinrich Himmler when he was a prisoner of the British forces at Luneberg, in northern Germany. While it is well known that Himmler committed suicide on the evening of 23 May 1945, by swallowing cyanide while undergoing a medical examination by a Royal Army Medical Corps doctor, the suggestion that he had been murdered was entirely novel, but Allen claimed to have uncovered proof of a conspiracy involving Brendan Bracken, the Minister of Information in Churchill's War Cabinet, Sir John Wheeler-Bennett and Robert Bruce Lockhart of the Foreign Office, and two members of the Political Warfare Executive (PWE), Richard Crossman and Leonard Ingrams. The evidence consisted of an enciphered telegram from a 'Mr. Thomas' in Luneberg, addressed to Bruce Lockhart, initialled by him and copied to the Prime Minister, and then correspondence, from Bracken to Lord Selborne, then head of Special Operations Executive (SOE). Apparently this unlikely group of murderers had decided to silence Himmler so he would never reveal under interrogation by the Americans, that months before the end of hostilities the British had been conducting secret peace negotiations with Himmler through intermediaries in Sweden. The existence of these talks, incidentally, had been omitted from the Cabinet Office official wartime histories of both SOE and PWE.

The first clue to the plot was discovered by Martin Allen, in the form of a memorandum from Sir John W. Wheeler-Bennett, dated 10 May 1945, addressed to 'Sir Robert Bruce-Lockhart KCMG':

> We cannot allow Himmler to take to the stand in any prospective prosecution, or indeed allow him to be interrogated by the Americans. Steps will therefore have to be taken to eliminate him as soon as he falls into our hands.[1]

This is rather an unusual document, for three reasons. Firstly, Bruce Lockhart's double-barrelled surname was not hyphenated, and since the two men knew each other well, it seems an odd mistake for Wheeler-Bennett to have made. Secondly, the language is very strange as the English invariably speak of 'going into the witness box' in preference to the American equivalent of 'taking the stand.' Also, the choice of the word 'eliminate' is a curiously modern one, but most peculiar of all is the fact that Bruce Lockhart is supposed to have added, and initialled 'R B-L' a sentence in manuscript, 'I agree, I have arranged for Mr Ingrams to go for a fortnight.'

The 'Mr Ingrams' mentioned was Leonard, a peacetime merchant banker who had served in PWE during the war, but also apparently an assassin who had travelled to Germany under the alias 'Mr Thomas' and somehow had administered cyanide to Himmler. He had then cabled Bruce Lockhart:

> Further to my orders we successfully intercepted H.H. at Luneberg before he could be interrogated. As instructed, action was taken to silence him permanently. I issued orders that my presence at Luneberg is not to be recorded in any fashion and we may conclude that the H.H. problem is ended.[2]

For a clandestine operation without any record, it evidently did not strike Martin Allen as contradictory that 'Mr. Thomas' should not only send such a signal, but that it should have been copied to the Prime Minister. And then, in the same vein, that Brendan Bracken should have written, on his official departmental letter-heading, in similar terms to 'My Dear Top', his affectionate form of address for Lord Selborne:

> Further to the good news of the death of Little H, I feel that it is imperative that we maintain a complete news black-out on the exact circumstances of this most evil man's demise. I am sure that if it was to become public knowledge that we had a hand in this man's demise, it would have devastating repercussions for this country's standing. I am also sure that this incident would complicate our relationship with our American brethren; under no circumstances must they discover that we eradicated 'Little H', particularly so since we know they were so keen to interrogate him themselves. I am of the opinion that the special S.O.E./P.W.E. Committee and team now can be dissolved, even though Mallet is still negotiating with W.S. in Sweden. Perhaps you could let me know your opinion on this matter.[3]

This uncharacteristically inelegantly-phrased letter, dated 24 May 1945, essentially served to provide the motive for the murder, and raised the issue of *SS-Brigadefuhrer* Walter Schellenberg's continued contact with the British ambassador in Stockholm, Sir Victor Mallet. However, by the date of Schellenberg's mission to Sweden, an attempt to negotiate the surrender of the German occupation forces in Norway, had been completed a fortnight earlier. Having had his last telephone conversation with Admiral Dönitz's headquarters on 10 May, Schellenberg had taken refuge at the home of the Swedish diplomat, Count Folke Bernadotte, where he remained until June when he was extradited to the British zone to face war crimes charges. Having appeared as a witness at the trials of Hermann Goering and Joachim von Ribbentrop, Schellenberg was convicted on two minor charges by the International Military Tribunal in April 1949, and sentenced to six years' imprisonment.

Upon his release Schellenberg had moved to Italy where he had written his memoirs, and included a lengthy account of how in April 1945 he had attended talks held by Himmler with Count Bernadotte who had been asked to act as an intermediary with the Supreme Allied Commander, General Eisenhower, for the complete surrender of all German forces. However, this attempt to open talks with Eisenhower failed when the latter refused to deal with Himmler. So why were these efforts considered so secret that it had been necessary to have Himmler murdered? The logic is hard to follow, especially as there had been other, equally well-documented examples of Himmler having sought to make private contact with the Allies. One had been through Ronald Seth, an SOE agent who had parachuted into Silesia in 1942, only to be captured almost immediately. Seth experienced many adventures while in German captivity, but in March 1945 had met Himmler and Schellenberg in Hamburg and had been entrusted with a personal message for Winston Churchill, proposing peace terms, and he had delivered these to the British embassy in Berne in April. Accordingly, there were plenty of people who knew that Himmler had been attempting to make contact with the Allies to negotiate a separate peace with the British and the Americans, but there was no obvious reason why the British government should have wanted to prevent anyone, and especially Himmler, from revealing these abortive attempts at opening talks.

Closer scrutiny of the three incriminating documents found by Martin Allen in the PRO's Foreign Office files revealed some unusual similarities. All three had started with the same words, 'further to', and although they had originated in different departments, being John Wheeler-Bennett's in the Foreign office, the deciphered telegram and the Ministry of Information, all were found to have been typed on exactly the same typewriter. A forensic document examiner, Dr Audrey Giles, also reported that the 'Ministry of Information' letter-heading had been printed by a high resolution laser printer, a machine not available in May 1945, and that Brendan Bracken's signature had been written over a pencil tracing of the name. Clearly all three documents were forgeries, so how could they have found their way into the Foreign

Office files in the PRO? That is a mystery that has yet to be solved, although the security on the building is intended to prevent visitors from leaving with documents, and there are no measures to stop anyone taking papers into the reading rooms.

Clearly Martin Allen had been duped by the forgeries, as had Peter Padfield, a PRO researcher and former journalist who had authenticated them for the BBC during a radio interview broadcast to publicise the book, but it turns out that as a historian Allen had experienced quite a run of bad luck, as his two previous books, *Hidden Agenda*[4] and *The Hitler-Hess Deception*,[5] had both been reliant on documents whose authenticity had been questioned.

Allen's first book, subtitled *How the Duke of Windsor betrayed the Allies*, purported to reveal that the former King Edward VII had been a Nazi spy who had passed military secrets to Germany through a French collaborator, Charles Bedaux, acting as an intermediary. But could such a sensational charge really be true? Allen claimed to have uncovered an incriminating letter, dated 4 November 1939, addressed to 'Leiber Herr Hitler' in the Duke's handwriting, among his late father's papers, in which Edward said he had 'recently returned from a trip to the north and observed some very interesting views. I have described my holiday in great detail to your acquaintance, Mr. B.' This document, according to Martin Allen, had been given to his father Peter by Albert Speer in July 1980, and it amounted to confirmation that the Duke had supplied Bedaux with military intelligence following his well-publicised tour of the Maginot Line. Although born in Paris, Bedaux was a business efficiency consultant who had developed a reputation as a German sympathiser, and he would eventually be arrested in North Africa by the Free French, and be taken to Florida, where he was investigated by the FBI, and where he eventually committed suicide in February 1944. That Bedaux had been a notorious Nazi collaborator is not in doubt, nor is his acquaintance with the Duke, who had borrowed his home, the Chateau de Candé, near Tours, to marry Mrs. Wallis Simpson in June 1937. However, there was quite a difference between being lent the home of a Nazi collaborator, and being a spy, and although the manuscript letter appeared to bridge that gap, there were immediate doubts about its authenticity when it was produced. While forensic examination showed the paper to be of the right age, experts expressed reservations about the handwriting which appeared to display strange pauses in the construction of German words that the Duke would have been very familiar with. As a fluent German speaker and writer, what was the explanation for these distinctive lapses, usually associated with someone writing in a language unfamiliar to them.

Aside from doubts about the authenticity of the document, there was also the issue of its provenance. Allen said it had been a gift to his father from Speer, but if so he had opted not to include it, or even refer to it, in his book on the Duke of Windsor, *The Crown and the Swastika*, which was published three years later, in 1983. In this book Allen senior's central thesis was that the Duke had intrigued with the Nazis in July 1940 while in Portugal, and had held secret meetings with Hess to negotiate peace, thus allowing Hitler to attack the Soviet Union. Hess subsequently had been lured to England, Allen argued, so as to silence him and to conceal the Duke's treachery, which was a continuing embarrassment for the royal family.

The problem with this thesis is that Hess never went to Portugal in July 1940, but that did not deter Martin Allen from adapting the idea for his second book, *The Hitler / Hess Deception*, which was released in 2003, based on the proposition that Hess had conducted secret peace negotiations with the British ambassador to Spain, Sir Sam Hoare, in Switzerland, and that British intelligence had cooked up a Machiavellian plot to encourage Hitler to launch his disastrous attack on the Soviets. Once again, Allen had 'unearthed many documents previously undiscovered by historians,' but the Public Record Office files cited do not contain the key letters and memoranda quoted in the text. For example, Rex Leeper is identified as the author, in August 1940 of a note addressed to Hugh Gaitskell of the Ministry of Economic Warfare, in which he stated 'recent attempts to find an accord' had been made by the Germans, and suggested that this weakness should be exploited, on the authority of the Prime Minister, by the use of black propaganda prepared by Leonard Ingrams and Richard Crossman. This is obviously a crucial document for, according to Allen, it would 'germinate into one of the most successful and best-kept British Intelligence secrets of the Second World War,'[6] yet it is not only hard to find in any archive, but nobody seems anxious to claim the credit for its success. The operation is not mentioned in David Garnett's recently declassified official history of PWE, and Ingrams' subordinate, Ellic Howe, who wrote a detailed account of PWE's black propaganda activities, also omitted any reference to it. Thus it would seem that Martin Allen has had tremendous bad luck in being the victim of disappearing documents and reappearing forgeries, all of which mysteriously support his father's theory that Hitler had been tricked into making the strategically disastrous error of opening the Russian front in June 1941.

If the implications for the integrity of archives were not so serious, the issue of elusive documents, or counterfeit letters, would be mildly comical, and certainly an area worthy of research to find the motives of the perpetrators, but evidently someone has gone to considerable trouble to find suitable paper, usually obtained through the expedient of cutting blank pages from the endpapers of books published contemporaneously, and then converting them into minutes, memoranda and letters with a typewriter of suitable vintage. For Allen to have been caught by the same ruse in all three of his books must be very dispiriting for the historian, but although he was interviewed by the police, and recommended for prosecution, the Attorney-General announced in 2007 that no further action would be taken against him because of his poor health, and the public interest. Accordingly, one is left wondering who else, apart from his readers, have been deceived in much the same way?

One such individual taken in by a far less serious scam was Richard Brooks, the culture editor of *The Sunday Times* who was saved from considerable embarrassment in 2005 by his more perspicacious colleagues when he detected a scoop with the imminent release of *The Moneypenny Diaries*.[7] Brooks, unpopular with his fellow journalists for his ruthless quest for headline-grabbing stories, fell for an ingenious tale peddled by 'Dr Kate Westbrook', supposedly a respectable Cambridge academic who allegedly had inherited an astonishing legacy from her late aunt. Jane Moneypenny. According to Dr Westbrook, her aunt had worked in the Secret Intelligence Service and had been the model for Ian Fleming's famous fictional secretary in his 007 thrillers. Sensing a potential exclusive, Brooks accepted the story as authentic and opened negotiations with the publishers, John Murray, to serialise the imminent book in which Jane Moneypenny revealed how 007 had really existed, and had played a key role in the Cuban missile crisis of October 1962. Convinced that the diaries had only been edited by the niece, Brooks fell for the scam until he was tipped off that the entire project was nothing more than an elaborate publicity stunt organised by the author with the approval of her sponsors, the Fleming estate. In reality 'Dr Kate Westbook' was Samantha Weinberg, a South African journalist and award-winning crime writer married to a BBC wildlife documentary-maker. Her success was such, even if she did eventually break the news of her ruse to Brooks, that in 2006 she wrote a sequel, *Secret Servant*,[8] in which she perpetuated the claim that the publication of the diaries had led to threats of prosecution and the loss of her teaching job at Cambridge. Of course, all this was nothing more than a light-hearted way of continuing the Bond tradition, although the implications for the gullible Brooks might have been more serious if he had not been warned in the nick of time.

Such scams are quite harmless, and in the case of *The Moneypenny Diaries* the publishers never made any false claims about the origin of the material, leaving it to their ingenious author to perpetrate the hoax. When challenged she promptly acknowledged that the exercise had been imaginary, a rare example of refreshing candour in a field inhabited all too often by authors with rather different motives.

References and Notes

Chapter 1: Official Assassin
1. Anthony Kemp, *The Secret Hunters* (O'Mara, London, 1986).
2. Captain Bernard Knox, Jedburgh Team GILES.
3. Peter Mason, *Official Assassin* (Phillips, New York, 1998).
4. *ibid*, p.11.
5. *ibid*, p.17.
6. *ibid*, p.23.
7. *ibid*.
8. *ibid*.
9. *ibid*, p.27.
10. *ibid*, p.41.
11. *ibid*, p.62.
12. *ibid*, p.73.
13. *ibid*, p.74.
14. *ibid*, p.76.
15. *ibid*, p.77.
16. *ibid*, p.93.
17. *ibid*, p.101.
18. *ibid*, p.121.
19. *ibid*, p.122.
20. *ibid*, p.130.
21. *ibid*, p.131.
22. *ibid*, p.132.
23. *ibid*, p.141.
24. Peter Wright, *SpyCatcher* (Heinemann, New York, 1987).
25. *Official Assassin, ibid*.
26. *ibid*, p.31.
27. *ibid*, p.57.

Chapter 2: Nemesis in Northern Ireland
1. Harold Wilson, House of Commons, 12 January 1976.
2. Ken Connor, *Ghost Force* (Cassell, London, 2006).
3. Raymond Murray, *The SAS in Ireland* (The Irish-American Book Co., 1993).
4. Fred Holroyd, *War Without Honour* (Medium Publishing, London, 1989).
5. Shaun Clarke, *Soldier E: SAS Sniper Fire in Belfast* (Ted Smart, London, 1994).
6. *ibid*, p.17.
7. *ibid*, p.21.
8. Michael Paul Kennedy, *Soldier I SAS: Eighteen Years in the Elite Force* (Osprey, London, 2011).

9. Nick Curtis, *Faith and Duty* (Andre Deutsch, London, 1998).
10. *ibid*, p.66.
11. *ibid*, p.69.
12. *ibid*, p.73.
13. *ibid*.
14. *ibid*, p.80.
15. *ibid*, p.81.
16. *ibid*, p.84.
17. *ibid*, p.87.
18. *ibid*, p.101.
19. *ibid*, p.103.
20. *ibid*, p.121.

Chapter 3: Sir Ranulph and the Feathermen
1. BBC Radio 4 interview, 11 September 2015.
2. Sir Ranulph Fiennes, *Here Soldiers Fear to Tread* (Mandarin, London, 1995).
3. Sir Ranulph Fiennes, *The Feathermen* (Bloomsbury, London, 1991).
4. Gary Murray, *Enemies of the State* (Simon & Schuster, London, 1993).
5. *ibid*, p23.
6. *ibid*, p.37.
7. *ibid*, p.40.
8. *ibid*, p.51.
9. *ibid*, p.59.
10. *ibid*, p.61.
11. *ibid*, p.62.
12. *ibid*, p.91.
13. *ibid*, p.92.
14. *ibid*, p.97.
15. *ibid*, p.105.
16. *ibid*, p.111.
17. *ibid*, p.115.
18. *ibid*, p.119.
19. *ibid*, p.151.

Chapter 4: Espionage in Korea
1. Lawrence Gordella, *Sing a Sing to Jenny Next* (E.P. Dutton, New York, 1981).
2. *ibid*, p.11.
3. *ibid*, p.15.
4. *ibid*, p. 21.
5. *ibid*, p.83.
6. *ibid*, p.84.
7. *ibid*, p.91.
8. *ibid*, p.98.
9. *ibid*, p.103.
10. *ibid*, p.109.

11. *ibid*, p.121.
12. Arthur Boyd, *Operation Broken Reed* (Carrol & Graf, New York, 2008), p.14.
13. *ibid*, p.5.
14. *ibid*, p.16.
15. *ibid*, p.28.
16. *ibid*, p.40.
17. *ibid*, p.91.
18. *ibid*, p.122.
19. *ibid*, p.146.
20. *ibid*, p.xvii.
21. *ibid*, p.31.
22. *ibid*, p.253.
23. *ibid*, p.33.
24. *ibid*, p.244.
25. *ibid*, p.xxi.
26. *ibid*.
27. *ibid*, p.259.
28. *ibid*, p.xviii.

Chapter 5: The Soviet Conspiracy
1. Stewart Steven, *Operation Splinter Factor* (Hodder & Stoughton, London, 1974), p.47.
2. *ibid*, p.55.
3. *ibid*, p.56.
4. *ibid*, p.68.
5. *ibid*, p.104.
6. *ibid*, p.121.
7. *ibid*, p.123.
8. *ibid*, p.131.
9. *ibid*, p.151.
10. *ibid*, p.153.
11. *ibid*, p.154.
12. *ibid*, p.159.
13. *ibid*, p.161.
14. *ibid*, p.164.
15. *ibid*, p.166.
16. *ibid*.
17. *ibid*.
18. *ibid*, p.168.
19. *ibid*, p.172.
20. *ibid*, p.173.
21. *ibid*, p.174.
22. *ibid*, p.181.
23. *ibid*, p.187.
24. *ibid*, p.188.
25. *ibid*, p.193.
26. *ibid*.
27. *ibid*, p.197.
28. *ibid*, p.198.
29. *ibid*, p.199.
30. *ibid*, p.203.
31. *ibid*.

32. *ibid.*
33. *ibid*, p.207.
34. *ibid*, p.208.
35. *ibid*, p.209.
36. *ibid.*
37. *ibid.*
38. *ibid*, p.212.
39. *ibid*, p.214.
40. *ibid*, p.215.
41. *ibid*, p.217.
42. *ibid*, p.219.
43. Bernard Hutton, *School for Spies* (Neville Speaman, London, 1961).
44. *ibid*, p.33.
45. *ibid*, p.35.
46. *ibid*, p.36.
47. *ibid*, p.41.
48. *ibid*, p.51.
49. *ibid*, p.87.
50. *ibid*, p.88.
51. *ibid*, p.91.
52. *ibid*, p.95.
53. *ibid*, p.97.
54. *ibid*, p.101.
55. *ibid*, p.103.
56. *The False Defector* (Baker, London, 1970).
57. *ibid*, p.27.
58. *ibid*, p.33.
59. *ibid*, p.41.
60. Nicholas Elliott, *Never Judge A Man by his Umbrella* (Michael Russell, London, 1991), p.26.
61. Harold Macmillan and Peter Quennell, *The Macmillan's Diaries: The Cabinet Years* (Macmillan, London, 2003).

Chapter 6: Greville Wynne's GRU Defector
1. Andy J. Byers, *The Imperfect Spy: The Inside Story of a Convicted Spy* (Vandamere, St. Petersburg, 2005).
2. Victor Sheymov, *Tower of Secrets* (Naval Institute Press, Annapolis, 1993).
3. Phillipa Kennedy, 'The Spy Who Deserted Me', *Daily Express*, 27 March 1985.
4. *ibid.*
5. Greville Wynne, *The Man from Odessa* (Robert Hale, London, 1981) p.40.
6. *After the War – What Then Soldier?*, Author's Collection.
7. *The Man from Odessa*, p.86.
8. *ibid*, p.80.
9. *ibid*, p.78.
10. *ibid*, p.98.
11. *ibid*, p.154.
12. *ibid*, p.197.
13. *ibid*, p.10.
14. *ibid*, p.139.
15. *ibid.*

16. *ibid*, p.112.
17. *ibid*, p.113.
18. *ibid*, p.156.
19. *ibid*, p.146.
20. *ibid*, p.144.
21. *ibid*, p.222.
22. *ibid*, p.144.
23. *ibid*, p.164.
24. *ibid.*
25. *ibid*, p.116.
26. *ibid*, p.202.
27. *ibid*, p.208.
28. *ibid.*
29. *ibid*, p.209.
30. *ibid*, p.210.
31. *ibid*, p.197.
32. *ibid.*
33. *ibid*, p.223.
34. Greville Wynne, *The Man from Moscow* (Hutchinson, London, 1967), p.78.
35. *The Man from Odessa*, p.195.
36. *ibid*, p.196.
37. *ibid*, p.189.
38. Peter Wright, *SpyCatcher* (Heinemann, New York, 1987), p.202.
39. *The Man from Odessa*, p.195.
40. *The Man from Moscow*, p.130.

Chapter 7: Helga's 'Red Spy at Night'
1. Helga Pohl-Wannenmacher, *Red Spy at Night* (Leo Cooper, London, 1977), p.58.
2. *ibid.*
3. *ibid*, p.64.
4. *ibid*, p.66.
5. *ibid*, p.95.
6. *ibid*, p.118.
7. *ibid*, p.121.
8. *ibid*, p.122.
9. *ibid*, p.139.
10. *ibid*, p.144.
11. *ibid*, p.156.
12. *ibid*, p.161.
13. *ibid*, p.166.
14. *ibid*, p.122.
15. *ibid*, p.127.
16. *ibid*, p.122.
17. *ibid*, p.121.
18. *ibid*, p.122.
19. *ibid*, p.110.
20. *ibid.*
21. *ibid*, p.100.
22. *ibid.*
23. *ibid*, p.170.
24. *ibid.*
25. *ibid*, p.121.

Chapter 8: The Vietnam Experience
1. Frank Dux, *The Secret Man* (Regan Books, New York, 1996), p.51.
2. *ibid*, p.55.
3. *ibid*, p.56.
4. *ibid*, p.71.
5. Gayle Rivers, *The specialist*

Corgi, London, 1986).
6. *ibid*, p.23
7. *ibid*, p.47
6. *ibid*, p.23
7. *ibid*, p.47
8. *ibid*, p.44
9. *ibid*, p.61
10. *ibid*, p.67
11. *ibid*, p.81
12. *ibid*, p.82

Chapter 9: Tom Carew's 'Jihad'
1. Tom Carew, *Jihad!* (Mainstream, London, 2000), p.17.
2. *ibid*, p.21.
3. *ibid*, p.25.
4. *ibid*, p.27.
5. Ken Connor, *Ghost Force* (Cassell, London, 2006), p.81.

Chapter 10: Spooky 8: The Final Mission
1. Bob King, *Spooky 8* (St Martin's Press, New York, 1999), p.16.
2. *ibid*, p.71.
3. *ibid*, p.75.
4. *ibid*, p.77.
5. *ibid*, p.80.

Chapter 11: The Patriot
1. Oliver Upton, *The Patriot* (Frederick Garnder, London, 1989), p.3.
2. *ibid*, p.90.
3. *ibid*, p.173.
4. *ibid*, p.3.

Chapter 12: Sixteen Killers
1. John Unwin, *The Sixteen* Blake Publishing, London, 2004).
2. *ibid*, p.11.
3. *ibid*, p.43.
4. *ibid*, p.45.

Chapter 13: Was The Prime Minister Really A Spy?
1. Anthony Grey, *The Prime Minister Was A Spy* (Weidenfeld & Nicolson, London, 1983).
2. *ibid*, p.37.
3. *ibid*, p.38.
4. *ibid*, p.11.
5. *ibid*, p.22.
6. *ibid*, p.27.
7. *ibid*, p.44.
8. *ibid*, p.45.
9. *ibid*, p.47.
10. *ibid*, p.61.
11. *ibid*, p.61.
12. *ibid*, p.67.
13. *ibid*, p.71.
14. *ibid*, p.72.
15. *ibid*, p.85.
16. *ibid*, p.86.
17. *ibid*, p.87.

18. *ibid*, p.91.
19. Anthony Grey, *The Hostage Handbook* (Tagman Press, London, 2012).

Chapter 14: Sins Of The Father
1. Larry Kolb, *Overworld* (Transworld, New York, 2011).
2. Harold Lloyd Goodall, *A Need to Know* (Left Coast Pres, 2006).
3. Lucinda Franks, *My Father's Secret War* (Findaway World, 2009).
4. *Overwold*, p.43.
5. *ibid*, p.37.
6. *ibid*, p.51.
7. Miles Copeland, *The Game of Nations* (Simon & Schuster, London, 1970).
8. Miles Copeland, *The Game Player* (Aurum, London, 1989).
9. Miles Copeland, *The Real Spy World* (Sphere, London, 1978).
10. Roland Haas, *Enter the Real Past Tense* (Potomac Books, Washington DC, 2007).
11. *ibid*, p.11.
12. *ibid*, p.19.
13. *ibid*, p.23.
14. *ibid*, p.24.
15. *ibid*, p.71.
16. *My Father's Secret War*, p.12.
17. *ibid*, p.56.
18. *ibid*, p.77.
19. *ibid*, p.78.
20. *ibid*, p.85.
21. *ibid*, p.87.
22. *ibid*, p.91.
23. Valerie Plame, *Fair Game* (Simon & Schuster, New York, 2007).
24. David Doyle, *Inside Espionage* (St Ermin's, London, 2001).
25. James Waste, *Don't Shoot the Ice Cream Man* (Ringwalt, New York, 2010).
26. Nicholas Anderson, *NOC: Non-Official Cover: British Secret Operations* (Miurai, 2011).
27. *ibid*, p.23.
28. *ibid*, p.26.
29. *ibid*, p.27.
30. *ibid*, p.41.
31. *ibid*, p.44.
32. *ibid*, p.45.
33. *ibid*, p.66.
34. *ibid*, p.67.
35. *ibid*, p.72.
36. *ibid*, p.73.
37. *ibid*, p.75.
38. *ibid*, p.55.
39. *ibid*, p.111.
40. *ibid*, p.112.

41. *ibid*, p.121.
42. *ibid*, p.122.
43. *ibid*, p.123.
44. *ibid*, p.137.
45. *ibid*, p.138.
46. *ibid*, p.44.
47. *ibid*, p.56.

Chapter 15: Gestapo Müller
1. Gregory Douglas, *Gestapo Müller* (R. James Bender Publishing, San Jose, 1995).
2. *ibid*, p.19.
3. *ibid*, p.21.
4. *ibid*, p.22.
5. *ibid*, p.27.
6. *ibid*, p.44.
7. *ibid*, p.45.
8. *ibid*, p.51.
9. *ibid*, p.52.
10. *ibid*, p.56.
11. *ibid*, p.67.
12. *ibid*, p.88.
13. *ibid*, p.89.
14. *ibid*, p.127.
15. *ibid*, p.128.
16. *ibid*, p.131.
17. *ibid*, p.17.
18. *ibid*, p.21.

Chapter 16: Brigadier Alexander Wilson
1. Alexander Wilson, *Wallace of the Secret Service* (Herbert Jenkins, London, 1933), p.9.
2. *ibid*, p.22.
3. Michael Chesney, *Callaghan of Intelligence* (Herbert Jenkins, London, 1938); Michael Chesney, *"Steel" Callaghan* (Herbert Jenkins, London, 1939); Michael Chesney, *Callaghan Meets His Fate* (Herbert Jenkins. London, 1939).
4. The National Archives, KV/FO 1093/263, 18 June 1943.
5. Tim Crook, *The Secret Lives of a Secret Agent* (Kultura, London, 2010).

Chapter 17: Operation Vengeance
1. David B. Tinnin, *Hit Team* (Little, Brown, Boston, 1976).
2. Richard Deacon, *The Israeli Secret Service* (Sphere, London, 1988).
3. Elaine Davenport, Paul Eddy and Peter Gillman, *The Plumbat Affair* (J.B. Lippincott Co., Philadelphia, 1978).
4. Stewart Steven, *The Spymasters of Israel* (Macmillan, London, 1981).
5. Michael Bar-Zohar and Eitan Haber, *The Quest for*

the Red Prince (William Morrow, New York, 1983).
6. George Jonas, *Vengeance* (HarperCollins, New York, 2010).
7. Sam Green, *Flight 103* (Endevour, New York, 2008).
8. Grace Stoddard, *No Cloak No Dagger* (Wheatmark, London, 2009).
9. *ibid*, p.14.
10. *ibid*, p.17.
11. *ibid*, p.21.
12. *ibid*, p.22.
13. *ibid*, p.41.
14. *ibid*, p.44.
15. *ibid*, p.61.
16. *ibid*, p.62.
17. *ibid*, p.80.
18. *ibid*, p.83.
19. *ibid*, p.84.
20. *ibid*, p.87.
21. *ibid*, p.16.
22. *ibid*, p.25.
23. John Cottell, *Codename Badger*, p.11.
24. *ibid*, p.19.
25. *ibid*, p.31.

Postscript
1. Martin Allen, *Himmler's Secret War* (Robson, London, 2005).
2. *ibid*, p.27.
3. *ibid*, p.44.
4. Martin Allen, *Hidden Agenda* (Macmillan, London, 2000).
5. Martin Allen, *The Hitler – Hess Deception* (HarperCollins, London, 2003).
6. Peter Allen, *The Crown and the Swastika* (Robert Hale, London, 1983).
7. *The Moneypenny Diaries* by Kate Westbrook (John Murray, London, 2005).
8. *Secret Servant* by Kate Westbrook (London: John Murray, 2006).

Bibliography

Abraham, Tom, *The Cage* (Bantam, London, 2002).

Allen, Martin, *Hidden Agenda* (Macmillan, London, 2000).

_____, *The Hitler–Hess Deception* (HarperCollins, London, 2003).

_____, *Himmler's Secret War* (Robson Books, London, 2005).

Allen, Peter, *The Crown and the Swastika* (Robert Hale, London, 1983).

Anderson, Nicholas, *NOC: Non-Official Cover: British Secret Operations* (Miurai, 2011).

Asher, Michael, *The Real Bravo Two Zero* (Cassell, London, 2011).

Barnes, Scott, *BOHICA* (Daring Books, London, 1987).

Burd, Kai, *The Good Spy* (Crown, New York, 2014).

Boyd. Arthur L., *Operation Broken Reed* (Carrol & Graf, New York, 2008).

Burkett, B.G., and Whitley, Glenna, *Stolen Valour* (Verity Press, New York, 1998).

Butler, Josephine, *Churchill's Secret Agent* (Methuen, London, 1983).

Byers, Andy J., *The Imperfect Spy: The Inside Story of a Convicted Spy* (Vandamere, St. Petersbueg, 2005).

Carew, Tom, *Jihad! The Secret War in Afghanistan* (Mainstream, London, 2000).

Chesney, Michael (Alexander Wilson), *The Mystery of Tunnel 51* (Longmans, Green and Co., London, 1928).

_____, *Callaghan of Intelligence* (Herbert Jenkins, London, 1938).

_____, *"Steel" Callaghan* (Herbert Jenkins, London, 1939).

_____, *Callaghan Meets His Fate* (Herbert Jenkins, London, 1939).

Clarke, Shaun, *Soldier E: SAS. Sniper Fire in Belfast* (Ted Smart, London, 1994).

Connor, Ken, *Ghost Force* (Cassell, London, 2006).

Constantinides, George, *Intelligence and Espionage: An Analytical Bibliography* (Westview Press, Boulder, 1983).

Copleand, Miles, *The Game of Nations: The Amorality of Power Politics* (New York: Simon and Schuster, 1969).

_____, *The Game Player: Confessions of The CIA's Original Political Operative* (Aurum Press Ltd, London, 1989).

_____, *The Real Spy World* (Weidenfeld and Nicolson, London, 1974).

Cramer, Lennox Gordon, *Slow Dance on the Killing Ground* (Dramatists' Play Service, 1965).

Crook, Tim, *The Secret Lives of a Secret Agent* (Kultura Press, London, 2010).

Curtis, Nick, *Faith and Duty* (Andre Deutsch, London, 1998).

Davies, Nicholas, *Ten-Thirty-Three* (Mainstream, Edinburgh, 1999).

Douglas, Gregory, *Gestapo Chief: The 1948 Interrogation of Heinrich Muller* (James Bender Publishing, San Jose 1995).

_____, *Gestapo Chief: The 1948 Interrogation of Heinrich Muller* (James Bender Publishing, San Jose 1997).

_____, *Gestapo Chief: The 1948 Interrogation of Heinrich Muller*. (James Bender Publishing, San Jose 1998).

Dulles, Allen, *Germany's Underground* (Macmillan, New York, 1947).

Doyle, David, *Inside Intelligence* (St Ermin's Press, London, 2001).

Dux, Frank, *The Secret Man: An American Warrior's Uncensored Story* (Regan Books, New York, 1996).

Elliott, Nicholas, *With My Little Eye* (Michael Russell, London, 1993).

Fiennes, Ranulph, *The Feathermen* (Bloomsbury, London, 1991).

Franks, Lucinda, *My Father's Secret War* (Miramax, New York, 2007).

Gardella, Lawrence, *Sing a Song to Jenny Next* (E.P. Dutton, New York, 1981).

Garnett, David, *The Secret history of PWE* (St Ermin's Press, London, 2002).

Green, Sam, *Max* (Random House, New York, 2006).

_____, *Flight 103* (Century, London, 2008).

Grey, Anthony, *The Prime Minister Was A Spy* (Weidenfeld & Nicolson, London, 1983).

_____, *The Hostage Handbook* (Tagman Press, London, 2012).

Grose, Peter, *Gentleman Spy* (Houghton Mifflin, Boston, 1954).

Haas, Roland W., *Enter The Past Tense* (Potomac Books, Washington DC, 2007).

Hersha, Cheryl and Lynn, *Secret Weapons* (New Horizon, New York, 2001).

Hersh, Seymout, *The Samson Option* (Random House, New York, 1991).

Holroyd, Fred, with Burbridge, Nick, *War Without Honour* (Medium Publishing, London, 1989).

Horos, George H., *Show Trials: Stalinist Purges in Eastern Europe, 1948-1954* (Praeger Publishers, New York, 1987).

Hutton, J. Bernard, *Danger From Moscow* (Neville Spearman, London, 1960).

_____, *The Traitor Trade* (Neville Spearman, London, 1963).

_____, *Struggle in the Dark* (Harrap, London, 1969).

BIBLIOGRAPHY

_____, *The Great Illusion* (David Bruce & Watson, London, 1970).
_____, *The Fake Defector* (Howard Baker, London, 1970).
_____, *Women Spies* (W.H. Allen, London, 1971).
_____, *The Subverters* (Arlington House, London, 1972).
Kemp, Anthony, *The Secret Hunters* (O'Mara, London, 1986).
Kennedy, Ludovic, *Presumption of Innocence* (Littlehampton Books, London, 1967).
Kennedy, Michael Paul, *Soldier I: SAS Eighteen Years in the Elite Force* (Osprey, London, 2010).
Kennedy, Robert, *Thirteen Days* (W.W. Norton, New York, 2000).
King, Bob, *Spooky 8: The Final Mission* (St Martin's Press, New York, 1999).
Klein, Aaron J., *Striking Back* (Random House, New York, 1995).
McNab, Andy, *Bravo Two Zero* (Island Books, London, 1994).
McPhilemy, Sean, *The Committee* (Richard Rinehart, London, 1998).
Mason, David, *Shadow over Babylon* (Bloomsbury, London, 1993).
Mason, Peter, *Official Assassin* (Phillips Publication, London, 1989).
Murray, Gary, *Enemies of the State* (Simon & Schuster, London, 1993).
Murray, Raymond, *The SAS in Ireland* (The Irish-American Book Co., Dublin, 1993).
Pohl-Wannenmacher, Helga, *Red Spy at Night* (Leo Cooper, London, 1977).
Rivers, Gayle, *The Specialist* (Sidgwick & Jackson, London, 1985).
Ryan, Chris, *The One Who Got Away* (Potomac, Washington DC, 2006).
Sheymov, Victor, *Tower of Secrets* (Naval Institute Press, Annapolis, 1993).
Smith, Warner, *Covert Warrior: A Vietnam Warrior* (Posket Books, New York, 1998).
Spencer, Geoffrey, (Alexander Wilson), *The Confessions of a Scoundrel* (Werner Laurie, London, 1933).
_____, *The Sentimental Crook* (Herbert Jenkins, London, 1934).
Steven, Stewart, *Operation Splinter Factor* (Hodder & Stoughton, London, 1974).
Stoddard, Grace, *No Cloak No Dagger* (Wheatmark, London, 2009).
Suvorov, Victor, *The Aquarium* (Hamish Hamilton, London, 1985).
Urwin, John, *The Sixteen* (Vision, London, 2002).
Waste, James, *Don't Shoot the Ice Cream Man: A Cold War Spy in the New World Disorder* (Ringwalt, New York, 2010).
Welham, M.G., and J.A., *Frogman Spy* (W.H. Allen, London, 1990).
Westbrook, Kate, *The Moneypenny Diaries* (John Murray, London, 2005).
_____, *Secret Servant* (John Murray, London, 2006).
Wilkomirski, Benjamin, *Fragments* (Schocken Books, New York, 1996).
Wilson, Alexander, *Murder Mansion* (Longmans, Green, London, 1929).
_____, *The Death of Dr. Whitelaw* (Longmans, Green, London, 1930).
_____, *The Crimson Dacoit* (Herbert Jenkins, London, 1933).
_____, *Wallace of the Secret Service* (Herbert Jenkins, London, 1933).
_____, *Get Wallace!* (Herbert Jenkins, London, 1934).
_____, *The Sentimental Crook* (Herbert Jenkins, London, 1934).
_____, *The Magnificent Hobo* (Herbert Jenkins, London, 1935).
_____, *His Excellency, Governor Wallace* (Herbert Jenkins, London, 1936).
_____, *Microbes of Power* (Herbert Jenkins, London, 1937).
_____, *Mr Justice* (Herbert Jenkins, London, 1937).
_____, *Double Events* (Herbert Jenkins, London, 1937).
_____, *Wallace At Bay* (Herbert Jenkins, London, 1938).
_____, *Chronicles of the Secret Service* (Herbert Jenkins, London, 1940).
_____, *Double Masquerade* (Herbert Jenkins, London, 1940).
_____, *Wallace Intervenes* (Herbert Jenkins, London, 1939).
_____, *Scapegoats for Murder* (Herbert Jenkins, London, 1939).
Wilson, Gregory (Alexander Wilson), *The Factory Mystery* (Modern Publishing, London, 1938).
_____, *The Boxing Mystery* (Modern Publishing, London, 1938).
Wright, Peter, *SpyCatcher* (Heinemann, New York, 1987).
Wynne, Greville, *The Man From Moscow* (Hutchinson, London, 1967).
_____, *The Man From Odessa* (Grafton, London, 1983).

Index

INDEX

INDEX

251

INDEX